The New Ego

Pitfalls in Current Thinking About
Patients in Psychoanalysis

The New Ego

Pitfalls in Current Thinking About
Patients in Psychoanalysis

Nathan Leites, Ph.d.

With an Introduction by
Robert Stoller, M.D.

Science House

Library of Congress Catalog Card Number: 74–160165
Standard Book Number: 87668–046–5

Designed by Jennifer Mellen

Manufactured by Haddon Craftsmen, Inc.
Scranton, Pennslyvania

Acknowledgments

I am grateful for the support given by the Gender Identity Research Project, Department of Psychiatry, University of California at Los Angeles, and by the Foundation for Research in Psychoanalysis in the same city.

To Fred Iklé I am indebted for comments on my introduction.

N. L.

Table of Contents

PART III: The New Ego

Author's Note

In Parts I and II, I examine a substantial fraction of the pertinent writings in the field; in Part III, only the basic texts of Heinz Hartmann, Ernst Kris, and Rudolph Loewenstein ("the authors") are considered.

In discussing what seem to me to be debatable modes of speech, I often speculate on why they were adopted and usually submit that certain advantages accrue from doing so—advantages incompatible with "science." At no point do I allege that the pursuit of such advantages is conscious—nobody's good faith is questioned here.

When citing, I have often put between quotation marks only the words crucial for the point I am making, so as to ease reading. The context will, I trust, make it clear when I am transcribing the author's words.

Frequently I have pruned the texts under examination—without, as far as I can see, changing the relevant meaning. These excisions are indicated by ellipsis points within the quoted material.

All emphases are mine, unless there is a parenthetical statement to the contrary.

N. L.

If critical examiners find no subjects on which to exercise their powers of vituperation, they have no joy.

Chuang Tzu

Once upon a time there was a traveler drawing for the King of Ch'i. "What is the hardest thing to draw?" asked the King. "Dogs and horses are the hardest." "Then what is the easiest?" "Devils and demons are the easiest. Indeed, dogs and horses are what people know and see at dawn and dusk in front of them. To draw them no distortion is permissible . . . Devils and demons have no shapes and are not seen in front of anybody . . ."

Han Fei Tzu

Introduction

If this book frightens psychoanalysts, as it should, psychoanalysis could be refreshed, something it badly needs.

Although most analysts are deeply concerned about the present state of analysis, they hope that the tree itself, still growing vigorously, can be properly shaped by trimming and pruning a piece of theory here and there. This pruning, it is suggested, should take the form of improving procedures for selecting candidates, improving the atmosphere in which the training analysis proceeds, improving the curriculum, getting psychoanalysis more into the community (or out of it), improving techniques of graduate education so that more members will participate, changing criteria for membership in analytic associations (or holding the line against such changes), improving public relations (possibly even by keeping watch over what is said in public media about psychoanalysis), modifying theory (ego psychology, for example, or Kleinian concepts), and even modifying technique (or fighting to prevent modifications). Behind such suggestions lies the belief that the issues, while real enough, are irritants on a fundamentally sound science.

Other analysts, who do not believe all is so sound, feel analysis has been wounded from outside—that society, as it changes, is unwilling to live in the heady atmosphere of truth required of the person committed to analysis; or else they suffer a gentle sadness and forebearance, most gratifying of pains, as they contemplate the inability of others to recognize the truths of psychoanalysis. At worst, it is said, it is the sick or villainous who wound us, but if only we band together, confident in the goodness of our intentions, we can hand our torch to the select of the future.

Agreeing with the above (including even the incompatible opposites), I disagree in believing none fully accounts for the trouble psychoanalysis is in. Along with Professor Leites, I think that the trouble is our trouble, the sickness our sickness, and that the return to health will not come by modifying society or our position within it, by modifying our educational methods, or by further distilling our theory.

If the problem is really ours, not the problem of those outside, the task of débriding psychoanalysis will be as difficult and painful as is the shifting of character structure in our patients. Here too, the voice of reality will have to be strengthened in the psychic functioning of this rationalizing, intellectualizing, brilliant, imaginative, and creative patient—who does have a good prognosis if not permitted to think he can analyze himself, or worse, permitted to insist there is nothing so askew as to require fundamental treatment.

The first step in this reformation could be confrontation, wherein we are forced to look at and beyond the rationalizations, denials, and fantasies, that "improve on" reality, and be shown what we really are doing. Leites has now done this, and he has done it as it has never been done before. He has done it not by bringing new data or theory to psychoanalysis but by simply, insistently, maddeningly, relentlessly arguing for the application of good sense to psychoanalytic thinking.

Charming he is not, nor is he graceful or tactful. But, if one can stand to read him, he is extremely effective.

Certainly, this is not to say that the job of invigorating psychoanalysis would then be complete, for Leites has tried only to reveal the extent of treatment of the pathology, not to do the creative work that might then follow.

His technique is simple and can be taught to any psychoanalyst in a few minutes; what is uncertain is whether the attitude can be instilled. But if made part of a candidate's training, it would be a great contribution to the future of psychoanalysis.

The trouble is, he is difficult to read. He never lets up, no softness, no imprecision, no catering to the reader—just a steady rapping at our heads, each blow equally hard, equally spaced, none even vicious enough that, while more traumatic, would at least change the rhythm and style. (However . . . when I first read the manuscript, it seemed without humor; the second time it was a bit wry. Now, for me, it is filled with humor.) So I, who also feel hammered, am here now to ask the next reader, because this is important, to suffer the miseries.

In an important way, it is a shame he has chosen as special targets some of our finest people, for the work that has sprung from these

4

workers has been enriching to psychoanalysis. But, undoubtedly, to have taken on smaller game would have been to risk being brushed aside. Having gone for some of the best, Leites must be confronted on his own terms. The reader should not suppose that it is only these workers, or even identity, identification, and ego psychology against which Leites is railing but against the glorification of psychoanalytic theorizing. (He is not concerned here with psychoanalysis as practice— as a method for treatment and for learning about human behavior, or even as a strategy to be employed in the intellectual joys of applied psychoanalysis.)

Leites speaking:

Renaming a more or less plainly described event by a "concept" may give the impression of having explained it. (p. 132)

Fancy dress may hide not only familiarity but also weakness. (p. 135)

The obscure is surrounded by the familiar, and the multiplication of words militates against the awareness that their referent is in doubt." (p. 55)

Increasingly so, as time passes: "progress" in psychoanalytic theory has led to "a better integration, an ever clearer connection" of its parts: a point repeatedly asserted, but not proved, not even illustrated. (p. 165)

Focusing on intellectual operations may help in reducing one's awareness of not yet having formulated a hypothesis. (p. 170)

Central words of analytic theory . . . may be joined by terms from the advanced vocabulary of the human sciences at large . . . (p. 236)

It seems natural that pertinent evidence, though easily accessible, will just not be perceived or presented as long as it would overthrow a reigning sentence: attention to it has to wait for a revolution in the palace of theory. (p. 244)

The dreadful rigor he applies to the authors he investigates can equally well be applied to all the syntax of psychoanalysis; in doing so, we may be humbled. It would certainly be painful for me to have him do the same with what I write—and he could. (It is easier to see the flawed logic in others' works.) If he would make us so careful that we would at first be inarticulate, at worst we shall only lose our addiction to rotund phrases.

Leites yearns for clarity above all else; he does not complain because the findings of psychoanalysis are incomplete, the treatment techniques still being discovered, or its theory unfinished. What pains him is that analysts do not say what they think, or worse, do not know what they think.

One may—as with nonconstructs—declare one's indecision: without indicating to what it is due, hence what would render decision possible. When Hartmann, discussing in a passage quoted above one of his "assumptions" ("the use, in countercathexis, of energy withdrawn from the drives is more general if they are of an aggressive than if they are of a libidinal nature"), declares that "I would not dare to decide whether or not it will prove to be correct." One may add that he does not even dare to decide *how* one should decide that question. (pp. 190–191)

Or:

When clarity is so hard to achieve, obscurity may come to appear as an advantage one claims rather than a defect one strives to reduce. "The term 'identification,' Loewald announces, "is used here in . . . loose fashion, so as not to prejudge what might be implied in the concept"—which is presumably as harmful as disclosing one's fallback positions is foolish when negotiating. From the plain fact that many and obscure meanings are currently being given to our words—"when we ask for precise definitions . . . of incorporation, introjection, identification . . . we are not . . . likely to come up with . . . precise agreements"—Berezin seems to conclude to the propriety of this situation: "We have to leave these useful constructs in some kind of hazy balance of understanding"—a contention that might sound less plausible were it made starkly: we ought to leave these words hazy.

Yet what is odd, and rather a problem—his own writing reveals the other side of the coin: if one tries to be scrupulously precise, letting no word hang in ambiguity, then one so riddles a thought with parentheses or footnotes, interruptions in midair for additions, quotes within quotes—a tangle of clarifications—that clarifying thoughts become unclear. Happily, one can reread until the complications are overcome. If one cares, Leites can be understood—whereas one can read and reread words like identity, or neutralization, or narcissism indefinitely and never be sure what an author means. Perhaps, reader, like me you will find Leites hard but not impossible, while you might come to suspect that most psychoanalysts' theoretical writing is impossible but not hard.

This study is unique. Although there have been sporadic yelps of pain before—both in and out of psychoanalytic writings—at its defective logic (tautologies, syllogisms, nondefining definitions), Leites is the first to subject a particular body of data—actual writings in a representative area—to such an extensive (and devastating) analysis.

Leites' focus on logic and syntax and my complaining tone may irritate the reader who thinks of the worlds that analysis has discovered. But that central fact he and I take for granted; it is precisely that which should impel us to perfect the formulation of truths so important. This book is one-sided and can safely be left so only because the other side is vast—the data of analysis and much of the conceptualization that orders these data.

In the best of all intellectual worlds, it would make no difference who makes a statement. If Copernicus said that the sun was the center of a celestial system and not the earth, confirmation would not be denied were he mad. It may make it harder or easier for us to accept an observation if we know the man who is speaking, but that is all there is to it; it makes it easier or harder, it does not make the statement more or less true. And so I am troubled anticipating readers who will read this monograph in the same disreputable manner with which I sometimes approach an author if I know a little about him. Still, in a manner antipathetic to all that this work of Leites stands for, let me attempt to disarm the reader by saying that Leites is not trying to bite one of the hands that feed him. Least of all is he one of those members of psychoanalytic organizations who, no longer feeling that analysis (in any meaning) has anything to offer, tells us that his arguments are reasonable because he is a member of a psychoanalytic organization. Let us not even psychoanalyze Leites in absentia, as we analysts tend to do (when we disagree). If Leites had horns and cloven feet (worse, were a Professor of Political Science rather than a practicing psychoanalyst) such information would not affect the possibility that his arguments are valid.

In other words, I beg you to read and meet Leites head-on: with his data. Show him (don't simply declare it) that he is wrong when he says that Hartmann *et al.* do not indicate what clinical evidence would define "neutralization" or separate it out in the real world from "sublimation" (p. 202). Argue with him that it is not true that they and, sadly enough, almost all of us who write or think psychoanalysis are too concerned (the critical word is "too," not "concerned") with nonexistent "things" like "identity" or "cathexis" without saying what aspects of people's conduct we have decided to name thus.

Most of us know that psychoanalysis was founded upon and still

7

founds itself daily upon observation. While this, for Leites (and me), is the core of an optimism for the future of psychoanalysis as theory and practice, as research tool and contributor to an understanding of man's psychology, this optimism is minuscule as compared to that of analysts who say psychoanalysis is now a science. They may base their belief on the fact that, valuing science, they would like to be scientists; or because of some inflated idea that every psychoanalysis is an experiment; or because of consensual validation: we think we are right when we tell each other so frequently enough; or because, as we all agree, the heart of psychoanalysis—and its glory—is an unrelenting search for precise observations, as uncontaminated as possible by bias or faulty methodology. I believe it is especially the last that gives the sense of conviction that one is a scientist if an analyst.

Why are analysts so damned insistent on being considered scientists? Artists do not claim to be, and yet their careers are honorable, they stir us, cure our pain, and, on occasion, overturn history. All that should be satisfying, but not so for us analysts. What we must be, apparently, is scientists. I suppose this means that we would rather be right than good.

And that is the essence of science: to be accurate (right). A field becomes a science when it develops techniques that have feedback mechanisms in them to guarantee ever-increasing accuracy. Those well-known thoughts apply to the ideal of the analyst—but not to the performance so far. What is implicitly troubling Leites—and me explicitly—is that while analysts idealize precise observation, predictability, control of variables, sharing of data with others to rule out misperceptions and misinterpretations, laboratories for the creation of models, and methods for correcting defects, none of these exists in psychoanalysis; more than that, the analyst seems not only not to miss them but, when an attempt is made to introduce them, he is apt to feel they are unnecessary—or even harmful—to his "science."

One has to be careful, of course. Science is not a terminus at which one arrives but a process moving toward infinity. Each of the sciences has shaped itself in the past with the above criteria, only to find itself in a tighter and tighter bind of orthodoxy in which only the known was proved, so that there was no way out except by an "unscientific" explosion of intuition (Kuhn, Koestler). So, thank you, but I know already that science is not an absolute. That is still no excuse for saying that anything we choose to call a science is one because it shares with science the quality "tentativeness." Not even good intentions make a field a science. Fenichel's phrase in this regard is just right: "By opposing the idea that 'mind is brain' and by emphasizing strongly the existence of the mental spheres and the inadequacy of physical and scientific methods to deal with it, he [Freud] *won this terrain for science"* (Fenichel, *Psychoanalytic Theory of Neuroses,* page 4) (my italics). That is right: he won the terrain for science. But it still has to be populated by science. Of course, whether one labels psychoanalysis a science or not has no importance. The purpose of this discussion is not to apply a label but to get at what should underly it: are the methods of inquiry now favored by psychoanalysis likely to lead to the answers to our questions?

No field accepted as a science:

1. Has such a high amount of reference to authority to bolster an argument.

2. Can demonstrate its data as little to others.

3. Has a higher ratio of theory over observation.

4. Prefers as much to refine concepts by reference to other concepts rather than observations.

5. Uses metaphor and analogy so profusely.

6. Has such disagreement among peers to so many key words.

7. Strings together to such an extent one unproved statement after another, using the devices "it seems," "probably," and the like to arrive at a conclusion worded with the same assurance one would use if he had strung together a series of demonstrable facts to arrive at a new conclusion.

8. Has such a lag in publication (proving that what is "new" is not new enough to cause editors to rush).

The psychoanalytic writer is an essayist, not scientist; there are few scientific papers in the literature, but many, many essays.

We all agree that at the beginning of the process called science is precise observation; yet we also agree that observation must be refined and synthesized, for it is blind without concepts that unify and focus. Conceptualization has power for improving observation and prediction, but it fatally attracts intellects to exalt their concepts and so distort their vision, i.e., propagandize. This is too often true with some analysts, who, with minimal data, attempt to soar, powered by theory alone. The speed with which some leave observations behind and begin theorizing can be so fast that one suspects that, with an extreme of efficiency, facts would become completely superfluous.

The temptation to theorize without data is increased by the privacy and trust without which analytic treatment cannot proceed. As a result, no analyst has ever reported what he observed, nor has anyone else seen it. What science can make *that* claim? This is not our fault. What is our fault is that so many of us do not admit to regretting it. Some have argued cutely that in astronomy and theoretical physics one also cannot observe or experiment directly; but that is about all that psychoanalysis and such fields have in common; for the latter have been intent on precision about *what* evidence is required in any given case much more than analysts. To act in science is to be implacably oriented on returning to events, perhaps not right away but after a measured span of indirection. There is no such adamant drive in the psychoanalytic credo. (There was in Freud.)

Might there not be something wrong if, after 30 or more years of labor on ego psychology, there are no generally accepted definitions of such words as ego, ego functions, self, self-representation, identity, ego identify, self-identity—no way to know precisely which properties in the real world (i.e., behavior) an author has in mind when he uses one of them? That there were problems in definition when ego psychology moved into focus 30 years ago was fine. That these problems are still unsolved—for all the back-slapping about advances in theory— indicates disorder. Leites mercilessly demonstrates (not merely asserting without evidence) that an analytic concept is more likely to be tested by another analytic concept than by reality.

The crucial challenge in Leites' monograph is this: "How much does it matter what a word means, precisely?" That is the test for any science, and one does not become a scientist simply because he *says* he would like to be precise.

Our marvelous pneumatic vocabulary; reading the psychoanalytic literature is like reading art criticism. If an author uses these words, will you know what he is talking about?: libido, narcissism, cathexis, internalization, instinct, active, passive, neutralization, psychosis, neurosis, acting-out, identity, ego identity, self-identity, ego adaptation, aggression, fixation, homosexuality, unconscious, Unconscious, countertransference, incorporation, phallic phase, fetish, psychic apparatus, masochism, introjection, insight, hysteria, identification, projection, bisexuality, psychic energy, castration anxiety, instinctual drive, drive, need, sexuality, sexualization, self, self-image, self-representation and, even, psychoanalysis. These terms *are* our "science," and in some manner they refer to events in reality. They are terribly important, for they grope to make sense of the most complicated of realities, psychic functioning. My point is not that it is useless to develop a technical vocabulary but rather, as with Leites, that the way this vocabulary develops is leading us to "mythology disguised as reporting."

Astonishingly, on the one hand, analysts declare they do not agree on the meanings of these words, and on the other, continue to use them. To accept such a vocabulary is to walk on water. One wants to cry out, as Moses does in the joke when St. Peter, thinking to imitate him, steps on the waves and sinks: "Schmuck! Step on the stones."

What kind of business is it where a worker can build his reputation on inventing a word or redefining an old one?

10

Where would we be without "cathexis," "psychic energy," "libido"; suppose each author were forced, at the point where he would have used such a concept, to use instead simple descriptive words, immediately related to the events for which the Greek or Latin is applied? Why did psychoanalysts ever think that writing in the erudite style adds substance to one's thoughts? Yes, most ideas are more acceptable when made decorative, as in poetry, where ideas are often subordinate to style and beauty. In addition, psychoanalysis, like all of psychology, is the child of philosophy, and, rather old-fashioned, still prefers stately ponderousness ("sentences of large scope and low cost") to modest clarity. Some analysts seem to believe that por-tentousness demonstrates profundity, objectivity, and scientific attitude. How else can one explain the universal habit among analysts of talking about "the" mother and "the" father when the clinical data being reported would justify saying "his" mother and "his" father?

In a different age, the following would be recognized as a parody (Leites speaks):

"A man who sits reading the evening newspaper and then gets up and walks into the dining room to eat"—this is the deceptively simple event boldly chosen by Gaarder to exhibit the power of modern theory. In fact, this man "can be seen" as "having gone through a set of stages": "(1) He initially had a relatively high cathexis of the visual apparatus, a relatively high attention cathexis attached to the internal representation of the newspaper, and a low cathexis of the body image. Then there is a shift, with a relative decathexis of the visual apparatus, a relative decathexis of the attention capacity, increased cathexis of the sense of dimensional space, and a cathexis of the automatic muscu-lar function of walking. Also, there is probably a change in the thought cathexis as well as the thought content as it changes from the newspaper to the meal and the internalized representations of those with whom the meal will be eaten (why not the inter-nalized representation of the newspaper and meal?—N.L.)." It is thus that "an economic model of ego function" masters "something which we could formerly take for granted, but were not able to fit into a theoretical framework." Such feats are within the reach of our four words—identification, internalization, introjection, incorporation—as well as of "ego function."

As certain early findings become stale, and new insights hard to come by, there is a temptation to procure the sensation of freshness by a change of language.

Instant generalization, the quick grab for the universal, is a disorder of analysts. One would almost think that we are trying to disguise what we are really saying, which is usually interesting but not earth-shaking, converting it, not by data but by language, into profundities that substitute philosophy for science, thus:

Since all ego actions aim at gratification of the self on the outside (personal or inanimate) object, they represent at the same time object-related and narcissistic pursuits which must involve temporary changes in the cathexes of self and object representations and in the process of discharge of self-directed as well as of object-directed (libidinal, aggressive, and neutralized) psychic energy. Normal ego functioning presupposes a sufficient, evenly distributed, enduring libidinal cathexis of both object and self-representations. The action will arise from an initial hypercathexis of the specific object image and of the intended function with libidinal, aggressive, and neutralized energy. Besides, ego action requires the spur of a concomitant libidinal hypercathexis of the self-representations, which will encourage and guarantee the success of the action. This libidinal cathexis extends to the representations, on the one hand, of the intended function, and of the body parts and organs to be employed for it, and, on the other hand, of the whole self as an entity. The rising cathexis of the latter manifests itself in general feelings of self-confidence preceding and stimulating first the cathexis of the executive organs and then the action.

The increase of object cathexis puts the drive in motion, determines its direction, and leads, by way of drive-discharge processes, to completion of the action. In the course of successful actions, intense, rich feelings of identity are frequently experienced. After successful action, whatever excess libido is left is withdrawn from the object image and is turned back to the other objects and to the self-representations. Their rising cathexis finds expression in feelings of satisfaction in the body (or mental) parts used for the action, and in the general increase of self-esteem. I may add that libidinal hypercathexis of the self-representations, along with an aggressive hypercathexis of the object representations, is characteristic of narcissistic, aggressive, or sadistic attitudes toward the object; furthermore, that an insufficient libidinal object cathexis or an insufficient initial narcissistic cathexis may result in the partial inhibition of ego functions. A libidinal hypercathexis of the object—along with an aggressive hypercathexis of the self-representations—is bound to produce failure, and corresponds to masochistic or self-destructive behavior. But a major withdrawal and shift of cathexis from the object representation to the self-representation, such as occurs mostly in normal and pathological forms of regression, eventually leads to inactivity or to general inhibition of ego activity.

Leites says (p. 200), "In the rare case when a definition is given, it may consist in replacing a word by a nobler synonym." As you shall see, his monograph is a listing of varieties of this subtle sinning of psychoanalysts, of intellectuals, wherein style (imaginative foreplay) substitutes for the full experience. Intellectuals, in this sense, are fops, more concerned with the elegance of their dance steps and with the inhabiting of salons. This is certainly not to say that graceful writing, cleverness, high intelligence, or even erudition (the capacity to quote authorities aptly) are not marvelous when used to adorn good data. However, we must not forget that the data are not strengthened by good presentation but merely made pleasanter for the audience to receive and, when it comes to data (rather than art), in the long run not better than dull honesty.

Rich or flat in delivery, the ultimate test for a psychoanalyst is honesty and the desire to be clear, as opposed to being brilliant or poetic so that these effects draw attention away from lack of data or weak argument.

The inexorable conversion of hunch to hypothesis to theory to law to "concrete observation" is frightening. If only the words would stay put and concept remain concept. That they all too often do not contributes to the odd atmosphere one sometimes senses when reading at the highest level of psychoanalytic thinking. (We could as well be talking now of anthropologists, historians, sociologists, political scientists, and others. But of course we shall not.)

Too frequently, an analytic author strings together what he believes to be one proved law after another, while I am getting the impression that each affirmation, so taken for granted by the author, is really the title of an experiment yet to be performed, any one of which would be a revolutionary contribution to the world of science if only it could be demonstrated. When these run one upon the other without hesitation or uncertainty, the effect is deafening. Take the following:

The first form of anxiety is of a persecutory nature. The working of the death instinct within—which according to Freud is directed against the organism—gives rise to the fear of annihilation, and this is the primordial cause of persecutory anxiety. Furthermore, from the beginning of postnatal life (I am not concerned here with prenatal processes) destructive impulses against the object stir up fear of retaliation. These persecutory feelings from inner sources are intensified by painful external

13

experiences, for, from the earliest days onward, frustration and discomfort arouse in the infant the feeling that he is being attacked by hostile forces. Therefore the sensations experienced by the infant at birth and the difficulties of adapting himself to entirely new conditions give rise to persecutory anxiety. The comfort and care given after birth, particularly the first feeding experiences, are felt to come from good forces. In speaking of "forces" I am using a rather adult word for what the young infant dimly conceives of as objects, either good or bad. The infant directs his feelings of gratification and love toward the "good" breast, and his destructive impulses and feelings of persecution toward what he feels to be frustrating, i.e., the "bad" breast. At this stage splitting processes are at their height, and love and hatred as well as the good and bad aspects of the breast are largely kept apart from one another. The infant's relative security is based on turning the good object into an ideal one as a protection against the dangerous and persecuting object. These processes—that is to say splitting, denial, omnipotence, and idealization—are prevalent during the first three or four months of life (which I termed the "paranoid-schizoid position" [1946]). In these ways at a very early stage persecutory anxiety and its corollary, idealization, fundamentally influence object relations.

The primal processes of projection and introjection, being inextricably linked with the infant's emotions and anxieties, initiate object relations; by projecting, i.e., deflecting libido and aggression on to the mother's breast, the basis for object relations is established; by introjecting the object, first of all the breast, relations to internal objects come into being. My use of the term "object relations" is based on my contention that the infant has from the beginning of postnatal life a relation to the mother (although focusing primarily on her breast) which is imbued with the fundamental elements of an object relation, i.e., love, hatred, phantasies, anxieties, and defenses.

One usually can see clinical data behind the jargon but is never sure just what the observations are. Granted it is impossible to reproduce any moment of a psychoanalytic hour. Still, that is our problem, and if we do not solve it, we remain outside of science, and our statements, no matter how positively phrased, can only be accepted by others as possibilities, not as laws. When we listen to a patient, the slightest inflection, pronunciation, hesitation, drawing in of breath, or even shift of a finger can change a meaning. *These* are our observations, and in reporting them, they are susceptible to our distortions. We all know this, and it should make us modest.

14

Probably Leites' most painful technique is to take a sentence with an apparently heavy load of meaning, cross out the words that are only fillers, transform other words into their synonyms, and have the sentence then collapse before our eyes. This reduction of the hot air content is desolating and at the same time fascinating (especially when done to someone other than oneself).

"As *ego development* proceeds, abstraction from the concrete situation becomes possible": Did it not, would the ego still enjoy "development"? (We are, as in an instance cited above, left with a homely truth: as time passes, abstraction . . . becomes possible—unless it does not.) (p. 217)

"The recognition of inner demands," the authors propose, "broadens *the field of objective* cognition of inner reality, *of self-knowledge*": cross out the unnecessary (to meaning) words I have italicized, and you may no more want to pronounce the sentence. (p. 219)

Words whose omission would not seem to impoverish the meaning of a sentence may facilitate its being pronounced. That the oral, anal, and phallic phases influence the superego may be taken for granted; yet it is worth recalling that "*on the side of the drives* the phallic phase as well as the *earlier* oral and anal *libidinal* phases influence *the general and individual features of the system* superego." (p. 233)

That, enraged by another, I may proceed to hurt myself if I do not lash out at him, is classical; but it is worth recalling that "the *economic function* of the *external source* of unpleasurable feeling is . . . [in part] its *function* as *catalyst*, i.e., . . . [as rendering possible] the discharge of otherwise self-destructive energies aroused by the existence of this *external source*." The more I believe I am living up to my aspirations, the better I feel about myself? Yes, and Edith Jacobson has shown that "the degrees of self-esteem *reflect* the *harmony* or *discrepancy* between *self-representation* and *the wishful concept of the self*." All men are talkers (except those who aren't). Rather, "*verbalization* is part of the *function* of the *apparatus* of all men . . . ." It matters to know just what it is in me that I feel so good about: "In this *context* [which is not pertinent here—N.L.] another point might become *relevant*, though little is known about it so far, namely, the habitual or *situational representation* of the various *localizations* of *narcissism* in the *self-image*." (p. 234)

In another mode, an event too obvious to be enunciated starkly may become speakable if one also alludes to the acts of mind supposedly connected with its being mentioned. One might not want to bother recalling that education aims at socialization, and still desire to affirm that "*from the general biological point of view* . . . education aims . . . at . . . socialization." That education may have goals beyond preventing neurosis seems all too plausible; less so, perhaps, that "the goal of education *cannot be satisfactorily defined in terms of the concept of* neurosis-prevention alone." Though the discovery that hurting is fun has been made by many laymen, it is for the specialist to arrive at "the realization that the discharge of aggression and the destruction of objects *may be considered* pleasurable per se." Recalling that the superego has not been there from the beginning, while the drives and the ego have, the authors do not infer that this is why regression of the superego has less of a span, but rather that "this is one reason why regression is *harder to conceptualize* with respect to the superego than with respect to the drives and the ego." We would readily believe that the adult's pleasures would be smaller than they are had he not, apart from maturing, also learned since birth; but it seems worth noting that "since the formation of the ego *can in part be described as* a learning process . . . *one might say that* in man the gratification of . . . drives is guaranteed by learning." The ego aims, among other things, at interfering with the expression of drives? That is, "a large sector of the ego's function *can also be described from the angle of* its inhibiting nature"—a focusing on the activities of the theorist, which is, in this case, balanced by an envisagement of essences: "Defense is a . . . *expression* of . . . [the ego's] inhibiting *nature*." The child develops not only in psychosexual respects, but also with regard to aggression, object relations, ego functions? Yes, to be sure. But it can be put differently: "*Descriptions of* developmental *problems will not only have to refer to the data concerning* psychosexual development; *they will also have to include data on* the development of aggression, on that of object relations, and at least some of the key functions of the ego." Adult character is determined by the development of ego, of drives and of object relations? This is not the only way it can be said: ". . . *a satisfactory description of genetic considerations must simultaneously take into account* the development of the ego, the instinctual development and that of object relations. *Only on this basis does characterology become valuable.* . . ." If I am infatuated with myself, I may so be with regard to something other than my sexual prowess—or: As narcissism may be either instinctual or neutralized, "*a description from the angle of* narcissism *does not*

16

account for the distinction between 'sexual overestimation' [why the quotes?—N.L.] of the self, as we find it, e.g., in megalomania, and other forms of self-cathexis." (pp. 237–238)

The environment acts upon the ego? No, *"differences* in the environment act *directly* upon the *development* of ego *functions."*

Object relations are affected by the ego? Rather, "satisfactory 'object relations' *can only be assessed if we also consider* . . . ego development." (p. 245)

Defense influences and is influenced by ego? Yes, *"there is no doubt, and I mentioned it before*, that defense is . . . under the influence of other processes in the ego and, on the other hand, that defense intervenes in a . . . variety of . . . processes in the ego; *this I discussed as an essential aspect of developmental psychology."* (p. 245)

One mustn't lose perspective, however; Leites does not believe psychoanalysis has no substance. In fact, he takes it for granted that its substance is crucial for understanding psychic function. However, it is not his task to review the data or to develop a more efficient theory on which to hang the observations. He has set himself the job only of clearing away debris; he wants to show that words that talk about words cannot substitute for words that talk about events. So, he leaves for practicing analysts the gathering of better data.

A caution to those who would misunderstand: Leites knows that clarity is not enough. He does not say his preciseness must be used all the time. He reminds us how to test an idea but knows his technique generates no originality, only tempering originality with caution. It serves in that less romantic category of scientific endeavor called confirmation, and, like prediction or statistics only checks out possibilities to see if they might have an existence in reality.

His technique is used in all the sciences accepted as sciences. To the extent that science requires one to be logical, Leites is telling us to do so in order to make more science out of what now, and at that, too rarely, is art. (Since we all know that taking the art out of science kills science, I need not expand on that.) Leites is not implying by his example that the psychoanalytic literature should never break forth out of the rigid correctness that he delineates. One must begin somewhere, and poorly defined words are a beginning. In addition, there are events and ideas in psychoanalysis so elusive that they can still be handled only by analogy and metaphor. We come upon danger only when we believe metaphor is the reality for which it fumbles.

"Green in nature is one thing, green in literature another. Nature and letters seem to have a natural antipathy; bring them together and they tear each other to pieces." (Virginia Woolf, *Orlando*). Psychoanalysis imagines itself to be, could be, almost is, in a beautifully tense position between the "two cultures" (C. P. Snow), the sciences and the humanities. And yet psychoanalysis has so far failed to put itself in this position because its pretentions to be a science were not backed by the practices mentioned above.

In a recent essay on this subject, Bennis (1969) ("A Psychoanalytic Inquiry into the 'Two Cultures' Dilemma") quotes Graves: "The scientist concentrates on analysis and classification of external fact even if fact be beautifully disguised as mathematic relations; whereas the poet concentrates on discovery of internal truth . . . [the scientist] is healthy, sober, cooperative, reliable, industrious; though with little perception of the magical and emotionally underdeveloped."

We analysts would like to be both, should be both, and probably could be both. We shall not be unless, at the very least, we do as Leites indicates.

Leites recently wrote the following: "Modes of thinking that are of questionable validity, such as those examined in my monograph, *may* be 'factors of production' of high 'productivity' (to use the language of economics): they may *cause* the discovery of certain insights, which, once obtained, can be separated from their faulty initial derivation and be given a sound one. This is the case with some of Freud's theorizing, as a study would, I believe, reveal. But there the clinical payoff (product) is never far off and almost always major. In contrast: recent theorizing, as exemplified in *Ego*, but also in *Identity*. With the passing of time, theorizing in psychoanalysis has probably become both more faulty and less productive. It is that which may justify the kind of analysis I've attempted."

We need more like Leites; he is too alone (not completely—but let us leave it at that without citing the others). Although there are people outside psychoanalysis who are also dismayed at our untidy habits of arguments, they are too easily brushed aside as being inconsequential for lack of analytic training (not always for lack of correctness). If Leites were questioning techniques of analytic practice or challenging the accuracy of reported findings, one would ask that his challenge come from his own skill in technique, but he has not questioned technique, findings, or the fundamental postulates (e.g., unconscious processes, conflict, resistance, transference). These can defend themselves with quiet success.

If it were up to Leites, the rules of our game would change so that an explanation that is simple, logical, even superficial, or—worst

18

sin of all—a cliché would *not* be discarded, unless it does not fit the facts. Conversely, while it may be enjoyed, an explanation should not be accepted only because it is poetic, beautiful, imaginative, or even original:

> In reality two dangers threaten the cell in the process of reproduction. On the one hand, the conjugation of two cells implies the penetration of one substance by another which remains active and alive and has not, as happens in nutrition, first been rendered innocuous by the digestive juices and its prior death. And, on the other hand, the act of fission involves a disintegration of the substance which if continued would result in its annihilation.
>
> Now I think that the substance is biologically aware of these two dangers, that they are transmitted throughout the whole course of evolution down to man himself and that they thus constitute the most primitive sources both of the perforation complex and the castration complex which we discover at work in women and in men.
>
> The fear of penetration of the protoplasm is reflected in the dread of penetration felt by so many virgins and is no doubt at the root of many cases of frigidity in women. It can provide the foundation of the imposing edifice (to which all the accretions of the superego contribute) that we know under the form of symptoms.
>
> The fear of disintegration of the protoplasm would in turn be found to underlie the castration complex. In order to perpetuate its existence every individual must abandon a part of its substance, which becomes detached from it. But the narcissistic integrity of the substance suffers in consequence. And this narcissistic aversion to fission, transferred to the executive and representative organ of procreation, can serve as the foundation of the castration complex, with all the accretions derived from phylogenetic and ontogenetic experiences.

Such unashamed theorizing is an occupational hazard of psychoanalysts. Perhaps our practicing in the midst of fantasies and wishes must be balanced by noble thoughts. Perhaps our practicing in the midst of bewildering detail makes us yearn to leave this disorder for theory that reduces the confusion. And yet, as we create such theory in words of seeming clarity (which however are secretly known to be vague), our language will permit the infiltration of hidden wishes. Perhaps we ease the strain of refraining from—and yet still immersing ourselves in—our patient's infantile drives by replacing daytime deprivation with evening indulgence. Not that this indulgence is as instinctual as what our patients would get us into, but nonetheless, we

19

may feel a right to omnipotent speculation after a day's work at renunciation.

In the daytime practice, one is aware of the limitations of his powers, but at night he can regain his magnificence. By day, he is at times silent in his creative puzzlement, humbly subordinated to his patient's facts, while at night he becomes lord of concepts. By day, he swims, resisting the undertow from the patient, which can endanger the analysis; at night with his theory, he is back on shore.

The daytime analyst is humble, the nighttime writer grandiose. The daytime analyst is attacked, the nighttime theorist the attacker; pressure built up in the daytime is released at night. If one had to be as scrupulously skeptical at night as he is during the day, he would have to be his own attacker, and one needs relief from that. In our practice we try very hard to say what needs to be said exactly right so that our patient can comprehend and not be bullied into agreeing; if only the same care were taken in developing theory as in making just the right interpretation.

At this point we again differ from the true sciences: the distance between the narcissism of the first creative thought and the demonstration of the validity of the general rule is far greater there. In them, the creative moment may occur in the same way as in psychoanalysis, but thereafter the rules of the game are different: in the sciences, after one makes his claim, he states what can be done to prove the claim wrong so that the theory can be related to evidence. Then a decent interval of time passes in which the test is made, and all the world can see if the theory has withstood the test. Without this, there is, as Leites has once put it, "a breach in the wall through which primitive tendencies can flow in."

In all three parts of this monograph, the results are rather similar: Leites leaves a residue of tested and still surviving material, which, when one recovers from the shock and loss of the rest, is in fact a solid foundation on which to build further. To exemplify how his technique can help, let me note what he has done to an area of "philosophic nobility: identity."

I read the first report on "gender identity" about eight years ago. The term "identity" was used in innocence, for I thought everyone knew what identity was. In time, a definition really was needed in order to support a heavy load of data—and then a review of the literature revealed the following terms, not one of which was defined: ego identity, inner identity, fixed identity, behavioral identity, existential identity, primary identity, real identity, self-identity, entity and identity, sense of identity, personal identity, identity principle, identity consciousness, identity pattern, identity formation, identity theme.

Are they synonyms or not; how much do they overlap; what observations is each meant to designate? "The new words—familiar in their resonance and excitingly obscure in their significance."

What I had been looking for was a simple but nonetheless communicating word with which to enclose certain data. In trying to find sources of masculinity and femininity in relatively normal people, my research has been for years aimed at some of the most abnormal: transsexuals (people who are convinced, despite normal anatomy, that they belong to the opposite sex). In studying such people (primarily by treating them), I had found that certain fundamentals of their masculinity or femininity, as expressed in behavior and fantasies, including dreams, were clearly present and unalterably fixed long before the classical oedipal phase, long before that time when, according to classical psychoanalytic theory, unequivocal masculinity or femininity should occur. In addition, I noted the obvious, which practically everyone else has also noticed but which some analysts denied for theoretical reasons: the same is true for more normal people. For instance, little girls are not simply blighted little boys until, by means of the most incredible patchwork, they salvage a broken femininity, but rather little girls are prone to decided femininity as early as a year or so of age.

I postulated that the earliest stage in the development of a sense of masculinity or femininity was a sense of maleness in normal males and of femaleness in normal females. I called this sense "core gender identity," by which I meant the conviction that one belongs either to the male or female sex. Since this conviction is present throughout life, coloring all that one does, I, again innocently, used the word "identity."

I further postulated that the core gender identity—this usually subliminal, ever-present awareness of one's sex—was produced by:

1. Biological factors
   a. embryological
   b. CNS Centers
2. Genital anatomy, which signals to parents they have a boy or a girl.
3. Sex assignment and rearing
   a. parents' personalities
   b. parents' attitudes (conscious, preconscious, unconscious) about *this* son or daughter's maleness and masculinity or femaleness and femininity
   c. other people's (society's) attitudes about maleness and masculinity or femaleness and femininity
4. "Imprinting," "conditioning," "shaping": the effect of being raised from birth by a female (mother).

21

Later events, such as the phallic phase, penis envy, and oedipal conflicts were considered crucial for later stages in the development of masculinity and femininity but not in creating the core gender identity.

While it is not appropriate to review the findings that lie behind each of these factors or the degree of assuredness one can have in accepting them as contributory, these data are considerable. Certainly, it looked like I was in pretty good shape with the term "identity," for not only did it have the sanction of many of the great minds of psychoanalysis and other careful, nonanalytic thinkers, but when I used the term, I was referring to replicable data.

At around this time, Leites wrote his manuscript on identity. Let me quote extensively so that you can see what he has done to all of us who have needed that word.

> Neither the producer nor the consumers of such normal phrases seem to query the proliferation of close-by words, the appearance of a variety of which reassures rather than bewilders: It might indeed be the stark repetition of a naked noun such as "identity" that finally would make one demand that rules for its use be indicated. (pp. 110–111)

> Given this manifold of implicit definitions, the stable letters and sounds of the word itself may come to be seen more important than its shifting and uncertain meanings. (p. 114)

> Intending a word to *designate* a certain class of events, one may be dismayed by discovering to how many other classes it has already referred in previous usage. But if one desires, usually without consciousness, a word to be *an entity in its own right*, one may delight in the progressive revelation of its riches. (p. 121)

> Instead of rejoicing in the plentitude of "identity" as comprising, say, both the sense of permanence and the sense of difference that may thus already seem furnished with a common ground, we might have to deplore the poverty of our knowledge of their relationships; for the discovery of which, once the verbal provided by the rich concept is broken, we are thrown back on the arduous observation of events, in the place of the reverent contemplation of a word. (p. 122)

> When Erikson chooses the words "ego identity" to designate the growing child's "conviction that the ego is learning . . . steps towards a tangible . . . future," one might be tempted to replace the two words "ego identity" with the five "sense of adequacy

about growth." Again, it might be difficult to prove that this increment of three words would make formulations unmanageable, but easy to show that the (by some) valued sense of possessing a precious verbal entity would be lost: once more, the five words are all too clear and much too humble. (p. 123)

Though renouncing "concepts" is apt to entail pronouncing (a few) more words, it is also likely to save energy: compare, for each of the cases cited, the disquisitions stimulated by a portentous word and inhibited by a humble one. But that is just the trouble: simple terms make it difficult to expend one's ardor on them; they direct it toward the world itself, a notably less tractable object. (p. 123)

It is, observes Erikson about what disturbs young people, primarily the inability to settle on an "occupational identity"—or, simply, an occupation? ("Settling" on it, I am apt to think of myself as one having done so.) I could name several pairs of passages belonging to the class of which the following is a member. The author's text: "Men whose *ego identity* thrives on military service sometimes break down after discharge, when it appears that the war provoked them into the usurpations of more ambitious *prototypes* than their more restricted peacetime *identities* could afford to sustain." (my emphases) My version: Men who thrive on military service sometimes break down after discharge, when it appears that the war provoked them to higher ambitions than they could sustain in peacetime. . . .

Familiar points in fancy dress: The author's text: "In the *remnants* of the Sioux Indians' *identity* the prehistoric past is a powerful psychological reality. The conquered tribe behaved as if guided by a life plan consisting of passive resistance to the present which does fail to *reintegrate the identity remnants* of the economic past; and of dreams of restoration in which the future would lead back into the past, time would again become ahistoric, space unlimited, activity boundlessly centrifugal, the buffalo supply inexhaustible." (my emphases) My version: The conquered Sioux engaged in passive resistance to the present, which stood in contrast with the economic past; and entertained dreams of restoration in which life would again become changeless, space unlimited, activity boundlessly centrifugal, and the buffalo supply inexhaustible.

I have attempted to eliminate—I abstain, for reasons of

space and tedium, from showing why and how in every case—all words that I believe to be unnecessary for the meaning to be conveyed, and to replace fancy language—particularly "identity"—by plain terms. While the point made is thus unchanged, the flavor of the passage is altered: where "identity theory" seemed to be applied, ordinary perception is revealed to be reigning. When Erikson remarks that for a psychoanalyst, a cornerstone of his existence may be provided by a particular psychoanalytic "identity"—a word that he himself puts between quotation marks; thus expressing what misgivings?—I would propose substituting, say: orientation; and the sentence would be harder to pronounce, as its truth would be distressingly evident. The author's text: "Individual students of Freud . . . found their *identity* best suited to certain early theses of his which promised a particular sense of psychoanalytic *identity*. . . ." (my emphases) My version: Individual students of Freud found themselves best suited to certain early theses of his which expressed particular psychoanalytic orientations. (p. 125)

What is happening in such cases would be more readily recognized if one kept in mind an admission (not consciously felt as such, I am sure) made in passing by Jacobson when she speaks of "the building up of a person's character, of his individual personality, *in short of his identity*" (my emphasis). Why, then, the last synonym? Because, still young, it fascinates as the words preceding it did when they had its age; while they are now old, and, hence, merely designative (of a domain rather than of events about which hypotheses are formulated: in how many statements of analytic characterology does the word "character" appear or need to be present?) "Identity," however, being still young, attracts, being a live "concept," as an object of inquiry by itself: to prepare another article on *The Concept of Identity* is still respectable, while to write one more piece on *The Concept of Character* is provincial or odd. (p. 127)

"You would expect," Lichtenstein further affirms, "that man, whose instinctual drives are no more than 'innate dispositions to act in a certain manner,' but no longer automatisms, must find means to 'acquire' an identity." Disregarding the attractive but puzzling quotation marks around "acquire," and guessing from the context that "identity" here stands for "regularity of conduct," the sentence may be thus translated: "Man is acting in fairly regular fashion, because he would perish if he were not"—

a point that seems much less acceptable or interesting than when it puts on "identity" dress. (p. 128)

A sentence . . . may be proffered and received all the more eagerly when it seems difficult to conceive that it be false: what is a sign of malignancy—tautology—is then taken for a token of health.

When Erikson maintains that "there is no feeling of being alive without a sense of ego identity," this, right away, seems all too true. Yet, for the sentence to state a relationship among events rather than words it must be possible to indicate what it would look like to have, for instance, a *low* feeling of being alive together with a *high* sense of ego identity, or a *high* feeling of being alive together with a *low* sense of ego identity. (p. 131)

I would call the "gross product" of "identity's" rise to prominence during the last ten years the totality of hypotheses formulated in that period that (a) contain the word, (b) refer to clinically observable events, (c) were novel in content, and not only in wording, (d) do not seem clearly false. . . .

In my guess this gross product—which I have not attempted to aggregate here—is exceedingly low.

I would call the corresponding "net product" of "identity" theory that fraction of its gross product that could not without notable loss of convenience be reformulated in the language of analysis *minus* "identity."

At this time I believe *that* to be zero. (p. 141)

Finally, Leites extracts qualities implied in the term "identity": (1) the sense of existing; (2) the sense of separateness; (3) the sense of quality; (4) the sense of difference (from others); (5) the sense of permanence; (6) the sense of unity (as against that of being fragmented into several entities); (7) the sense of cohesion (concerning the elements comprised within what is sensed as unity); (8) the impact of beliefs about the self upon senses of self; (9) desires for constancy and variance.

Contemplating this, I wonder what terrible thing Leites has done. Need "identity" be such a big deal? Have we, "the producers and consumers" of this marketable catchword, lost much, rather than gaining some, if we use more specific terms? If these words—like "identity"—are meant to be algebraic sums condensing a multitude of *observable* parts, then, for the sake of those with whom we talk (including our own self), we should be able to identify those observable parts. Only when we have done so can we safely use the big word—"identity"—and have its meaning clear to each of us. And if we never can, let us discover that and so be freed to find new paths of investigation. Isn't something wrong if a word that names a concept rather than a thing has become so precious that we cannot give it up? Especially when one recalls what has happened to the word "identity" after it has gone out into the world, one can see that its lack of definition has fitted all too well the purposes of people who have wanted to persuade rather than understand.

Nonetheless, all of us who have used the term or have contributed related terms believe there is a sense, an awareness, a huge if dim quality in our personality that is an essence of our being. And we know that terms like "ego," "id," or "superego" do not quite cover that sense of being. It is not quite fair to be sitting up front here in an introduction agreeing with Leites on the logical weaknesses in the theoretical structure of the sentences of pyschoanalysis—and at the same time getting great nourishment from these same weaknesses. And, with a corrupt disregard for Leites' cautions, I still admire, use, believe I understand, and remember data that make me use concepts he holds up to us as examples of poor logic. A need for the ideas of Erikson, Greenacre, Lichtenstein, and others he has cited sometimes overrides my agreement with Leites' discipline (for instance Lichtenstein's "identity themes": those lifelong bonds of fate into which parents may lock their children).

I still haven't resolved this—and that is a debt owed to Leites: he forces us to stop thinking we have settled problems we have not settled. In the meanwhile, I am chagrined to discover that the old familiar terms, "masculinity" or "femininity," work well, giving the reader a bit more information than the vaguer "gender identity." Sometimes it takes longer, as when I would have to say regarding a "bisexual" person that "He had a mixed sense of masculinity and femininity," rather than say "He had a mixed gender identity." However, I think, you will know better what I am saying if the former sentence is used rather than the latter, if "the opaque screen of 'identity' " that stands between author and reader can be removed.

In other words, Leites has subjected "identity" to examination and has shown, not just exhorted us to believe, that it has been mismanaged. We owe him a great deal, first because he is willing to review the literature so meticulously and energetically, and second, because, on laying out his data for display, he allows us to make our own decision about the concept.

What Freud says about the splitting of the ego in the process of defense, or Richard Sterba about its splitting in analysis, observes Hartmann, are "examples of intrasystemic *thinking*," rather than *findings* about what goes on within the ego. And thinking is more attractive than observing, even if one is capable of perceiving the unsuspected. (p. 173)

That a sequence of sentences is a repetition of just one point can be hidden from awareness. . . .

If the language of the first sentence is common, what follows is technical. "One distracts a child best by loving attention," the authors observe, only to continue: "Cathexis directed towards action is thus [a dash of causation?—N.L.] transformed into object cathexis." (p. 230)

Such is the attraction of fancy words that they easily cohabit with simple ones that might have sufficed. When a patient, who has come for analysis complaining that he lacks interest in his work, shows affect in the hour when discussing events in the office, and when the analyst then draws his attention to the "contradiction" thus displayed, it might appear all too evident to note that "the patient has been stimulated to observe similar contradictions." But it is stimulating to say and to hear that when this happens "*the structure of the field* is changed." (p. 134)"

One may be plain to start with, on condition of then becoming learned. Having observed that "a healthy ego must . . . allow some of its . . . functions . . . to be put out of action occasionally"—something not too difficult to translate into an evocation of common experience—Hartmann continues for specialists only: "This brings us to the *problem* . . . of a *biological hierarchy* of the ego's *functions* and to the *notion* of the integration of *opposites*. . . ."

Inversely, after expressions that are difficult one may permit oneself to simplicity. Having observed about the "verbal element" in the analytic situation that one "structural function of . . . [this] process" is due to the fact that in the development of the child the "fixing of verbal symbols" is one main road toward "objectivation," Hartmann can say about the similar role of such "fixing" for patients: "It facilitates the patient's way to a better grasp of physical as well as psychic reality." (p. 234–235)

One may avoid the awareness of saying something obvious by alleging a cause of it which on inspection turns out to be a renaming of it. (p. 239)

If an obvious point is linked with one less so, the quality of the latter may be diffused onto the former. (p. 240)

I think a rivalry has existed between writers and psychoanalysts, the result of their arriving at similar insights by both similar and different techniques. Both use observations of the external world shaped by introspection, but each uses different language to report his findings. I am biased and think the writers (the good ones) tend to do better. Novelists, poets, and essayists will throw away in a phrase an insight over which we sweat for a whole paper, if not a book. And, for all our pomposity about communicating, the writer has been clearer, shorter, simpler, and no less profound. Not only that, he reaches us; our own discussions rarely do. Even when correct, we are tedious.

And, so embarrassing, when Leites translates some of our profundities into English, they are not impressive.

One concludes from Leites' sweeping of the stables that, if we refrain from excessive intellectualization, we can commit ourselves more heavily to observations—not only to making them but, second, to developing better techniques for communicating them to others for verification and, third, to being able to judge better others' reports of data. Leites is of course not the only one seeking this, though, regretfully, like most who are, he is not a full member of the analytic community. Among those sympathetic voices is that of Lindzey, whose related paper appeared some months after Leites' manuscript was written. He is worth quoting:

> There is only a tiny quantity of research existing today that is directly relevant to the theory [psychoanalytic] and is considered of reasonable merit by trained investigator and clinician alike. True, there is a considerable bulk of "psychoanalytic research" but it consists largely of delimited, semi-experimental studies that are frequently so remote from the operations implied by psychoanalytic theory as to strain the credulity of the most sympathetic reader. . . . Or else the research consists of clinical reports or observational accounts that are faithful to the theory and its implied method, but are accompanied by so many empirical flaws as to provide evidence only for the devotee. . . .
>
> Formal problems within the psychoanalytic theory are many and manifest. The investigator who wishes to use psychoanalytic theory as a proposition mill to grind out empirical predictions is destined not only to encounter little encouragement from his peers and a maximum of frustration from the slippery world of reality, but also to find little solace in the theory itself. The absence of a clear and explicit axiomatic base, the scarcity of adequate empirical definitions, the ever abundant surplus meaning, the metaphorical excursions, and the almost nonexistent syntax—all of these could be explored at length. Their presence, however, is

undeniable. Almost no one would deny that the theory at present is in a very crude state of development and looks scarcely at all like any theory we would hope to possess eventually. Indeed Nagel, distinguished philosopher of science, was recently moved to characterize psychoanalytic theory in the following terms:

> . . . the theory is stated in language so vague and metaphorical that almost anything appears to be compatible with it. . . . In short, Freudian formulations seem to me to have so much "open texture," to be so loose in statement, that while they are unquestionably suggestive, it is well-nigh impossible to decide whether what is thus suggested is genuinely implied by the theory or whether it is related to the latter only by the circumstance that someone happens to associate one with the other. . . .

It seems to me that revision of the theory at present can be justified more appropriately by means of results secured within the "context of confirmation" rather than the "context of discovery," and this implies empirical control, experimentation, statistical analysis, and other tools of analytic reasoning.

It is a lamentable fact that the distinction between competent observation and controlled experimentation is seldom appreciated by those working within a psychoanalytic framework. Freud himself never appreciated this difference and the following statement by Arlow (1959) illustrates the persistence of this pervasive astigmatism:

> Because of the principles that underlie psychoanalytic technique, those who are acquainted in a practical way with the psychoanalytic method are convinced that it constitutes the closest approach to a controlled experimental situation that has yet been devised to study the total functioning of the human mind. . . . Although the analytic situation corresponds most closely to the experimental laboratory of other sciences, psychoanalytic methodology is hardly comparable to that of chemistry or physics (perhaps with the exclusion of physiological chemistry). . . . The fact is that analysts are always making predictions, which they submit to confirmation or invalidation by the further study of their data. . . .

What we need, of course, are instruments that can be used for something more than demonstration studies—studies where negative findings, in effect, reject the instrument rather than the theoretical prediction. We need validated instruments that lead to studies where negative findings introduce a readiness to say the theory is infirm and that with further failures of confirmation should be amended to conform with what is regularly observed under well-controlled conditions. As Popper (1935) has argued, in order for a theory to qualify properly as an empirical theory, it must not only generate synthetic statements that are confirmable but also empirical predictions that are "refutable." The major shortcoming of psychoanalytic research is not absence of confirmation, but rather the difficulty of securing agreement among sophisticated proponents of the theory in regard to the precise conditions under which a derivation is to be considered disconfirmed.

Each time clear-cut observations are introduced into the argument, the effect is profound. To be sure, given observations will usually not resolve all arguments for which they are pertinent; multiple interpretations will still be possible. But these then call for further observations to decide among them, and even if it is not immediately feasible to make them, orienting oneself on them confers a new quality on theory. . . . It is exhausting to think that we are still fussing about this.

An example. For how long has the discussion of the development of female sexuality been turning round and round, in and upon itself. And what strange assertions have sprung from the minds of psychoanalysts (men) regarding what is happening in the anatomy and physiology of that most feminine experience—a woman's sexual excitement. (What had to happen supposedly happened because theory demanded it, not life.) Not only did none of us collect data on female sexual excitement as Masters and Johnson have; but we rarely admitted that our assertions left it unclear which observations could decide the issues. In contrast, while the relationship between female genital excitement and mature femininity is not settled by the work of Masters and Johnson, their research has produced a shift in the level of the discourse; beliefs have become questions that are now open to study.

Likewise, in the work of Mahler and others who are observing infants. How can we have believed that we could *know* what went on in a particular mother-infant relationship if the information we had came from the history gradually revealed in an analysis and the myriad expressions of the transference manifested by this now adult patient, removed from those events by so many years and so many defenses? We really thought that we were magicians, that the ordinary procedures of science were unnecessary for us; could we be so astute, so imaginative, so blessed by the Gods that we could not only make out the dim outlines of mother-infant or father-infant relationships but could build substantial theories of growth and development without minute observations of parents and their infants?

Once again, we do not yet have many answers, but once again we can be hopeful because we are developing procedures that will make available, not simply more speculation, but answers . . . approximations.

Of course, not everything will be answered; of course, many theoretical questions will be left uncertain; of course, we will freeze this new methodology and its implications into a new orthodoxy that others will have to break open. But, whatever may make the future of psychoanalysis viable, we will now have access to the findings and even the theories of nonanalytic workers.

Leites suggests that Hartmann did this years ago by permitting the obvious to become acceptable to psychoanalytic theoreticians. "One may proclaim truths that common sense has presumably never doubted, but that were—as a rule, implicitly—denied when analysis was young. One may do so without either recalling the earlier denials or what has made for their cessation: the arrival of evidence or the onset of sobriety." And I wonder: How often has one read in an analytic paper, "I was wrong" or "I made a mistake"? That Freud did so has become more a matter for deification than identification. While that thought is saddening, one can just as well say that the resistance of psychoanalysts is no more severe than that of any other committed group and that, sooner or later, we will accept anything, even the obvious. Example:

Rapaport says of Hartmann's epochal *Ego Psychology and the Problem of Adaptation*, "The concept of 'conflict-free ego-sphere' is perhaps Hartmann's most important single contribution among the many in this rich and sweeping paper. This concept actually condenses two ideas: (a) ego-development has conflict-free as well as conflictual sources; (b) though any of these conflict-free sources, and any of their maturational products, may at various times become involved in conflict, they form the nucleus of that group of structures and functions within the ego which is at any given time 'conflict-free.' "

The influence of that monograph on subsequent psychoanalytic history has been perhaps more important than any single work in the last 30 years: Hartmann shifted the course of psychoanalysis. Yet even in 1939, psychologists might have shrugged at such an announcement, for, using a different language but *the same observations*, they had long known these two ideas and had hurt feelings that analytic writings ignored their work.

My purpose is not to defend academic psychologists; that would

31

be presumptuous. Besides, I do not wish to; their obstinate refusal to recognize the role of conflict and unconscious fantasy is a historic blunder easily as fascinating and by an order of magnitude more stultifying as our not taking account of nonconflictual forces sooner.

As to why it took 40 years after the *Interpretation of Dreams* before a major work would open psychoanalysis up to "the obvious," as Leites calls it, here is Hartmann:

> The close connection between theory and therapeutic technique, so characteristic of psychoanalysis, explains why the ego functions directly involved in the *conflicts* between the mental institutions commanded our interest earlier than others. It also explains why other ego functions and the process of coming to terms with the environment—except for a few pertinent problems which played a role in psychoanalysis from the beginning—did not become the subject matter of research until a later stage of our science. Psychoanalytic observation has frequently come upon facts and considerations related to these other ego functions, but rarely subjected them to detailed study and theoretical reflection. I believe it is an empirical fact that these functions are less decisive for the understanding and treatment of pathology—on which psychoanalytic interest has been centered so far—than the psychology of the conflicts which are at the root of every neurosis. I am not inclined, however, to underestimate the clinical importance of these functions, though here I shall deal mainly with their theoretical significance, and even with that from only a single point of view. We must recognize that though the ego certainly does grow on conflicts, these are not the only roots of ego development. Many of us expect psychoanalysis to become a general *developmental psychology*: to do so, it must encompass these other roots of ego development, by reanalyzing from its own point of view and with its own methods the results obtained in these areas by nonanalytic psychology. This naturally gives new importance to the direct observation of developmental processes by psychoanalysts (first of all the direct observation of children).

The last two sentences are especially gratifying, but in the 30 years that have passed since this monograph was written very few of "these other roots of ego development" have been encompassed in the heralded general developmental psychology; in fact, the resistance of psychoanalysts to such "encompassing" has been fractious indeed.

Freud and the early analysts had to establish their radical findings and defend them against the brutal simplicities of the philosophers and academic psychologists. The price for this was the belittling of huge areas of the psychologists' work. It was only at the end of his life, in "Analysis Terminable and Interminable" (1937) that Freud called for the study of the ego's "original, innate distinguishing characteristics," its own "individual dispositions and trends" with which it is "endowed from the first." And only when this was followed by Hartmann's monograph in 1939 and when then the enlightening scholarship of Rapaport legitimized academic psychologists was the work of even a handful of the latter finally made palatable to analysts. It was not until 1939, then, that even Hartmann could admit that "pure phenomenological description of the details of the mental superficies, which one could disregard previously, is essential for and attains a special importance in ego psychology."

With the ease hindsight provides, I can remark petulantly that while they could have been disregarded before, they should not have been, and that what analysts might haughtily call "superficies" may be just as fundamental as, say, the primary process.

Fundamental for what? For normal personality development.

We do not know to what extent the study of the earliest phases of normal personality development will require not only the work with which we are familiar: (1) conflict—the study of trauma, separation anxiety, loss, cruelty, defensive identification, etc., and (2) non-conflictual forces—biologically originating, autonomous ego functions; but also (3) nonconflictual—a vast area still unfamiliar to psychoanalysts but known to students of learning theory (e.g., conditioning, positive reinforcement, imprinting, nondefensive identification). These other conflict-free processes ought to be (are beginning to be, e.g., Bowlby, Mahler, Spitz, Winnicott) fully dealt with into analytic theory. Do these forces, such as a happy mother's hovering, blissful, and gentle preoccupation with her infant, contribute to personality development? Of course; we all know so. Are there repetitive acts, invariably reinforced by a mother's joyful smile and cooing, which set patterns of behavior permanently into the personality? Are there behaviors of mothers which, when applied during a critical period in infancy, imprint patterns of behavior, as occurs in other species? Do such "learned" patterns, implanted in the first year of life, function as much as unalterable drives as do the biological (genetic and constitutional) forces that we more comfortably and traditionally call "id"? (Perhaps such "learned" responses, now fixed as character—"identity"—are as responsible for analysis interminable as are faulty technique, transference resistance, repetition compulsion, or death instinct.)

Perhaps the more normal one is—that is, at ease with himself, day and night, even while dreaming—the more his character structure is the result of such nonconflictual forces; it may be impossible to discover them by means of the psychoanalysis of adults.

All this has meaning to me, being at present in the midst of a struggle within myself while studying learning theory. I have found that essential aspects of the development of masculinity and femininity cannot be accounted for only by considering conflict, the permutations of anxiety (especially castration anxiety), and the issues surrounding the oedipal conflict and its resolution. There is no question that these latter, with which we are familiar from our patients, shape the final forms that masculinity and femininity take. Yet I was surprised that some of the earliest and most fixed gender qualities (for instance, the sense of maleness or femaleness) can be established in a nonpainful, nonconflictual manner. Still not having good enough data, I am forced to manage primarily by means of theory, and so am struggling to decide to what extent these processes might be viewed from the perspective of learning theorists. There are extensive data showing that masculine and feminine behavior can be powerfully and permanently influenced by parents' attitudes "shaping" or "moulding," that is, by parents' reinforcing certain behavior with high rewards. (We already know that this business of "positive and negative reinforcement" is permanently memorialized in the identifications and other fixed modes of function which we call "the superego.")

We need not consider these issues, which have been important to psychologists for the last half century or more, superficial any longer. It is not that the academic psychologists' studies were inadequate, though how pathetic these workers could not include *fantasy* as a variable in their theories. That is their problem. I am concerned with ours: We have failed to the extent we did not absorb nonanalysts' studies of nonconflictual sources of personality development. Although it was necessary early in analysis to concentrate on the unconscious and on the id, and while a study of the history of psychoanalysis can make us understand the motives for that concentration, that does not mean it was not a mistake. Happily, we need not be in a hurry; it is impressive enough that once the first discoveries were consolidated, Freud could move more and more to study the surfaces of the mind (surfaces are not necessarily superficial, except in geometry). But still, one may complain that 70 or more years is a long time to wait for "the ultimate conquest of the obvious."

In this regard, Leites' work may come to mark a major shift in psychoanalysis. Our drifting in dispirited theory could be ending. The willingness to generalize to laws of nature from a few observations is less likely now to give one the feeling that he is sailing with an acrobat's grace. It is just not satisfying to be fleeced (at the cost of a terrible pun we may recall how painfully Freud discovered that) by a theory that purports to explain most things. We may be forever limited in what we understand; we may never know precisely what goes on inside an infant's psyche. But it will be a relief to mark out our limitations. If not, we shall continue fruitless arguments, for instance, whether infants at three months have fully formed fantasies, as the Kleinians insist, or whether infants are incapable of such fantasies, as the rest of us insist—both groups not only without proof but also—and *that* is a graver matter—without techniques to get proof.

If psychoanalysis is a science, it must furnish instructions on how to prove or disprove propositions. Try this:

> Here is my problem. (Let it be due to anything: stupidity, unconscious resistance, peevishness, ignorance, knowing stubbornness, mental illness, or whatever you prefer.) I keep seeing how much we take for granted, how many undemonstrated affirmations are compacted along with data in our analytic vocabulary and then—surprised —how I do not know if Hartmann, for instance, means the same as I think he does. Example:

>> Let us now consider more closely the relation of the function of thinking, this foremost representative of the internalization process, to the tasks of adaptation, synthesis, and differentiation. In this connection we will have to disregard much that we know about thinking—for instance, its being energized by desexualized libido, its conjectured relation to the death instinct, its role as helper (rationalization) or opponent of the id, its dependence on the cathectic conditions, its facilitation or inhibition by the superego and by drive—and affect—processes, and so on.

Hartmann says we *know* these crucial things about thinking. But, please. Wait.

Suppose, for instance, one takes the position that he does not know yet that thinking is energized by desexualized libido; he requests the data that others know so that he too can know. Suppose one says he has never been shown any part of the real world that can be measured, or even merely made manifest for a flickering moment, that energizes thinking (except carbohydrates, enzymes, and the like—and they are no more libido than they are death instinct). Suppose one says that he cannot grasp what form desexualized libido would take in the real world so that it demonstrated its existence. (Electricity is still a mystery to us; we do not know what it is—but the lights go on when the current —whatever that is—flows—whatever that is.)

Suppose one says that even if there were a "thing," libido, he cannot imagine either the nature of the process "to desexualize" or in what form a product of that process would materialize.

(John 20: 29. "Jesus saith unto him, Thomas, because thou hast

35

seen me, thou hast believed: blessed are they that have not seen, and yet have believed.")

It simply is silly to disregard such questions by reference to authorities with whom you agree but who also do not know the answers, or by dismissing the questioner, or by suggesting that someone else at some future time will take care of the grubby details of demonstration.

Yet most analysts, in vibrant self-satisfaction, would agree with Rapaport, who says: "Dr. Hartmann's work demonstrates . . . a cardinal requirement of the scientific method . . . namely his unswerving insistence upon precision in methodology, and upon logical consistency in theory." When inside the system, one may not even know there is a set of rules. Inside the system, there seems to be no system, and one feels he is free.

If Leites succeeds, it will be harder to play our game. How will we then accept at face value a statement about some fundamental aspect of human psychology, when it is reported that "This paper is based on experience gained from the more or less profound analysis of X cases . . .," when the author cannot help but leave us unclear what is the analysis practiced moment by moment in the unique situation of that analyst's personality and that patient's personality; and what do we do about the "more or less profound," since lack of profundity (incompleteness) is the argument each of us can throw at the other in order to discredit each other's observations and conclusions. Or, another typical psychoanalytic comment:

> There is, I believe, no clinical observation to confute the idea that the intensity with which a child is desired is entirely dependent on the intensity of the preceding wish for a penis; therefore, one may say that the stronger the wish to have a penis, the stronger will be the subsequent wish to have a child; and the more difficult it is to bear being denied a penis the more aggression will there be in the reaction to the thwarting of the wish for a child. Thus arises a vicious circle which often obscures the state of affairs for analysts; we find repeatedly that the very women whose violent psychic conflict was occasioned by the castration complex (i.e., by penis envy), are the ones who also have an ardent feminine wish for a child.

Or, if a "sadistic constitution" is offered as an explanation for the way someone habitually behaves, how will we ever find ways to prove that the person in question has one and also, once this is demonstrated, that it leads to the behavior alleged?

There is no question about it: after the Revolution things will be duller.

Once we are in principle dedicated to observation, we shall be in less danger from the single case study. The great richness of the single analytic case is probably the most powerful source of original ideas in the history of psychology. Unfortunately, in psychoanalysis, the excitement generated was not always tempered by our seeking confirmation from enough other cases. It depends, to be sure, on the nature of the conclusion drawn (e.g., Columbus discovering America). For certain conclusions, one need only find one occurrence for it to be validated, but other judgments require more. (Thus, to say that X may be found without specific hereditary cause, one needs only one set of identical twins, one of whom has X, the other not, both biologically identical in those factors essentially related to X.) Since by now we have enough theory to explain any finding, we are in especial danger if we do not confirm an impression with other data. For instance, in my research, the first boy studied in depth with a particular rare condition (childhood transsexualism) was found to be extremely active and fearless. We were all struck by this finding, and we attempted, successfully, to explain it by theories already developed regarding the special mother-infant relationship found in boyhood transsexualism. The finding was fascinating, its fit with theory gratifying. The second such boy had the same trait, and so we were even more pleased.

The next 10 failed to show it.

We just must restrain our enthusiasm and wait for those next 10—or thousand, or however many the statisticians tell us are necessary for sense of conviction to be transformed into validity of assertion. On the other hand, there are very few discoveries indeed in human psychology that have been made by statistical techniques; on the record so far, their generative power is low. Still, these techniques do act as a marvelous conscience.

But as galling as is the habit of generalizing from the single case it hurts even more to realize that once a psychoanalyst has learned his theory well, he need never see another patient and yet hardly be at a disadvantage with his colleagues in using the theory or in creating new theory. Theory is now a perpetual motion machine.

What psychoanalysis needs is a good editor.

ROBERT J. STOLLER, M.D.

37

Author's Introduction

In contemporary psychoanalytic thought words often do not function as they do in the sciences, namely, as vehicles to designate events, vehicles that refer to what they indicate by a stipulation that is neither true nor false but more or less ambiguous and convenient.

Psychoanalytic writers frequently employ a word that is important and yet obscure without presenting its definition, as if it had already been given in the discussion at hand or as if the word had a standard meaning of which only nonspecialists might be ignorant. Alternatively, they may present an obviously incomplete definition (for instance, one which also holds for another word that is not meant to be a synonym of the first) or one in which the *definiens* is hardly clearer than the *definiendum*, which may be obscured by the use of defining words that are clear in other contexts. In such fashion, by keeping a definition implicit, writers can more easily adopt another definition that is quite different from the word's ordinary usage and then violate it.

One (by "one" I mean the writers to be examined) may prefer an uncertain definition: Believing that a definition depends on insight, a writer might decide that the time for it has *not yet* come, without considering that he has *already* used the word in making affirmations, perhaps because he is more oriented toward highly charged words that are easily procurable than toward important insights that are difficult to obtain.

A writer may consider the presence of a multiplicity of definitions (frequently, implicit ones) for the same central word as a normal state of affairs. Since the word is so important, how could it not have numerous meanings? Similarly, one expects an important event to be designated by several words, which may then diverge in other usages. It then comes to be taken as normal that I (I am putting myself in the place of the writers examined) cannot be sure what a colleague means when he employs prominent words of our common language.

As if they were events, words (they themselves, not their usage in space and time) may be thought of as inexhaustible targets of exploration. A precious word will be a home for many things: It would be invidious to exclude any event within a wide domain from communion with it, that is, inclusion in its referent; it is appropriate for such a word to be rich in facets. When a writer proposes that a considerable variety of phenomena is to be called by the same word, he apparently assumes that they all share a property, yet what that is may not be obvious or specified. With a large word, I can glide from one sector of its vast referent to another and envisage something different from my colleagues; then, perhaps, I can engage in exciting, riskless, and indecisive combat with them.

Among the many meanings that an important word can decently accommodate, it is often felt that one is true. Deciding on a definition then resembles discovering the properties of an event, and a disagreement about the referent to be assigned to a word is similar to variance about what goes on in patients. Just because a word has been much abused, I may feel a special obligation to employ it in its true meaning, perhaps forgetting that others may very well attach their incorrect ones to my use of it.

Definitions, authors may believe, depend on insights. A perfect definition is the consummation of inquiry; a good resting place for a discovery is the definition of a relevant word. Obtaining more insights, then, may be viewed as a means to enrich such a word rather than to clarify what the word designates as an elementary condition for the proper formulation of knowledge.

But then, it may be thought that there is little difference between highly charged words themselves and the sentences in which they appear. One usually knows what "concept" is being discussed, but one often doesn't know what text is presenting the insight (and, it is to be hoped, the concept) the author is discussing.

A word may stay prized, though the insights for which it is used are few and will not multiply, despite claims for the concept's usefulness. It is probably easier at present to make discoveries about antecedents, concomitants, and consequences of one or another component of, say, "identity" (as currently used) than it is to discern the conditions, accompaniments, and effects of that word's full referent. Still, it is tempting to dwell upon the comprehensive concept, elaborate on it, and merely predict high productivity for it without much likelihood that anyone will check on this forecast.

40

In the meantime, I may feel a sense of achievement in merely naming events—superimposing a highly charged term on numerous ordinary and clear ones. I may feel that such a laying-on of a great word (it may not be easy to select targets because its meaning is uncertain) is a powerful act, elevating the level of my discourse right then and there. Without an explicit definition, I can overlook the fact that I am merely substituting one word for others that make up a definition. I may not be dismayed about erasing the particular reference given in the original account in favor of the less specific one of my concept, and about doing this without much compensating benefit from then being able to invoke laws in which the concept figures, for their inventory (usually not established) is meager, and the chances of enriching it are smaller than would be the case for each of the concept's components. Yet it is precisely these that I am eager to efface.

However, I may feel that I have no choice: How can one think without master concepts? Without the condensation provided by such concepts, wouldn't I drown in particular words? The very act of including numerous phenomena within the referent of a central word may make me feel that I have grasped the complex relationships among them.

In addition to this immediate achievement, I may be confident about the word's future productivity—a property to be maximized. Before events can be approached, complex calculations (apt to be alleged rather than presented) regarding the proper choice of words must be undertaken; it is not just a matter of choosing a vocabulary, where any one might do if there were no inappropriate meanings and if agreement could be reached.

Thus, attention is focused away from the objects of inquiry toward the inquiring mind; one thinks less about patients and more about one's conceptual "tools"—means, of course, to gain insight into patients, but, for the time being, rivaling them as objects of concern. And this concern is, as yet, little constrained by checks on whether, let us say, generous investments in the production of producers' goods around 1960 (the development of the concepts to be discussed) showed up in more consumers' goods (new insights about patients) ten years later. In fact, the more one is gladdened by an abundance of steel, the less one will be dismayed by a shortage of steak. Obscurely, the natural relationship between the two may be reversed: Instead of using concepts to understand patients, insight into the latter may come to seem important because it reflects on the status of concepts. Any direct discussion of patients with little help provided by concepts may, by that very token, seem of limited worth, no matter how novel the findings. Hence, there is a temptation to frame such discussions with concepts and not notice that such a scaffolding may inspire one to feel that it has high deductive power, a certainty which only a careful audit could dispel—the very procedure that would then seem otiose.

Being less concerned with the truth of what is found than with the "usefulness" of concepts, one comes to live in an eternal future of endless growth, although the actual rate of growth in knowledge about patients may be modest—a situation that is made more tolerable by one's very absorption in the perfecting of "tools."

The various "tools" accepted by a writer are often believed to form a "whole." Here again, the ordinary relationship of means and ends may be inverted—in visible feeling though not in declared thought: A discovery of relationships among events may be greeted as ending a painful lack of connection among concepts.

It may be thought so evident that one's assertions form a "system" that the precise nature of the relationships among them (which is thus affirmed) need not be indicated. While one has to admit, on occasion, that his affirmations do not all stand or fall together, the lesser degree of interpedendence among them is not spelled out. In any case, since there is no inventory of the given propositions, there is no basis for testing any contention in the matter, and desire can express itself freely.

Preoccupied with itself, the mind attempts in various ways to reduce its dependence on events. First, of course, it does so by an epistemology that stresses the dependence of observations on the mind's own products. Then it does so by ambiguity: To the extent to which it is not clear what evidence would disprove a certain affirmation, the latter becomes independent of the conduct of patients. A large and perhaps growing number of words are acceptable even though (or precisely because) their clinical reference is obscure.

It is also believed that points are reached from "theory," that is, presumably, by deduction (although there may have been none). Thus, there is a feeling that these points are not entirely at the mercy of observation.

Finally, one may magnify the role of "assumptions" or "constructs," devoid—by definition—of any reference to what is observable in patients. They are, then, not true or false—that is, verifiable by deductive chains or observations—but rather more or less "useful" with regard to payoffs, on which little checking is done. Creating constructs gives one a feeling of freedom and power; the battle among constructs is gratifying and riskless.

Apart from the mind turning in on itself, a slow growth rate of insight can be made more tolerable by inflation in a situation where it is easy not to perceive gross discrepancies between the movement of nominal and of real income.

One way to raise the nominal product is to increase the output of unrecognized tautologies. One may take advantage of circumstances and procedures inhibiting awareness of the fact that a point is true by virtue of the meanings assigned to the component words. When definitions are not explicit, it becomes more difficult to discern that this is the case; it is possible, for instance, not to notice that common words (of general or specialized speech) are being used in an uncommon fashion. When I feel that a certain meaning of a word is true, deductions from it may seem to be as important as a statement about events. I may mislead myself and others by inserting into a tautology words appropriate to sentences about events, using, for instance, the vocabulary of research. Excessive modesty—presenting a tautology as uncertain or not always true—may have the same effect; one may also be misled by the proximity between an affirmation that depends on words and one that relates to the world within the same grammatical sentence or by expressions that follow each other. Success in hiding a tautology is facilitated because people are not inclined to suspect an affirmation that seems to be both novel and true; it seems difficult to imagine patients' conduct that would improve it. This sign of vacuity—and, if unrecognized as such, of malignancy—is apt to be taken as a hallmark of excellence.

Another way to increase the nominal product is to raise the output of reformulations, unperceived as such, of previously acquired knowledge as well as the production of concealed truisms; practices facilitated by the same circumstances and procedures that lead to the acceptance of tautologies. A new word may become so highly valued that almost any expression in which it appears will be favorably received. At that point one may not sense that no information about patients will be lost if the cherished term is simply crossed out. However, it might then also become clear that what is asserted is too evident or familiar to be worth enunciating. Or, by boldly conferring a peculiar meaning on a familiar word, an affirmation may appear to be strikingly novel; it may be difficult for anyone to realize that the new sentence does not convey novel meaning. While appearing to show *how* two types of events are related, an assertion may, on close view, limit itself to affirming *that* they are—although few would suspect that they were not.

When psychoanalysis emerged, striking discoveries were accompanied, and perhaps facilitated, by denials of what was obvious or had been learned elsewhere. After one finally dispensed with exaggerations, he could celebrate the return to sobriety as a breakthrough to novelty.

With the passage of time a finding that had been exciting when it was first made becomes stale. If no new insights of similar magnitude are at hand to fill the void, one is tempted to satisfy himself by changing the language that had been applied to the aging object, for example by starting to use a word in a weak sense that had earlier been reserved for a strong sense.

Besides seasoning the insipid, there is a tendency to hide assertions that are striking but vulnerable. They will provoke less doubt when they are stated in rich rather than poor words (to use an Italian contrast) or when they are presented together with difficult references to intellectual operations rather than as candid statements of what is happening with patients.

If, instead of presenting outright a hypothesis that is both interesting and dubious, I enrich it with the definition of a concept, the damage from a dissenting reality will be limited: The hypothesis then cannot be destroyed; the enriched concept will merely not be applicable, yet it will still remain—with its enhanced substance—suggesting what has just been disproved. That we deal only with a definition makes us safe; that the definition will be sensed as being inspired by a bold (and, alas, erroneous) idea creates interest.

Often a key word in an affirmation has two meanings: a weak one that makes the statement tautological, truistic, or familiar; and a strong one that makes the statement both striking and dubious, or at least hard to swallow by the reader. The weak meaning will guarantee plausibility, and the strong meaning, excitement. Similarly, a statement may be truistic or familiar when made for *some* of the pertinent cases, while it is alluring and vulnerable when advanced for *all* of them. Dispensing with both of these qualifiers will once more prevent a trade-off between certainty and interest.

As the habit of considering hypotheses by themselves has not yet been fully established among us, it seems appropriate to say something about myself. If I were to employ the word "Freudian," I would call myself one—except for what this book is about, namely certain ways of thinking and talking about patients usually called "theoretical." Whatever their defects (or perhaps because of them), these patterns have powerfully stimulated insights, say, during the first third of this century. Less in recent decades, and by now the productivity of current modes of "conceptualizing" may have become negative. The original motor has turned into a fetter.

For a quarter of a century I have been aware—so, of course, have others—of the kind of points I shall attempt to make. I chose not to write about them. Then, a few years ago, analyst friends of mine asked me to do so, and I did.

N.L.

Part I
Identification

SECTION 1: USES OF CONCEPTS

1 | Some Meanings

1. "The terms introjection and projection," announces Edith
Jacobson, addressing herself to the task of elucidating the language
she is going to employ, "refer to psychic processes as a result of which
self-images assume characteristics of object images, and vice versa."[1]
Thus we are plainly told which easier words ("self-image," "to assume
characteristics," "object-image") may be substituted in her pages for
some difficult ones: "projection" and—to enter into the present
discussion—"introjection."

One might imagine that it would be standard practice to be *that*
explicit about words called upon to figure prominently in an author's
contentions, while their meaning is substantially in doubt. However,
the contrary is the case for the terms of interest to us here: Edith
Jacobson's simple sentence has few counterparts. "Identification" and
the words felt as close to it—mainly "internalization," "introjection,"
"incorporation"—have now for long belonged to the very core of
analytic vocabulary. To introduce a full definition of one of them into,
say, an article attempting to clarify a particular point in their sur-
roundings might, obscurely, seem as awkward as it would be to indicate
in exhaustive fashion what is meant by "proton" in a contribution to a
journal of physics today. After all, the reader is presumed to have
assimilated, years before, textbooks of elementary theory. To continue
providing complete definitions of crucial words in current additions
to existing knowledge might be to deny that the latter has already been
formulated in satisfactory fashion—a denial that may be avoided in

biochemistry because it would be untenable, and in psychoanalysis because it might be all too much to the point.

2. The reluctance to present one's definitions of the words in which we are interested coexists in apparent ease with the awareness that they are being reputably used in many senses—an event that, I imagine, would cause shock in the "sciences" (perhaps so much so that it rarely occurs), but is apt to be accepted as a fact of intellectual nature in analysis. "It would," observes Gaarder respectfully, "seem . . . rash at this point to assume that there is any great similarity in the way abstractions are conceptualized [I would have hoped: deconceptualized—N.L.] concretely by various observers."[2] "There is little agreement," notes Grinker in less difficult language about "identification," "among the countless people using the term"[3]—is it not natural that everybody will want to ally the word's precious substance to the humbler events with which he is concerned?

3. Such sentiments may lead not only to the same word hallowing many occurrences; they may also make several terms consecrate the same fact. There is, recalls Koff about "identification," "introjection," and "incorporation," a "tendency of . . . authors to use . . . these words interchangeably";[4] perhaps they shouldn't, the reader may feel, but that they do might be an expression of vitality rather than disease. In any case, it is normal—to take only a few pages of one author[5]—for us first to learn that the ego's "acquisition of adaptive techniques involves the process of *incorporation*," and immediately thereafter that "the ego develops by acquiring *introjects* that lead to more efficient functioning."[6] For a patient's "*introjected* analytic attitude" to become "the basis for transference resolution," "the *incorporation* must become an aspect of the ego's synthetic functioning"[7]—a sentence ruining a surmise that might have been made on the basis of the one preceding it, to the effect that words beginning with *incorp* are meant to designate a process, and terms starting with *introject* its result. In fact, statements frequently, though no doubt with little conscious design, conform to this pattern: "The fragmented ego is impaired in its ability to *incorporate* and form stable *introjects*";[8] "*incorporation* corresponds to the acquiring and synthesis of *introjects* in the infant,"[9] which is more interesting than to know that introjection stands in that relationship to introjects.

"This paper," announces Cameron, "presents materials from the . . . therapy of a patient. . . . These include . . . the . . . *introjection* of a therapist image. . . . I shall present clinical evidence of the *incorporation* . . . of therapist attitudes . . .":[10] The cost of repeating oneself is reduced, while its benefits are preserved.

4. "Commonly," Edith Jacobson recalls, "the idea of an . . . introjection of objects . . . pertains . . . to the process of introjection of

48

objects into the ego (the self) or the super-ego [but where else could they go?—N.L.], *i.e.*, to processes of identification";[11] it is in passing that one may declare two central words to be synonyms.

5. When it is, on the contrary, suggested that every one of several major words close to each other has a distinct meaning, the ease with which they may be viewed as synonyms after all allows one not to pay the price of differentiation. "Introjects," explains Giovacchini, "are formed by introjection, incorporation or identification."[12] The reader is unlikely to be disturbed by the fact that nothing follows about what difference it makes to introjects whether they arise in one or the other of these fashions.

6. There are meanings given to our terms that, while usually not made fully explicit, would, if they were, readily be acknowledged; that is, could tolerate coming out into the open. (I deal with them in Section 2.) But there are other meanings that lack this capacity.

7. Perhaps they lack this capacity because they are rather trite as well as little connected with what one feels to be the domain of the valued words at stake. The implicit definition of "*A* is identified with *X*" may simply by that *A* is unconsciously *X*, *without* thereby engaging in a relationship with another person. For a man to have a feminine "identification," or a woman a masculine one, now often means that he or she unconsciously believes himself or herself to be of the gender indicated by the adjective: the relationship to an other, essential to the avowed meanings of our terms, is absent here (or only marginally present as having played a role in the genesis of the attribute in question). "The mother cannot see the child as a separate individual, as the child becomes *identified* with a figure from the mother's past which is incompatible with the reality of the child . . ."[13] presumably means that the mother *displaces* traits originally attributed to somebody else onto the child. "A man . . . falling in love," explains Knight, "projects onto her [the woman] his own femininity and his own wishes." Then, "he is partially in love with himself as he sees himself reflected in his conception of her." Perhaps this is too simple as it stands; in any case the author adds that this state of affairs comes about "through" an "*identification*" that is "effected" by the "*projection*" he mentions.[14] But does the former term here not designate, in unusual fashion, precisely the event that the latter habitually denotes: not making the self resemble the other, but rather the other the self?

8. In yet other cases a meaning that does fall within the words' usual domain is difficult to admit, because it is too thin to make it avowable for a term that has strong referents in its core; and yet one desires to dilute the word covertly, so as to make it applicable to unexciting situations that are in need of its support. Having presented a patient who "made a forte out of . . . anticipating other people's

49

. . . every wish and thought, so as to be able to please," who "could always perform what the other person expected," Gruen concludes that "*identification* can be a defense against authenticity. . . ."[15]

9. "In previous studies," recalls Bychowski, "I have followed the vicissitudes of *internal* images within the ego":[16] an assertion preferable to one about just "images," though an inspection of the presumable meanings of the three words involved (internal, image, ego) would tend to show that by virtue of implicit definitions one may presume that an "image" is "internal" to a person and belongs to his "ego." Still, "internal" is too weak an adjective to guard against awkward questions —have you abstained from all observation of the vicissitudes suffered by external images (within the ego or outside)? Have you omitted all inspection of the vicissitudes undergone by internal images external to the ego?

10. "Internalized" does better than "internal." An "internalized image" seems to be a synonym of "introjected image," which in turn seems to mean the same thing as "introject," though here the accent (pertinent in verbal music) seems to be shifted from representation to cathexis. In any case, "introject" is a powerful concept of the fifties and sixties, a period seemingly willing, nay eager, to overlook that there may already have been a word for its frequent referent: unconscious belief. "A man," observes Knight, "will . . . be attracted to a girl . . . who seems to have the attributes of his introjected mother":[17] who seems to be similar to what he unconsciously believes his mother to be. Having shown that Toulouse-Lautrec's life was heavily influenced by his unconscious reactions toward his parents—which might have been surmised early in the century—Bychowski brings his findings up to date: "I hope that these . . . remarks suffice to show to what extent the drama of Toulouse-Lautrec was a[n] . . . illustration of the . . . struggle of the ego against the *introjects*."[18] It is not simply that psychotics are apt to be conscious about what remains in the neurotics' unconscious; rather, "the schizophrenic ego . . . [perceives] not the objects as such, but their *internalized image* which becomes . . . released from the unconscious."[19] Pollock contrasts "the *current ongoing reality* of the *existing* symbiotic tie" between a patient and her mother (presumably the three *italicized* adjectives all mean the same thing, which in turn is the referent of the noun emphasized) with the "archaic introjected tie"[20]—i.e., (presumably) her conscious with her unconscious reactions. Having avoided the simple and capital observation that his mother may appear to the infant "warm, pleasant and nourishing" in favor of the already technical formulation that his "memory traces" may lead to such a memory, Krupp takes one step farther by noting that "with deprivation . . . the same mother may be . . . *introjected* as a bad mother."[21] Having recalled that the representations of many objects

have to be repressed, Giovacchini notes that they may be so "in the form of introjects,"[22] without, however, indicating other such "forms" —perhaps because "introject" is, after all, but a synonym for "repressed object representation," as sentences such as the following seem to suggest: "The analyst becomes cathected and as a consequence there has to be a . . . withdrawal of cathexis from introjects."[23]

11. Why should only unconscious beliefs be elevated to the status of "introjects"? Let all beliefs share this privilege! Such a penchant seems often to prevail over Edith Jacobson's reminder that "it is . . . incorrect [whatever the meaning of this adjective with regard to words that are ambiguous and evolving—N.L.] to describe the object- or self-images of normal or neurotic adults . . . as 'introjects.' "[24] In fact, Koff, with exceptional clarity, may declare that "introjection . . . is defined as a . . . process by means of which an external object . . . is represented by an image."[25] Usually, however, it is left to the reader (or author) to combine an exhilarating sense of novelty with a reassuring perception of familiarity when he is told that in the "the medieval mind" the "introjections of the Redeemer have to be followed by the externalization of Satan [presumably, projections onto him—N.L.]";[26] or that in the same epoch it was "the introjects responsible for the ego ideal" which "were expelling out of the ego field the original instinctual impulses. . . ."[27] Desiring to repeat the not unknown contention that the patient is apt to entertain both correct and incorrect beliefs about the analyst, Giovacchini presumably finds helpful the concept "introject" so as to avoid the question by himself or others what this declaration adds to the analytic treasure trove. For if it is known indeed that, at a certain stage of analysis, "the patient has two views of the analyst," it may not yet be recognized that "one such view," the very one that makes possible a workable transference neurosis, is nothing but "the analytic introject" itself.[28]

In another nuance—shades replacing differences—the word "introject" refers to the charge rather than the content of beliefs. Curiously, it may then occur in a sentence where, had one already decided on *ject*, one might have wanted to preface it with "extra" rather than "intro": The "Indian sage," recalls Bychowski, "has divested himself . . . of all spheres of reality, that is, in our terms [sic], of all introjections."[29]

12. The sentence just quoted shows how well the concept tolerates proximity with the designation of its presumable referent in plain words: As long as faith is vivid, it does not shy away from confrontation with what to the unbeliever may seem reduction, if not to the absurd, then at least to the common. The low, incapable of dragging down the high, is elevated by its presence. All that may have to be avoided is a definition of the concept such as might dispel the sense of its unfathomable

51

plenitude; but, as we shall see, even that limitation need not always be observed.

The concept may be *followed* by the simple word, without suffering deflation. Speaking about "an organism," Bychowski mentions its "introjected imagery, *that is,* its own aspect of the world."[30] Having shown about one animal with regard to another that the "instinctual patterns" of the former "try to reestablish a . . . unity between the latter and a corresponding introject [in the former]; or . . . [that] one may say that in an instinctual act the animal tries to find an externalization of its . . . introject," the same author concludes: ". . . thus the young bird 'expects' to be fed by its parents, who in turn 'expect' to feed it"[31]—where only the quotation marks around a common word keep one above plain speech.

More frequently there is a *crescendo* from simple word to concept. "During this stage," says Krupp about the infant, "of forming 'good' and 'bad' images, representations of the outside world and the self, introjects are. . . ."[32] Speaking about "images of . . . outside reality," Bychowski continues: "If we describe the latter as introjects . . ."[33] the attachment to the concept makes it unnecessary to justify its appearance—in any case, is there not intellectual gain in replacing four words by one, twenty-one letters by nine? Having recalled that according to Lorenz "young geese (who follow their parents soon after being hatched) become attached to another bird or to a human being when they are removed from the parents before the young have had a chance to see them," the same author concludes (and perhaps explains): "In this instance . . . another introject can take its [the parents'] place." And when "Tinbergen reports . . . that five days after their fledglings are hatched, heron gulls will not accept any other fledgling of the same age and species, though the human observer is unable to distinguish among them," this mere observation gains theoretical status thus: "Apparently [sic] during this brief interval introjection of the images of the young has become complete."[34] "A boy of eleven," narrates Grinker, "closely attached to his mother through her neurotic and then actual malignant illness, experienced the death of the mother without mourning." But later "He wooed and had sexual relationships only with sick girls whom he then ran from. . . ." Though we might receive with but little surprise the point that these girls were, for the patient, unconsciously connected with his mother, we are apt to be interested in the affirmation that while in such a case "the object is not *introjected* . . . old *introjects* are reanimated."[35] Our attention is thus apt to be caught all the more as the connotations of the verb "to introject," as well as of the older nouns "introjection" and "introjected object" seem at present somewhat different from that of the newfangled noun "introject": While the latter increasingly appears to designate any

52

unconscious reaction, the former continue to evoke some extreme ones—what I shall in Section 2 call "mingling," in one or the other mode. "A young librarian," tells Brody, "was about to leave analysis for several days to visit her parents in a distant city. During the last analytic session before her holiday, she spoke at length of the college professor who wished to borrow more books from the library than the rules permitted. The patient was determined that under no conditions would she allow this . . . infraction. The professor, a female, had given the patient a gift. The patient was in conflict as to whether or not to accept the gift, fearing she might be tempted to allow the books to be borrowed." Again, we might appreciate less simply hearing that feelings toward early authority infiltrated into this reaction of the patient than to be told that "in anticipation of the visit to her parents, early introjects were revived. . . ."[36] Or take, once more, Grinker presenting a patient leading "a life of suffering from guilt feelings and . . . [of] constant . . . restitution. At the height of his oedipal feelings, when he was sneaking looks at his mother's body and feeling her naked back under her dress, the patient lost his father. The mother made the little boy of five a husband in miniature, even permitting him to take a superior position to her second husband. The patient all his life avoided success and continued to lose, share, or return all his earnings, so that he was continually bankrupt. . . . He could permit himself no pleasure in work, play, or family life, and acted, felt, and spoke as if he had killed his father and must suffer the consequences." As late as a few decades ago this plain account might have seemed of sufficient interest; now it apparently needs seasoning: It is "introjection" that "leads" to such a life that merely furnishes an "example" of what this process can do. And instead of letting us know that nothing was wrong with the patient apart from the massive pathology presented, we hear that "the introjected object influenced a pattern apart from most [sic] of his character structure. . . . The self-representation apart from this . . . introject was reasonably realistic"[37]—where "introject," as a synonym for unconscious reactions toward father, receives, once again, even more force through being preceded by "introjected object" with its stronger connotations. After all, even "introject" may still be used less harmlessly, as when Bychowski reports upon the typical depressive patient who "in his dreams may show himself filled with . . . introjects. . . . A female patient dreamt that her vagina was filled with books and phallic symbols as representatives of both her father and her analyst. She then proceeded to eliminate them, in fantasy, by the way of the genital, anal, and oral orifices."[38]

53

2 | Solitary Words Embody Ample Truths

13. Endeavoring to elucidate the meanings of preferred words, authors may stop short of furnishing indications that would enable readers (or themselves) to decide whether the term in question applies to any given event or not. Having observed that *"operationally* . . . the concept of the introject can be *sharpened,"* Giovacchini points out that "it . . . [is] a psychic formation characteristic of . . . early ego-states, which is of fundamental importance for psychic structuralization, but which may . . . also impede . . . development":[39] perhaps not quite sufficient if one wants to be able to ascertain which introjects, if any, a certain person possesses at a certain moment.

"Imitations of . . . love objects, which begin in the first year of life," advances Edith Jacobson, "probably emerge from *what we may call* primitive affective identifications":[40] but we are never told what it is, while the locution employed evokes the atmosphere of sciences where we would be. As "the child's desires to remain part of his love objects or to make them a part of his own self . . . give way to wishes for realistic likeness with them," "this goal," the same author points out, "[comes to] be achieved by virtue of . . . identifications [rather: The achievement of realistic likeness shall be called identification—N.L.], *based on mechanisms of 'partial introjection.'* "[41] Now it is not clear whether "introjection" is used here according to the author's explicit definition quoted above (paragraph 1); that is, whether it is asserted that every increase in the child's realistic likeness to adults is preceded by a temporarily unrealistic reduction in his estimate of the difference between

54

him and adults. Uncertainty about the meaning of "introjection" is both increased and obscured by the quotation marks around the word: why are they present, if it is simply a matter of applying a definition that has been presented? But then, do the quotation marks not allude to well-known usage, of which the reader should be cognizant? "Partial" and "mechanisms" may also contribute to subduing any sense of incomprehension: The obscure is surrounded by the familiar, and that multiplication of words militates against the awareness that their referent is in doubt. That the author is indeed making up for her exemplary clarity in defining "introjection" by being moved to forget her definition becomes even more probable when we read that "identifications," if induced by fear of losing a love object, may aim at "preserving" this object "by processes of introjection": Is there really an intention here to assert that becoming like the other—if this be the meaning of "identification"—"preserves" that other only if one has first come to believe, wrongly, that one has already become like the other ("introjection" according to Jacobson's definition)? "Identification," explains Grinker, "is an end result of transactions between . . . any human individual and . . . any other human individual," a "transactional memory residue"[42]—but is that not also true for "object relations," and if so, what is the common characteristic of those "end results" that it is proposed to call "identifications"? Is it that in them the "transactional processes" of the "object" with the "subject" are "internalized" by the latter?[43] But if so, which "processes" are to receive this appellation? "Identification," writes Brody, "refers to the assimilative process occurring after . . . object cathexes have been established";[44] but if the word "identification" is in need of elucidation to a certain degree, is that degree smaller for the term "assimilative process"?

When in the "opinion" of Edith Jacobson "the terms introjection and projection refer to . . . processes . . . where . . . the self may be *constituted in* the object representation (projection), or the object *in* the self-representation (introjection),"[45] the author seems to overlook that the locution "to constitute A in B" may be fairly well defined for objects in space—to constitute the government of Australia in Canberra—but hardly so for the relations between "self" and "object." "In internalization," explains Luquet, "the object is *reconstructed* in the self by the ego, which '*erects*' it as a replacement of the external object."[46] Again, while the verbs "to reconstruct" and "to erect" are well defined for physical acts, this is not the case with regard to the nonphysical act of having another reappear "in" the self. (It is a sense of this that is apt to be responsible for the quotation marks around the one of the two verbs that has been less used figuratively.) Still, the familiarity of the crucial terms from the tangible world may make one overlook that they are being employed here out of the reach even of their ordinary figurative uses.

14. When clarity is so hard to achieve, obscurity may come to appear as an advantage one claims rather than a defect one strives to reduce. "The term 'identification,' " Loewald announces, "is used here in . . . loose fashion, so as not to prejudge what might be implied in the concept"[47]—which would presumably be as harmful to thinking as disclosing one's "fallback" positions when negotiating. From the plain fact that many and obscure meanings are currently being given to our words—"When we ask for precise definitions . . . of incorporation, introjection, identification . . . we are not . . . likely to come up with . . . precise agreements"—Berezin seems to conclude to the propriety of this situation: "We have to leave these useful constructs in some kind of hazy balance of understanding"[48]—a contention that might sound less plausible were it made starkly: we ought to leave these words hazy.

That such "haziness" of words might make it difficult to decide upon the truth or falsity of sentences in which they occur does not seem an excessive cost to assume: Perhaps "concepts" or "constructs," all conviction of their "usefulness" notwithstanding, are not really felt as mere producers' goods to the end of discovering properties of events.

15. In less extreme fashion it might at least appear normal that I do not know for sure what my colleague is talking about when he employs a word prominent in the vocabulary we have in common. Viewing Edith Jacobson as a believer (one of the many, it would seem to me) in the proposition that "frustrations . . . stimulate . . . identification," Grinker has to ponder (for good reasons) on the latter word, and comes up with the following hypothesis: "By this Jacobson probably means internalization of object-subject transaction."[49] Probably.

16. As God in several theologies can be described only by analogies, so perhaps the referent of a concept. Noting that "there are many connections between . . . repression and introjection," Fenichel recalls that "repressed ideas . . . [may be] felt as if they had been swallowed," which, however, would merely create "a similarity to introjection,"[50] not yet show us introjection itself, something unexpressed even beyond eating.

17. The richness of a concept may appear as of intrinsic value. "We wish to emphasize," declares Malin proudly about his group (that of Melanie Klein), "that projective identification to us has come to mean many different things and embraces many concepts":[51] as God is sometimes enhanced by being perceived everywhere.

18. Such richness may be had at low cost: A variety of events may be designated by the same word, without any indication of the characteristic common to all of them calling for such treatment, but with an implied assertion that it does exist. "This communication," Koff

announces about his article, "considers"—is it not improper to object to anybody "*considering*" what he chooses, while it might not yet be amiss to tell him that what he *affirms* is not so?—"introjection, identification and incorporation to be aspects of a similar process":[52] of the same, presumably (as there is nothing, in the context, for it to be similar to); but of which, we do not learn. "Identification," observes Knight, "may result from several mechanisms. . . . It may occur by displacement . . . when we identify one object with another object . . .; it may occur mainly by projection as in the case of 'altruistic' surrender . . .":[53] No statement follows as to what it is, precisely, that these two movements of the psyche (as well as others to which the author proceeds to allude) have in common. "The ego's health," according to Kris as paraphrased by Wiggers, "depends on a replacement of . . . incorporative identifications by those which form the mechanism of acting like the object through an . . . understanding of it."[54] Just what it is that is in common between my feeling that I have somebody else within me and my adopting this or that trait of his is not indicated; but it must be something important, as both conducts are asserted to be varieties of that one capital phenomenon, "identification." "Jacobson," again paraphrased by Wiggers in a report on a meeting, "agreed [with Nunberg] that Freud does not say that 'the melancholic identifies with the lost or ambivalently loved object' in the sense of an ego identification. Instead, his identification is a narcissistic one, which is entirely different from the identifications made in the ego"[55]— entirely different and yet, by virtue of an identity not specified, "identification." "As one goes further into the manifold meanings of identification," Schecter shows, "it becomes apparent that they constitute a conceptual family whose members . . . are representatives of different levels of psychic development. . . ." In fact, "some of these conceptual relatives are . . . distant, claiming family membership more on the basis of analogous rather than homologous relationships."[56] Which degree of "analogy" to what ("homology") is required for an event to be called one of "identification" remains unmentioned.

19. Extending with no definite boundaries over events, a great word includes, in some sense, the meaning of its neighboring peers. Considering "the two concepts identification and identity," Schecter observes that "neither is . . . meaningful except in the context of the other."

20. The sense of the primacy of the word (of certain words) over sentences attempting (whatever sophistication in epistemology accompanies their utterance) to photograph reality (a hidden one perhaps, but reality still)—that sense is fostered by a lack of discrimination between terms and statements. Thus the definition of a word may (still) appear not as the mere indication of its referent (indispensable for

statements and yet entailing none of them), but rather as a distillate of what is known about the class of events in question (though it may not be clear what that class is as long as definition is eschewed). "There is futility," declares Grinker, embarking on an analysis of "identification," "in attempting to define my subject in advance, since the purpose of this presentation is . . . [the] definition of processes culminating in identification":[58] Inquiry ends with "defining," rather than starting with the designation of the classes of events the relationships between which one is trying to discover, that is, with defining one's terms. Thus sentences affirming connections between events serve the crowning enrichment of one or a few words, the central concepts, rather than words being clarified so as to elucidate the meanings of the sentences in which they appear.

21. But inquiry may endanger as well as enrich the meanings of the words it employs. "The question comes up," observes Knight about "projection" and "introjection" "as to whether or not these mechanisms, by definition unconscious, can actually be conscious. . . ."[59].

22. "The . . . process," declares Brody, "in which an alteration of the ego ensues, *resulting from the abandonment of an object choice*, is known as identification."[60] And what about an "alteration of the ego" that does *not* happen to "result from the abandonment of an object choice": Would the author refuse it the precious name? Presumably he would say that he knows a law that tells him that there is no such case: Every "alteration of the ego" in question "results from" the event mentioned. Even if belief in such a law could be entertained, it should be stated as such (which, however, would make it more vulnerable—more discernible) rather than encapsulated (and sheltered) in a definition. Similarly, Koff seems to define "identification" *implicitly* as an imitation of another that is rather faithful, and appears to convey, also *implicitly*, a law according to which the critical (unspecified) degree of faithfulness in imitating another is reached only when the ratio of favorable over unfavorable strivings toward him (an object, by the way, as we would by now suspect, to be "renounced") transcends a certain (unspecified) magnitude. But instead of declaring on the one hand a definition, modestly, and on the other hand a hypothesis, ambitiously, he presents an amalgam of the two in which the hinted-at definition seems rich, and the alluded-to law is sheltered: "Anna Freud used the concept of 'identification with the aggressor' to understand how a person could develop traits of character originally perceived in a hated object. . . . This resembles identification in that there are changes . . . to resemble the object . . . but it does *not* occur as a consequence of a true [sic] object relationship with a renunciation of that object in the external world. In fact, we do not see true [sic] identification, but a parody, a satire, a hostile mimicry of the object."[61] The author also seems to convey,

always implicitly, another law according to which the critical level of fidelity in imitation is reached only if the cathexis of the imitated object transcended (before its "renunciation") a certain (unspecified) level—which then permits another amalgam of the same type: "So-called psychotic identifications . . . [are not] 'true' identifications because there never was real investment in the external objects."[62] "Because" the author proposes that one *speak* of "identification" only if the condition in question obtains? Or "because" there is a *law* according to which it must obtain for that alteration in a person to occur, which it is proposed to call "identification"? Or perhaps (as long as the amalgam persists) "because" of both these points, lending each other their strengths to cover their weaknesses? "A 'true' . . . identification," the author sums up, "is a consequence of a 'true' object relationship, with a renunciation of that object . . .":[63] As long as it is a "consequence," never mind whether it is one by virtue of stipulated language—so what?—or by virtue of the mind's shape—a capital matter.

23. The passages just quoted illustrate the penchant for viewing a certain definition of a given word, such as "identification," as "true" (as well as the presence of misgivings about this inclination, which express themselves, for instance, in the quotation marks with which that adjective may be surrounded). Thus, there is a disposition to disregard the difference between sentences that stipulate substitutions between words in the author's language, and sentences about relationships between events. In fact, when Lewis Carroll points out that a word may mean just what one chooses it to mean, neither more nor less, he is, according to Koff, talking not as a philosopher of science but as a "satirical writer"; for to "science," in contrast, "each word has its own special meaning derived from the word itself, not the intention of the user"[64]—whatever this may mean, beyond the point of convenience (if not propriety) that new users should not deviate from established usage (if there is any—and, if so, it may of course be manifold). Having recalled near the beginning of an exposition that "identification . . . is frequently used in the literature as synonymous with introjection," Knight, at the end of his paper, looks back on the results achieved: "It has been the thesis of this discussion that identification . . . *is* not synonymous with introjection."[65] "In my opinion," Jacobson writes about two words as she might about two patients, "the terms introjection and projection refer to . . ."[66]—as if, regardless of the multiplicity of events they are *made* to refer to, there is, for each of them, just one to which they *do* refer: truly. (And yet, one may refuse to forego a decent measure of freedom with regard to words: "Since these terms," the author adds, "have been frequently misused or applied *too broadly*, I have refrained from employing them *too freely*."[67] "He believes," writes Koff about Hendrick, "that introjection and incorporation *are*

59

the same, *not to be* differentiated from identification":[68] The imperative
mode of the second verb makes it easier to accept the indicative mode
of the first (just as the quotation marks around the adjective "true,"
in a previously cited passage by the same author, render its application
to a noun other than "sentence," or its equivalents, less shocking).
"Incorporation," affirms Brody, contradicting Hendrick, *"can be . . .
differentiated from introjection and identification"*[69]—whatever this
means beyond either discerning nuances in current usage, or recom-
mending that the second (or third) word not be a synonym with regard
to the first (who would want synonyms anyway in a language fashioned
to designate rather than to express?). I wonder what rule for the
settlement of their conflict might be acceptable to these two opponents
in the matter of relations between our three words; we shall not know,
as it is characteristic for such a divergence not to issue in a confrontation. Hendrick notes that "identification" and "introjection" "have
come to be used . . . commonly . . . as synonyms," and he discusses
certain conditions from which this state of affairs "results." "Yet," he
affirms, "the conclusion that introjection and identification *are* synonyms is unjustified." For "introjection *is* a wish to incorporate a
fantasy," while "identification *is* . . .":[70] Never mind what; all that
concerns me here is that Hendrick seems sure that a term *is* in a way in
which a patient is. So is his antagonist. For from the finding that with
the child's maturation his "mental representations" come to be "more
in terms of objects than of pleasure-pain experiences," Brody concludes
that, as this happens, "it is *more descriptively accurate to speak* of
identifications than of introjections":[71] The author avoids the (by now
generally shocking) adjective "false," but conveys a mistake similar,
for example, to that of not perceiving the emergence of "objects" in
the child's development. Luquet having announced that "we call" by
the name of "assimilation" the event of a "complete fusion of . . . [a]
functional [sic] object with the ego," and by the name of "assimilatory
introjection," on the other hand, "the mechanism which leads to it,"[72]
Berezin comments: "Luquet *suggests the intriguing idea* that 'the
complete fusion of the functional object with the ego' *he would call*
'assimilation,' and the mechanism leading to it 'assimilative introjection' ":[73] The juxtaposition of the first and the second sequence
italicized by me does not appear weird. When Luquet envisages the
situation in which "the ego . . . cathects an internal image of the
object . . . but is not completely confused [sic] with it" and then goes
on to announce that "it is this phenomenon that we term *imagoic
introjection*" [italicized in the text—N.L.],[74] Berezin, once more,
reacts in the way just illustrated. First he speaks of "the central thesis
which Luquet proposes—i.e., the ego . . . 'cathects . . . an internal
image of the object which . . . is not completely confused with it.' "

Then he acquaints the reader with Luquet's nomenclature: *"This, he* [*Luquet*] *suggests, is* the *imagoic introjection* (the last two words italicized in the commentator's text, as they were in the author's—N.L.)":[75] The level of reality enjoyed by the meaning conferred upon a new word by its creator is hardly inferior to that possessed by the event thus designated.

24. The sense of freedom, frustrated with regard to definitions, may express itself in relation to propositions. Considering reactions of the type, "when I say 'if I were you, I would do so-and-so,' " and "the observation that a successful criminal might make a successful detective," Knight reflects: "Perhaps it might be more accurate to *view* the resulting identification as a more or less conscious affair [as if it were not observations that should decide on statements about degree of consciousness—N.L.] and still *regard* the processes by which it is achieved, projection and introjection, as unconscious mechanisms. . . ."[76]

25. While governed by reality, a concept is endowed with the power to penetrate it—so much so that one may warn against exaggerating its might. When one wants "to understand why an individual is 'selective' in his identifications," what is "clearly needed," observes Schecter, are "concepts beyond identification":[77] even a great word does not itself designate the causes of what it designates.

3 | Facilities Through Difficult Language

26. When cherished words are used in ways such as those described in the preceding chapters, it becomes possible to insert them into

61

sentences whose meaning would not be impaired by their absence, but whose force is enhanced by their inclusion. "Fantasies of introjections are found," observes Fenichel, "in which the penis is equated with an introjected woman"[78] or sometimes the penis is equated with a woman; a formulation which has the disadvantage of raising the reader's (perhaps even the author's) demand for a case. "In previous studies," recalls Bychowski, "I was concerned with parental images of certain individuals. . . . In these persons *the incorporation of* such images . . . had resulted in a split within the ego . . .":[79] As the italicized words are omitted, surprise is reduced. In analysis "*the incorporation of* an interaction that is based on primary process operation cannot become a basis for ego development," affirms Giovacchini:[80] Were the underlined words dispensed with, it might become easier to wonder whether this is not a tautology (what is of the "primary process" is not of the "ego") or a truism (conduct of the analyst "based on" the primary process, and not merely drawing on it, is unlikely to foster the patient's ego development).

27. "A man who sits reading the evening newspaper, and then gets up and walks into the dining room to eat": This is the event chosen by Gaarder to exhibit the power of modern theory. In fact, this man "can be seen" as "having gone through a set of stages": "(1) He initially had a relatively high cathexis of the visual apparatus, a relatively high attention cathexis attached to the internal representation of the newspaper, and a low cathexis of the body image. Then there is a shift, with a relative de-cathexis of the visual apparatus, a relative de-cathexis of the attention capacity, increased cathexis of the sense of dimensional space, and a cathexis of the automatic muscular function of walking. Also, there is probably a change in the thought cathexis as well as the thought content as it changes from the newspaper to the meal and the internalized representations of those with whom the meal will be eaten" [why not from internalized representations of newspaper and meal?—N.L.]. It is thus that "an economic model of ego function" masters "something which we could formerly take for granted, but were not able to fit into a theoretical framework." Such feats are within the reach of our four words—identification, internalization, introjection, incorporation—as well as of "ego function."

As certain early findings become stale, and new insights are hard to come by, there is a temptation to procure the sensation of freshness by a change of language (a penchant I already discussed in paragraph 12).

"Because of the relatively ineffective maternal introject," Giovacchini observes about a patient, "the capacity to assimilate other adaptive experiences was impaired":[82] Having been unable to learn much from his mother, he was incapable of learning a great deal subsequently. That the unconscious reactions toward her mother, in a woman patient who has remained highly dependent on her, are important, and not only the conscious ones, may be one of the well-known observations that can be transmuted into modern theory thus: "It is not just the external symbiosis that is significant. The internalized symbiotic connections . . . are the essential elements."[83]

What is more elementary in analytic theory and more important in analytic practice than a patient applying an unconscious phantasy about an early object to a present one? A readily understood, but, unfortunately, by now rather common word is available for this: displacement. Hence Bychowski in the pursuit of "the vicissitudes of internalized images encountered on many occasions . . . situations calling for their externalization. I shall call the process in question the 'release' of the introjects":[84] a new act about an old fact. A patient hardly went beyond what has been talked about for decades when, "starting with his tenth year . . . [he] used to beat the pillows in his bed furiously and then embrace them, throw spitballs at the wall and fight imaginary armies," allowing analysts to discern that "all these imaginary objects were substitutes for parental images." However, the classic turns modern when we learn that he "externalized his introjects," that he furnishes an instance of the mechanism whereby "real individuals serve as points of materialization of internal images. . . ."[85]

Continuing the sentence, the author proceeds to eliminate the distinction between "displacement" and "projection" by writing: ". . . images, including the image of the self." And elsewhere "projection" is used where one would expect "displacement." "In the . . . struggle against the . . . parental introject," the same author reports on another patient, "the ego used the mechanism of . . . projection." What did "the ego" in fact do? "For many . . . months the patient accused her mother and father . . . of . . . wanting to destroy her. In the transference reaction the analyst correspondingly became the object of these reproaches. . . . It was he who wanted her to become a dull housewife. . . . This transference illustrates" the usual displacement from parents to analyst? No, rather "the *projection* of the . . . paternal *introject*."[86] A patient of Malin's whose father "was described as . . . [a] martinet" developed a "perception of the analyst as rigid, autocratic and hard to please." As his mother "was a . . . martyr," "on still other occasions he would perceive the analyst as . . . supercilious, polite, ingratiating, insincere and martyr-like." So far, so known. But we begin to react more vividly upon understanding that the first set of beliefs "represented a projection of the father identification," while the second set of qualities "belonged to his mother identification."[87]

Is it that the outer (concerning the parents) had become the inner (of the patient) before turning outer (attributed to the analyst) again? Or is it that we now can afford to say "identification" and "projection"— without the reader (or perhaps even the author) knowing the rules of the new game; but that is perhaps a part of its charm—where a public definition hitherto obliged us to say: displacement? At any rate, Jacobson has found it useful to warn that "we must not confuse transference processes based on [consisting in—N.L.] displacement from one object image to another, such as from the mother onto the analyst, with projections."[88]

However, "projection" is attractive only where we do not (yet) expect it; where it belongs (in its traditional meaning) the urge to avoid it is as strong as that which opposes the perpetuation of "displacement." An "important concept that emerged in the course of . . . investigations" conducted by Bychowski "was the externalization of various aspects of the self."[89] For instance, "In the course of the analytic working through, the feminine image of the self becomes externalized and fastened on other men, including the analyst."[90] Grinberg affirms: "The essential aspect in the functioning of that mechanism is that the subject projects his own conflicts, emotions or parts into the object":[91] where the only novelty with regard to by now stale sentences containing the word "projection" is the affirmation of the existence and projection of "parts" of persons—a novelty, however, that does not concern the "mechanism" itself, but only the events to which it is applied.

So strong is the attraction of the new words, or of the new meanings infused into the old ones, that their employment does not always require silence about predecessors, as in the instances just mentioned. (*See* paragraph 12.) Having discovered that a certain patient "*externalizes*" some aspects of the image of his own self, Bychowski simply continues: "He *projects* what he calls the bad . . . image of his self on individuals who. . . ."[92]

Components of the two languages may even be present within the same sentence, at the bearable price of unperceived pleonasm; even pairs of words with presumably identical meanings may follow each other within the confines of one grammatical unit: "In the course of analytic working through of this *introjection*, these . . . *images* became *externalized* and *projected* onto. . . ."[93]

The new and exciting word may even, without apparent damage, be *presented* as the synonym of an old and dull one. ". . . the hyperenergized object representations (introjections) . . .," writes Krupp,[94] and also ". . . depressive introjections (depressions). . . ."[95] "Incorporation," declares Brody, "is . . . a . . . way of relating in which the self-representation becomes much like the . . . object representation."[96] Never mind that this powerful word's denotation is rendered so weak;

for its connotations—in happy contrast to the traditional proprietor of its new meaning, "identification"—remain, and the deviant definition will soon be forgotten (perhaps even by the author)—but not without having facilitated the word's ample and exciting employment.

28. "Incorporation," affirms Koff, "should . . . be used only when it refers to the concrete aspects of the object, such as behavior or appearance. . . . [It] avoids the abstract qualities of the object," the domain of "true identification." Here I had imagined that if somebody wanted to restrict the use of the word "incorporation," he would limit it to my unconsciously inserting something within me, and that if somebody wished to restrain the employment of "identification," he would confine it to my adopting somebody else's properties. Now I learn that the "true" dividing line is not that at all: It rather runs between the "concrete" and the "abstract." An original point—but one proposing merely a peculiar language; and also merely proposing it: The chances of others obeying are small, and the probability of the author himself disregarding his strange command high. Which may also be the case when Giovacchini notes about "internalization" that "this concept refers to the loss of the introject's *boundaries*. . . ."[98]

29. "The process of *incorporating the analyst with his* nonanxious *attitude* and willingness to understand . . .," writes Giovacchini,[99] when what he designates is, presumably, the patient's *taking over the analyst's attitudes*: The formulation chosen *evokes* reactions going farther than that, e.g., toward the feeling of being another. It is tempting to act thus when one handles words, such as our four, which have been used to name events spread over a wide range (*see* Section 2). "Near the beginning of one hour," Cameron recalls, "Grace became infuriated with me over a blunt comment. . . . I told her there might be some truth in what she said, but that my comment still stood. . . . Four days later, this usually timid patient, who had never been able to endure serious criticism, reported that an angry teacher had made a public attack upon her supervisory methods. 'She was so excited about it! And I was trying to find out what there was in what she wanted to say. I was encouraging her to be difficult instead of just smoothing things over.'" What is "obvious" here, the author comments, is "the use Grace made of my *incorporated* strength"; she was *taking over* a trait of the analyst—"if I could take her tonguelashing without . . . giving ground, she could stand fast in the face of another's attack."[100] When "incorporation" merely refers to unconscious imitation, "introjection" may suggest a farther-reaching reaction: This patient showed "*introjection* of the therapist image" so as "to further the process of forming new partial *identifications*";[101] or, in what I surmise to be other words for the same event, "introjection of my image as an internal object . . . [was] preceded and accompanied by the *incorporation* of my

attitudes."[102] But, "introjection," too, is not incapable of moderation in meaning. A patient accepts an interpretation: "The patient . . . introjects this insight as, so to speak a part of the analyst"[103]—where the "so to speak" may suggset that not every acceptance of an interpretation is here affirmed to be accompanied by the unconscious fantasy of having some of the analyst within one. "A housewife in her twenties," Giovacchini reports, "felt she knew nothing about mothering . . . she did not know how to feed, dress, care for, or play with her child. . . . The analysis revealed that she believed that she had never learned anything from her mother about mothering, since her early upbringing was in the care of a series of indifferent maids. . . . The patient believed she had never had the opportunity to learn the techniques of mothering, as one would by . . . experiencing them. . . ." What had happened here? "Lack of formation of a suitable introject . . . ."[104] "During one therapeutic hour," Cameron recalls, "the patient became increasingly apathetic and incoherent. . . . I said, 'Sit up!' " And now a "dream four months later. 'I was bleeding myself for a good cause. . . . I was holding up a bottle and filling it with blood. I was getting weaker and weaker (she felt she was dying) and somebody said, 'Sit up!' " What had been of the analyst had become of another in a dream—no, the analyst's command had been "introjected."[105] A patient, prior to analysis, has come to see himself in the image of certain others; in analysis he ceases to do so, but (at first at least) starts perceiving others in the image of himself he is abandoning—this story of moderate events is overlaid with evocations of extreme ones when Bychowski notes that "*incorporation* of the images of aggressive . . . boys of his childhood days and of strong adults have resulted in enhancing his . . . aggression and thus making him 'bad.' . . . In the course of analytic working through of this *introjection* these . . . images became externalized and [sic] projected onto various male figures, who then appeared as persecutors."[106] Recalling that "some mourners limit their grief by succoring another individual who has also been bereaved," Krupp paraphrases this point—but does he not entertain and convey a sense of enhancing it?—by judging that "such *projective identifications* aid in denying . . . loss."[107] As it was already well known to earlier analysis that "identifications" of the kind here involved are fostered by a similarity of condition between the one who "identifies" and the one with whom he does so, the novelty is in the adjective "projective." This, however, in its connotations—not disciplined by a statement of denotation—goes beyond the case thus "conceptualized": "projective *suggests* that the mourner, so as to become capable of unloading his grief onto somebody else, exaggerates (or fabricates, by allegation, if not provocation) that other's loss; which probably does occur (no such

66

box is likely to be empty), is more striking than what has been envisaged, and, precisely, has not been *affirmed*.

That more than making oneself similar to another is involved may also be suggested by *plain* words the literal meaning of which refers to something moving from an exterior into an interior. "If I . . . wish to imitate a certain person," Knight explains, "introjection is the main mechanism whereby I take *into* myself the . . . attributes of the object. . . ."[108]

When a word evoking extreme events within our four terms' zone of reference is chosen to designate a moderate occurrence, we would by now expect that this can be done despite a sober naming of the latter happening somewhere nearby. Affirming that "the male lyrebird is noteworthy for his . . . capacity for acoustic *introjection*," Bychowski goes on to explain: "He . . . *imitates* all manner of sounds of other birds, human beings, and even mechanical instruments."[109] Making the familiar point that the patient, in the course of analysis, may adopt attitudes of the analyst toward him, Giovacchini introduces and repeats it by speaking about the patient's "*introjected* analytic attitude." After that, he is free to be simple: "The analysand expects to be responded to in terms of . . . conflict, but the analyst scrutinizes his conflicts. . . . The patient, by *adopting* a similar attitude begins. . . ."[110]

30. Having defined "introjects" (as distinct from "identifications") as events of infancy, Brody still finds it possible and worthwhile to affirm that "the earliest relationship of the parents to the infant determines the kind of introjects that will be formed." He continues in the same vein: "In turn, these introjects will determine the kind of identifications and object relations that will be established."[111] But not only they: "Identifications are influenced by . . . the existing ego. The external world . . . and the instinctual drives . . . influence our identifications. The inborn characteristics . . . of the ego and their maturation . . . help to determine the identifications that will be formed." In its turn, "identification . . . is essential to the transition from primary to secondary process thinking. Identification is essential to learning and to the acquisition of language. The maturation and growth of the ego are dependent on the identifications that are formed, as is the character of the individual. The identifications that are formed determine how the . . . psychic apparatus will function."[112] Presumably attachment to the concept thus magnified has helped the author to avoid the sense that where two such factors as, say, "identifications" and "ego" are concerned, it may by now be superfluous to reaffirm the closeness of their connection, while it would be stunning to deny it, and productive to contribute to falsifiable knowledge as to what the precise relationships

(no doubt, numerous) between them are. In the absence of such discoveries, the currently frequent lack of such a sense does carry the advantage of furnishing a supply of sentences of large scope and low cost. "The future identifications that the infant makes," the same author advances with higher specificity, "will depend in large part on the affects evoked in surrendering his narcissistic position in favor of object relations":[113] But for that "part" really to be "large," those of numerous other aspects of the infant that are equally plausible determinants of "future identifications" will have to be small; and it would be the indication of the factors to be degraded rather than the enumeration of those to be confirmed that would enhance our knowledge. When we read, however, that "the nature of the developing ego will depend, to a great degree, on the personalities of the persons around the infant"[114]—without this being presented as a polemic against Melanie Klein—we recall that pleasure and assuagement from reaffirming acquired truth may reduce the urge, and dispense from the obligation to produce new insight.

31. As the awe felt toward a great word tends to make us tolerant, or unaware, of its obscurity, a sentence containing it may be left dangling without any indication of the operations required to establish its falsehood or truth. "It seems to me valuable," observes Knight about "sympathy," "understanding," "analytic insight," and "intuition," "to reduce it to . . . projection [always?—N.L.] and . . . *possibly* also introjection."[115] Reading the sentence thirty years after it was written one may find it difficult to say whether clinical observations made in the meantime have been favorable to it or not—or even whether the conduct of patients is at all pertinent to it, as its truth (if "possibly" be replaced by "certainly" and "valuable" by "true") may follow from the implied meanings of the first four nouns on the one hand, and that of "introjection" on the other hand. (*See* paragraphs 32–36.)

32. "All projection includes identification," declares Malin in a vein that encourages himself and his readers to take it for granted that he has discovered a law (an invariant relation between events): Apparently he does not sense that a statement of this sort, if it does not seem bold (until proof for it is furnished) is all too apt to be true: being true by virtue of the (as we will by now suspect, at least partially implicit) definitions of the words it contains.

When proof is attempted, this may become apparent. "A projection," the demonstration of the thesis cited above begins, is "meaningless, unless the individual can retain . . . contact with what is projected"—a sentence to which (so that *it* not be "meaningless") I can only give the following sense: The one who projects perceives what is projected—which indeed follows from the definition of "projection." "That contact," the proof proceeds, "is . . . loosely [sic] an identification"—but only if every perception, being by definition one of a perceiver, is, again by definition, accompanied by "a type of internalization," which, by a further definition, is, "loosely," an "identification." Here is the full text of the sentence just examined:

A projection, of itself, seems meaningless, unless the individual can retain some contact with what is projected. That contact is a type of internalization, or, loosely, an identification.[116]

33. "Identifications," declares Jeanne Lampl de Groot—after having defined the word as the realization of "the tendency to become like another person"—"make use of the mechanism of 'introjection' (or 'incorporation')." Is there another *conceivable* "mechanism" of which the one who identifies could "make use"? The suspicion that there is not rises when the author continues by setting forth that "the individual 'introjects' the image of the other person, he 'takes over' some . . . of the latter's characteristics":[117] Does the locution before the comma not designate the same event as the one following it?

34. Having reported that in a child patient "conscience . . . was experienced in terms of 'will Mother approve?' rather than 'do I approve?' " and having called this "externalizing the psychic image of the mother," Ritvo asserts: "When the psychic image is prominently externalized, *it may indicate* a limitation or restriction of internalization."[118] The author's manifest uncertainty strengthens the belief that we are dealing with the always contingent relation between two classes of events; but do not the two locutions "prominent externalization of psychic images" and "limitation or [sic] restriction of internalization" designate just one? Having decided to speak of "identification" only "after object cathexes have been established," Brody observes that "identifications arise *more* out of ego perceptions than out of primitive sensations"[119]—a sentence about a difference in frequencies, hence surely about the world! But is the author not excessively modest, thus garnering the advantage of being more convincingly empirical? Are sensations still "primitive" once there are "objects"?

35. "When we *review the material presented,*" declares Bychowski, "we can state that . . . the release of internal images represents a reversal of the original process of incorporation."[120] But is it really necessary, or even appropriate, to "review material" other than the words contained in this sentence in order to be assured of its truth? If "process of incorporation" designates the act of adopting from another an unconscious reaction (which may or may not be unconscious in that other); if "internal image" refers to the result of a "process of in-

corporation"; if "release" of "internal image" refers to either the breakthrough to consciousness and conduct of the unconscious reaction in question, or to its projection; if "reversal" is taken in its ordinary meaning—we then obtain that "the release of internal images represents [is—N.L.] a reversal of . . . incorporation." That "introjections are developed through experience with external objects, whose images are transferred to become part of the self" is, according to Grinker, a point "indicated" by "tenable theory"[121]—or does one obtain it by writing out implicit definitions of words involved?

36. If one avoids construing as a tautology a sentence that seems to call for it, the alternative may not be pleasant. "In later life," observes Grinker, "when boundaries [between self and nonself] have already been formed, introjection of the objects is no longer easily possible."[122] That is, if "forming" boundaries be a matter of degree: the more they have been "formed," the smaller the "ease" of introjection. But when we speak of boundaries that have been more rather than less "formed," do we not precisely mean (among other things, perhaps) boundaries that render introjection less rather than more "easy"? Now one might say that this demonstration of the sentence being a tautology derives from a feature absent in its manifest content: the "formation" of boundaries admitting of degrees. Let us drop this malicious addition. Then we learn that introjection is "easily" possible when there are *no* boundaries between self and nonself; that is, when there is no self. But "introjection," whatever its unknown complete definition, refers to an element of a nonself becoming one of a self. We do not have a tautology any more, but now a contradiction. According to Edith Jacobson both "projection" (meaning: the self being "constituted in" the object representation) and "introjection" (meaning: the object being "constituted in" the self-representation) occur "especially" when the "boundaries" between self and object representation are "dissolving."[123] But when we speak about a "dissolution of boundaries" between self and object, do we not designate (perhaps among other things) the very event to which we also refer by talking about the "constitution" of one of them "in" the representation of the other? However, if the truth of the sentence be not thus assured by its being revealed a tautology, it becomes dubious. If, for instance, "dissolution of boundaries" between self and object representation be taken to mean a reduction in the self's sense of separateness, how probable is the truth of a law affirming a negative correlation between that sense and the incidence of "introjections"?

37. "If we experience ecstasy or lust or sadistic feelings through witnessing, or reading about, or hearing about the activities of others who are experiencing these feelings," asserts Knight, "[this] is possible

through . . . projection of our own wishes onto the active object and *by* introjection of the object."[124] What about these causes? When, in the situation described, we say that we "project" our wishes on that other, do we not have in mind precisely the fact of feeling what we believe him to feel? That is, would it be conceivable to do the latter and yet not the former? Similarly, could we conceivably feel ourselves what we take him to feel without having "introjected" him? That is, are the words purported to refer to causes not merely other ways of designating an as yet unexplained effect? "Anna Freud," claims Koff, "used the concept of 'identification with the aggressor' to *understand how* a person could develop traits of character originally perceived in a hated object"[125]—or is it merely that the charge of the word fosters the illusion of having explained (whatever that may mean) that which it only designates? When the infant is "imitating the gestures of the persons around him," he does so, according to Fenichel, by "using the mechanism of primary identification"[126]—a word by which we presumably designate precisely such events as the infant's imitating the gestures of the persons around him. "Identification," affirms Brody, "may *cause* alterations in the ego, in the self-representation, or in the self"[127]—an act more important than that of naming them! "In Evelyne," observes Ritvo, "the processes of internalization were more successful because the mother, who was more loving than discomforting, lent herself readily to introjection in the formation of partial ego identifications."[128] But is it not the same event that is referred to by saying that "internalization was more successful" ("processes" might be omitted) and by speaking about the alleged cause of this, namely that "the mother lent herself readily to introjection . . ."? What is grammatically a subordinate clause (". . . who was more loving . . .") is thus, in substance, the principal one, the entire sentence affirming nothing more about events than that "internalization" is "more successful" when the mother is "more loving than discomforting." But that is a lot to assert; and one may feel less vulnerable in doing so when a falsifiable hypothesis is embedded in the suggestion that an event is its own cause.

38. Yet another way to avoid falsifiability is to introduce terms that sound familiar enough from other uses, but with regard to which it is far from clear what events they are now supposed to designate. Affirming that "all identification includes projection," Malin proves this law in two steps. First, whenever there is "identification"—substitute any of our three other words, for once accepted (though not avowed) as synonyms—there has been a state of being "receptive to the object for introjection." Second, for that state to obtain, "we must project out a part of our inner psychic contents": hence there is "projection"—

q.e.d.[129] The trouble is only that we are given no advice how to ascertain the presence or absence of the "receptiveness" in question, or of the "projecting-out" invoked—unless we confer on the latter term the ordinary meaning of "projection" (disregarding the "out"). This would establish clarity all right, but has the disadvantage of producing the almost certainly false contention that every "identification" is preceded by (ordinary) projection. The alternative is our being stuck with a term of unknown reference, "projecting-out"; that is, with a proof as incomplete as if it contained the unelucidated word *tuo-gnitcejorp*, our obscure acquaintance robbed of his deceptive familiarity by being arranged backward.

39. ". . . nor can," Schecter declares, "identification fully account for . . . one's identity."[130] How easy would a competent reader find it to sketch (not more than that) the look of a human for whom this statement would be wrong? And how likely are one reader's conditions of falsification (that is, the meaning he assigns to the sentence) to be the same as another's? All of which is obscured when it is weird to doubt that we do know which events are to be designated by "identification," "identity," and "A does (not) fully account for B."

40. Instead of (or in addition to) loosening the link between a sentence and the world so as to protect oneself from being proved wrong, one may reduce the claim one makes for the view one chooses. In advanced writing it has become rare for such-and-such a statement to be affirmed as true, and such-and-such a one as false. With increasing frequency one reads passages such as Pollock's according to whom "Marty's concept that identification is synonymous with fusion . . . seems too global and encompassing."[131] What about: "Marty's allegation that identification is synonymous with fusion is false"? We are now in ruder climate. That synonymity, according to Pollock, does not obtain in whose language? Does Pollock assert that Marty is concerned with the actual languages of analysts? Or is there no synonymity between the words in question in a language recommended by Pollock? But where is it expounded? And how is it superior to the ones now employed? Or is it a matter of the relations between two classes of events, one called "identification" and the other "fusion"? And if so, which relations are respectively affirmed and denied? Better stay with the concept.

41. "Projective identification," observes Malin, "seems to be the way in which human beings are able to test their own . . . psychic life by projecting . . ., and perceiving the environment's reaction to . . . [the] projected parts of oneself."[132] Whether the conduct in question is indeed to be designated by the fashionable term introducing the

sentence, it is impossible to say: that word is not sufficiently defined by the author to decide such a question. However, the "concept" does, precisely because of its ambiguity, offer shelter to the interesting and dubious assertion to which the author seems to tend, but from the bald enunciation of which he appears to shy away: that with a nonnegligible frequency the act of projecting is motivated by the desire to perform a "test" of the kind indicated. "When made aware of the amount of . . . aggression invested in the *maternal introject*," reports Bychowski about a patient, he "feels his stomachaches revive."[133] The moderate meaning —when made aware of how much he desires to attack his mother . . .— protects the extreme one: when made aware of how much his mother, now dwelling in his stomach, attacks him. . . . (At the same time, as we have seen above, the extreme meaning confers zest on the assertion.) If, as we have observed, the word "projection" may be avoided where it would render a sentence, while not less true, all too stale (paragraph 27), and if it may be employed where it rejuvenates old saws by assuming an unusual meaning (paragraph 27), it may also perform the service of masking a difficult credible contention. When Melanie Klein declares about Julien Green's hero in *If I Were You* that "the depleted part of Fabian . . . longs to be reunited with the projected parts of his self,"[134] to "project" means not so much (no explicit definitions are given, to be sure) to attribute properties of oneself to others, but rather to believe that one is the other. The striking assertion thus made is shielded by the traditional word with its moderate connotations.

42. Facilitating the expression of more than the reader might be ready to accept, the turn of speech I have just described may also induce an author to affirm more than he wants to maintain. Having made it plausible that he may mean by "introjection" the phantasy of eating—"we conceive of introjection as a psychological process akin to incorporation. In the earliest months of life, . . . introjection is associated with . . . salivation . . . and . . . increased gastric secretion." Grinker goes on to declare that "introjection is a process by which object representations and self-representations are created in the mental apparatus."[135] Does this mean that the emergence of *any* belief is accompanied by the unconscious phantasy of eating its referent?

43. "Fabian," affirms Melanie Klein, "*by becoming* Esménard, . . . *projected* into another person . . . some of his own destructive tendencies."[136] At first sight hardly novel. But what the reader is led to by formulations of this kind is the proposition not that I may attribute my characteristics to another when I become him, but that whenever I so attribute them, I so become; and conversely, that whenever I adopt another's characteristics (the traditional meaning of "identification"), he becomes me, or comes to dwell within me. (*See* paragraphs 63–66.)

It is rare for this bold statement to be expressed as overtly as by

Melanie Klein when she observes that "for the individual to feel that he has a good deal in common with another person is concurrent [implicitly: always—N.L.] with projecting himself into that person (and the same applies to introjecting him)."[137]

More frequently one takes advantage of words whose usual referents extend from the anodine to the extreme. "Sometimes," notes Fenichel, "certain persons, who serve as models for certain ideas, become 'introjected into the superego' in the same manner as the Oedipus objects have been introjected in childhood . . .":[138] Might this not merely mean that these persons become, precisely, models, and the ideas I attribute to them my own, just as "introjecting Oedipus objects" may not mean believing that I am they, or that they are within me?

Instead of frankly advancing that *everybody* is doing to his parents what Kronos almost did to Zeus, one may convey this extreme contention in a form that can be sensed as a harmless turn of speech. "Many persons," Fenichel recalls, "who have lost one of their parents early in childhood . . . tend to establish . . . extensive identifications, *that is,* to incorporate their objects."[139] Does "that is" join synonyms, or recall an established law that whenever I borrow much, I swallow the one from whom I do?

A law that may be hinted at more clearly when it is illustrated from psychosis: "*Incorporation* of everybody," observes Fenichel about mania, "has been confirmed by the findings of Lewin according to which multiple *identifications* are characteristic for manic states."[140] Grief can also serve as a starting point for the contention that there is no substantial borrowing from another without an eating of him. "It can often be observed," one may start uncontroversially, "that a mourning person . . . begins to resemble the lost object." In fact, one may proceed, "every mourner tends to . . . [engage in] building up a . . . substitute object within himself after the real object has departed"—an ambiguous formulation (*see* paragraph 11). But "building" is presumably preceded by "devouring," as we are reminded that "bulimia . . . which unconsciously means eating the dead person, and the refusal of food, which means the rejection of this idea, come within . . . normal grief." Thus the conclusion: "All this gives evidence" that the "identification with the dead person"—imitating him—"is subjectively [which here presumably means: unconsciously—N.L.] perceived as an oral incorporation":[141] eating him.

44. When a word that usually serves to shelter awkward assertions by virtue of its ambiguity is temporarily deprived of it in favor of an exclusive extreme meaning, one may have to restore the balance by going far in the opposite direction. "Introjection," writes Fenichel at one point, "that is . . . the fantasy that the . . . object has been devoured

and now exists within the body."[142] Immediately thereafter he mentions, for one configuration, "the fact that *in the superego* another *introjected* object is already present . . .,"[143] which perhaps already designates a less extreme event than a devoured body dwelling "in" that agency; perhaps only my now demanding of myself what somebody else had previously requested of me. In fact, a few pages later even the explicit (and episodic) definition of the word has swung toward the other end of the scale on which it moves: "Introjection . . . is the opposite of projection: . . . characteristics of an object which one dare not become aware of . . . are perceived in one's own ego [rather: self—N.L.] instead."[144] A bit later we hear, no doubt in this sense, about a patient that "by building a superego, he introjected the angry behavior of the father. . . ."[145]

45. Equilibrium can also be reached not by a sequence of sentences, as in the case just cited, but by the juxtaposition within the same sentence of words going in opposite directions. "The self-reproaches of . . . [a] patient," observes Fenichel, "*corresponded* to complaints made by an *introjected* mother about an introjected father."[146] Had Fenichel spoken about self-reproaches corresponding to complaints made by *the patient's* mother about *the patient's* father, what I have called the "moderate" possibility would have been clearly designated. Had he maintained that the self-reproaches *were* complaints made by an introjected mother about an introjected father, what I named an "extreme" event would have been unmistakably envisaged. Fenichel chose to allege an impossible world by combining elements of possible ones, sheltering the extreme by the moderate.

4 | From the Outer to the Inner

46. "Objects cannot be cathected," affirms Gaarder in characteristic fashion:[147] as if doing so were to have the cathexis, a part of the self, leave it and rejoin an other, the object; as if it were not directing that part of the self toward another.

"But," the author adds in equally standard manner, "their internalized representations can."[148]

The "internalized representation" of an object is, he explains, "that complex within the . . . mind which represents the external object."[149]

As "internalized" does not seem to have a counterpart in "externalized," and as a "representation," taken in its ordinary meaning, is a part of a mind, one might simply say: representation.

That representation—*of an (external) object*—has a cathexis: the cathexis (one might as well say) *of that object.*

That cathexis is joined to a representation of the object? To be sure, just as the representation is attached to the cathexis of the object!

47. Observing that "the thesis presented"—the one just cited—"can be illustrated by clinical vignettes," Gaarder announces that "the vignette I will use is from Engel and Reischman's film of 'Monica, an infant with a gastric fistula and depression.' . . . Monica, in the film, is an infant, hospitalized. . . . She has come to know one of the doctors who takes care of her. . . . She has through her experience acquired an *internalized representation of the object* [italicized by the author—N.L.] —the doctor [alternatively: she has cathected the doctor—N.L.].

76

Motion pictures of her taken in the doctor's absence show her . . . as . . . listless. . . . In the absence of the real object . . . the internalized representation of the object is relatively uncathected [alternatively: the object is relatively uncathected—N.L.]. . . . Then the beloved doctor appears. . . . Monica immediately 'comes to life' . . . the internalized representation of the object . . . [is] activated by . . . cathexis . . . [alternatively: the cathexis of the object is increased—N.L.]. . . ."[150]

What this characteristic passage shows is the preference for language where the accent is on something being part of the self rather than directed toward an *other*—an imbalance that, on one occasion, Edith Jacobson attempts to correct. When doing so, she starts out, however, with the currently orthodox assertion that "object images are 'endopsychic' formations"—but what are "exopsychic formations"? And whatever they be, what might "exopsychic images" (whether of objects or not) be? That is, what more is being said here than that an "image," by definition, is part of a self? The author goes on to claim that "object images" are "part of the inner world" of a self. But what might his "outer world" be? What is said here beyond, once more, that an image belongs to a self? It is only after having paid these obeisances to the current predilection for the "inner" that Edith Jacobson proceeds to recall that "object images" are "distinguished as objects"—isn't that going a bit *too* far in the direction opposed by present fashion?—"from the image of the self," are "separated and [sic] kept apart from it"[151]— whatever that adds to noting that images of nonself are not images of self.

48. Beyond satisfying a taste for the internal, the vocabulary in question allows sheltering the allegation that others, in my unconscious belief, reside within me (*see* paragraphs 13, 43–45). While affirming, as we now expect she will, that "precision suffers . . . from our failure to make clear distinctions between external objects and their endopsychic representations," Edith Jacobson recalls that "Melanie Klein . . . compounded this confusion by failing to distinguish the latter from what she and her followers called 'internalized' or 'introjected' objects, or simply 'introjects' "[152]—which is presumably also the meaning of Loewald's admonition: "A . . . distinction must be maintained between a relationship to fantasy objects and an internal relationship that is a constituent of ego structure."[153]

49. Loewald's singling out of "fantasy objects" hints at the fact that the less than fully declared allegation of somebody else being felt as living within somebody is best made when one starts one's considerations not with conscious orientations to present objects, but with unconscious reactions to past ones. "All his emotions," observes Melanie Klein about Julien Green's hero when he is attracted to a baker's wife, "apply also to the internalized mother"—which may still

(or already not) mean the real mother of the past to whom unconscious emotions remain attached. However, the author goes on, the hero's "jealousy of the man who, he believes, possesses the baker woman at night, refers also to an internal situation, for he feels that he can hear inside him the man's voice speaking to the woman."[154]

50. We have already seen several instances of the penchant toward affirming what I called extreme events within the domain of our words, instances where that disposition could be acted upon without benefit of the doctrine that cathexis pertains to the internal representation of an object rather than to the object itself. Let me add two examples at this point, one from the beginning and one from the end of the period (between the mid-forties and the mid-sixties) to which the illustrations in the present study belong; examples that may be thought to be minor, but seem to me all the more pertinent.

"The persecutions," avers Fenichel in discussing paranoia, "represent projections of the patient's . . . conscience." One may ask whether *all* persecutions do, which is suggested but not affirmed. In any case, once the sentence is accepted, it follows that "an introject"—"for the superego is the result of . . . introjection"—"has been reprojected." As the minor premise is familiar, interest, within this syllogism, would, one might expect, remain focused on the major one. Not so. Fenichel, on this occasion, is rather concerned with proving that "the persecutor . . . had been incorporated and reprojected"; that there had been what Anthony Burgess in *The Clockwork Orange* calls "the old in-out" rather than the simple "out" of old-fashioned projection. The fact that, as I suggested above, one might view as the most intriguing one in this context—that only conscience is projected—is viewed by the author merely as a "circumstance" that "corroborates" a "theory": namely, that "an introject had been reprojected." Fenichel even commits an error that makes the derivation of the desired conclusion more interesting than it should have been. According to him "the fact that the persecutor represents . . . [also] the subject's own features shows that this object, in the patient's fantasy, had been incorporated and reprojected": while it is only the replacement of "features" by "conscience" that would save the sentence from falsehood, and (as so often) make it dull. And when the author continues by recalling a mechanism that may "play a certain part . . . in normal love" and that "bestows upon the object features of the ego [rather: self—N.L.]" this, once more, is affirmed to be not simple projection—how naïve (and dull)!—but, within quotation marks, a "passing of an object through the ego":[155] the nonself will have dwelt within the self before leaving it!

"She . . . told me," reports Grinberg about a patient showing "rigidity and stillness," "that when she was six years old, her mother . . . had committed suicide." In fact, her mother "had hanged herself in her presence, and it had been . . . on account of her delay in warning the rest of the family that the death could not be prevented." Now, "I had the feeling that with her corpse-like rigidity the patient was . . . trying to show that she carried *inside* a dead object. . . ." Why even consider the possibility of the patient having become *like* her mother? Not unexpectedly, then, the author, observing that this patient was trying to "get rid of it"—the dead mother whom she "carried inside"—by "projective identification," affirms that she "tried to introduce it *into* me":[156] again, why even consider the possibility that to the patient the analyst *was* a corpse rather than having one *inside* him?

51. To the force that impels the nonself into one corresponds the impetus that propels it out of one again. Noting among promiscuous homosexuals "pseudo-objects created out of externalized introjects," Bychowski finds "their projection . . . explained by the strong . . . charge of the introjects and the weakened countercathexis. With the weakening of this encasement the . . . introjects are expelled . . . and fastened on . . . chance encounters."[157] The indication of particular motives for "introjection" and reprojection has been replaced by the taking for granted of an in-out profile of movement peculiar to psychic particles.

5 | The Mingling of Selves

52. When, in my belief (I shall in the paragraphs to follow repeatedly talk about reactions—which might be my own) an other *"immigrates into me"* (emphasis together with quotation marks shall indicate that the term in question appears to me suitable for standard usage), he may be *"added onto me"*; when I *"emigrate into him,"* I may be *"added onto him"*; as perhaps in "certain feelings of well-being" that "are felt as a reunion with an omnipotent force . . . brought about either by incorporating parts of . . . [the] world or by . . . being incorporated by it."[158] This, of course, may be feared as well as desired; and one may alternate between the two movements sketched: "Grace," Cameron observes about a patient, "often felt at conscious levels that she was . . . an extension of mother, and sometimes that her mother was an extension of herself."[159]

The self that is added onto another may be believed to be a particular part of that other, which he is himself already not lacking (as in the case of a man for whom a woman is his penis), or which is absent in him—as in the case of women who believe themselves to be "mother's penis."[160]

The state where one is added onto another may be reached by a variety of movements: for example, one may surrender to the other who receives one; or one may seize the other.

53. Instead of merely becoming a part of a different self, one may penetrate into it: the other may be *"inserted"* into me, or I into him.

81

("Incorporated" would have been the obvious word, had it not suffered the fate described above.)

Fantasies going in one direction may of course be defenses against those of the other sort. "He came for an interview one year after the . . . end of his analysis," Blumstein reports about a patient. "He said . . . he was eating too much, and was . . . affected by a fear that he might have cancer. His associations led to the idea that cancer . . . eats the body. . . . After a suggestion that his cancer phobia might represent a self-preparation for being eaten and protected by an omnipotent figure, he felt . . . relief. The . . . process was . . . an unconscious reaction to . . . the analyst, the basic unconscious wish being to incorporate the analyst. The excessive eating and the cancer phobia were . . . defenses against the . . . wish to incorporate the analyst." [161]

What is inserted? It may be a part of the other. "The rigidity of posture, absence of gesture and inflection of voice," Lois Munro notes about a patient, "[was] the representation of himself with his father's catheter inside him."[162]

What movements result in insertion? "Masochism," observes Blumstein, "is associated with fantasies and acts of *self-preparation* for being incorporated." In one patient "the central feature of the masochistic fantasy "was "the self-preparation for being eaten, swallowed or inhaled."[163] In one case Melanie Klein perceives "the fear of being *imprisoned* inside the mother . . . the fear that the lost part of the self will never be recovered because it was buried in the objects."[164]

By what routes does insertion occur? Through all the body's apertures, the eyes, and the skin.

Where does "*the insert*" dwell?

All I may know is that there are inserts of me somewhere: a patient, according to Melanie Klein, may entertain the feeling that "he does not know where the parts of himself, which he has dispersed into the external world, have gone to." [165]

Or only the body within which the insert resides may be specified: "I feel," Hendrick quotes a patient, "as though my eyes reached out and took him inside me."[166]

When the part of the body where the insert dwells is indicated, the insert itself may be a whole other. "If I could get him in my anus, I could keep him there," muses another patient of Hendrick's;[167] "my husband is inside my abdomen," discloses one of Brody's.[168]

Finally, a part may dwell in a part: A patient of Bychowski's "feels an alien body in his stomach which contracts and quivers like a vagina."[169]

What does the insert *do from the inside*? Any of the things he may have done from the outside.

What happens to the insert? A patient of Bychowski's—to illustrate one of many possibilities—keeps his mother's breast inside him so as to "eat himself up," in his own words, "like a hibernating animal feeding on his own resources."[170]

If an insert is ultimately removed, the possibilities of movements and routes are of course the same as with regard to its establishment.

Insertions and removals of inserts may succeed each other. Thus in Ruddick's patients suffering from the common cold "there were oscillations between incorporation and ejection, i.e., swallowing and, spitting, sniffling and blowing the nose. . . ."[171]

54. Beyond inserting the other into me, or myself into him, I may feel that I have changed into him (*"metamorphosis of self into other"*) or that he has changed into me (*"metamorphosis of other into self"*): a difference that is not stressed in Khan's "becoming the object rather than modeling . . . some . . . function . . . [on] an object,"[172] or when Lois Munro declares about a patient that "he was his mother,"[173] but which is made explicit by Margaret Little: "He [the analyst] experiences him [the patient] at times as himself, *or* himself, at times, as the patient. . . . Conversely there are points at which the patient experiences the analyst as himself, *or* himself as the analyst."[174]

When Anna O., as Krupp recalls, looked into a mirror after her father's death, it was him she saw.[175] "The nine-year-old," the same author reports about a patient's reaction to her sister's death, "handled it by saying to herself, '. . . I will carry her around with me. . . .' "[176] There are patients, Annie Reich observes, whose whole body becomes "a part of the parental body," particularly "a glorified phallus."[177] "She developed," Pollock tells about a patient, "an itching of her left antecubital area . . . [which] revealed itself to be her . . . wish . . . for contact with an infant. When she nursed and held her baby, its head was cradled in the left antecubital area. . . . While this was being understood, she developed neurodermatitis of the back of her head and neck as well as of her inner antecubital area. The wish to be the cradled infant as well as the comforting mother . . ." was thus expressed, I might have concluded, while the author leads the full and simple facts to the empty and majestic concept: ". . . indicated the . . . identification as mother and as child."

In contrast to such instances of the other now being where previously only the self was are the cases of the self now dwelling where before only the other existed, e.g., in the unconscious phantasies that may accompany "altruistic surrender."

The two movements may be combined. "While pregnant," Pollock reports about a patient, "Mrs. C greatly desired to have a little girl. She insightfully commented about this when she said, 'I probably wanted to . . . repeat the relationship with my mother. I even wanted her [the child] to look like me' "[179]—perhaps she unconsciously wished for a metamorphosis of herself into her mother, and of her child into herself.

When I change into another, I am apt to feel my original self reduced. But not always: "He felt," Bychowski reports about a patient, "he was both himself and a fellow student."[180] Even more so, when an other changes into me, I need not feel less myself, though I have quoted Melanie Klein about the case where this event depletes me (paragraph 41).

55. Short of changing the other into my self, there are the varieties of *"putting myself into his place"*: too obvious to need exposition. (There is an asymmetry here to the stark—unconscious or psychotic—putting of another into one's own place.) Thus there are, for example, in Jacobson's formulation, "the parental identifications with the child," which are "born of memories of the infantile past [of the parents, revived by the present of their children—N.L.]" and "limited to . . . fantasy and feeling . . .";[181] indeed "at any developmental stage the parents identify with their child's needs by reviving their own experiences of this phase."[182] Particularly "the mother," affirms Winnicott, rejoining the common belief, "knows what the infant feels like"; he adds: "through identification of herself with her infant"—which is a case of an event causing itself (*see* paragraph 30), unless "identification" here designates (how can one tell?) an unconscious metamorphosis of the child into the mother (for her). "Her concern," reports Pollock, again, on a matter close to common insight, "about leaving her small son in order to come to the analytic sessions . . . resulted from . . . her . . . identification with her son as the helpless child being left alone. . . ."[184] "She could not fully encourage and enjoy his [her son's] growing independence," the same author tells in a similar vein about another patient, "yet in her identification with him she derived much pleasure from his increasing accomplishments."[185] Silver's "[seeming] to indicate that . . . (a) patient learned adaptive techniques from the therapist," makes Giovacchini ponder: "This implies that the analyst is able *to introject* the patient's conflicts"—an ability that may appear less heroic when the concept is replaced by ordinary words: "react to . . . [the patient's] problems as if they were capable of producing similar anxiety or other effects within him [the analyst]."[186]

Taking an other's place may of course be less acceptable to oneself, or to the other, than in the obvious cases cited. "A physician," reports Brody, "attended a scientific meeting where a relative, another physician, delivered a lecture. The first doctor, the patient, reported that he . . . literally squirmed every time the relative made a grammatical error. . . . He had no strong positive feelings towards this relative. The relative . . . [had in fact] delivered a good lecture. . . ."[187]

56. The degree to which I am capable of taking the other's place,

and moved to do so, seems, often and all too obviously, related to the degree to which I experience a *"sense of sameness"* with regard to him. Such a sense may include my believing myself and him related to the same entity—God, value, leader or group; or it may not.

57. The sense of sameness, in its turn (and, again, all too obviously) often fosters *"the sense of communion,"* that is, a reduction in the sense of separateness between myself and the other (though it is easy to think of cases where the opposite takes place). "Normally," notes Jacobson, "the experience of . . . 'identity' [having become a concept, the word apparently needs quotation marks to indicate that it is used simply— N.L.] of pleasure in the sexual act may harbor elements of happiness derived from the feeling of return to the lost, original union with the mother."[188]

I may increase my resemblance to another by adopting some properties of his (*see* Chapter 6) so as to reinforce my sense of communion with him. "Like his mother," Krupp reports on a patient, "he complained of stomach pains which radiated to his back, and once, in describing these pains, he said: 'Her pains were my pains.' "[189]

Or a patient may develop an exaggerated belief in the degree of sameness between himself and his analyst so as to render possible the level of communion with the analyst that he desires. "She painted three portraits of me," reports Margaret Little about a psychotic exacting in this regard, "all of them with large dark eyes, like her own; and she told me that her mother, whom she was said to resemble, had also had them. I drew her attention to the eyes in the picture, and asked if she thought mine were really like that. She looked intensely into mine and said, 'That's how your eyes *are*.' (I would contrast this with a neurotic patient, who got up off the couch, after spending an hour talking about my white hair, and laughed at his picture of me.)"[190] Observing that a patient may project a part of himself on the analyst so as to foster a "feeling of relatedness" to him, Malin, characteristically, is not content with this finding stated baldly: it gains worth when one recalls that "Rosenfeld . . . and Bion . . . have applied the concept of projective identification" to it.[191]

However, a high sense of communion may arise precisely from a low sense of sameness. "She had understood," Margaret Little says about the patient just discussed, "my need of a patient and her need of a doctor to mean . . . identity of person between us."[192]

In fact, to her "acceptance of . . . [an] interpretation also meant identity of person, as did my acceptance of her for treatment, whereby I tacitly confirmed her in her belief, asserted that I too believed it, and was therefore, once more, one with . . . her":[193] belief in mutually favorable sentiments obviously fosters the sense of communion.

So does of course closeness of touch between selves. "Handshaking," notes Fenichel, "means . . . letting one's substance flow into the other person."[194]

58. When such flowing is integral, that is, any sense of separateness from the other abolished, one might want to speak, for short, of a *"sense of fusion,"* a return to "the child's feelings that he is part of his love objects and vice versa."[195]

In the case of a widow described by Jacobson whom Krupp paraphrases, her "painful thoughts turned into . . . preoccupation with the activities which her husband had particularly enjoyed. . . . She behaved as if by doubling her own efforts in those areas she could make up for what he had lost":[196] perhaps sensing that she had become her husband —and/or that they were one.

6 | The Resembling of Selves

59. Characteristics of mine *"adopted"* from an other—for short *"adopts"*: the first barbarism, I believe, proposed in these pages; and which I would not have dared suggesting were it not for "inserts"— need not, of course, reproduce the reality of that other: they correspond to my beliefs about him. "Ego identification," Hendrick points out, "is not restricted to reproducing the real powers of the . . . object; it also achieves powers attributed to the object by the infant's fantasies."[197]

In fact, the unconscious intent to adopt may be accompanied by the resolve to deform (e.g., to caricature).

The faithfulness of adopts may also be reduced by lack of capacity. "Their gestures," Fenichel observes about catatonic patients, "frequently are intended as imitations of other persons' gestures; but the failure of this intention makes the gesture 'empty' and 'meaningless.' "[198]

An adopt may be ego-dystonic. "He feared," Gruen observes about a patient, "his father's rages, and felt contemptuous towards him for them. . . . He rejected such behavior consciously. . . . The father's hated characteristics were secretly identified with. . . . In secret, he was all that which his mother complained about in his father. . . . Everything was secret, and . . . despised by a part of him"[199]—a type of observation that lends itself to the construction of a hidden tautology (*see* paragraphs 32–36): when there is "depersonalization" and "an 'as if' existence," the author advances, "there is lack of genuine identification": Is this a statement about patients, or not rather a (partial) indication of what the new word "genuine identification" shall serve to designate?

Short of taking over somebody else's conduct (as I perceive it), I may develop the (false) belief that I have. Thus, with regard to envied properties of his parents, the child may acquire, in Annie Reich's phrasing, "a feeling of identity with the ideal, without achievement."[201]

The achievement may follow. Having recalled that the melancolic treats himself as if he were the worthless love object "without assuming its characteristics," Jacobson notes that "in her depression . . . [a] patient had become as selfish . . . as she described her husband."[202]

A certain act of adoption may be a defense against others, already performed or dreaded.[203] "[The] image of the all-powerful pregenital . . . mother," Annie Reich discerns in a patient, "was used to counteract the . . . later image of the sick, suffering, pregnant mother with whom . . . he was also identified. When he . . . could no longer feel . . . a man, he could at least identify with the powerful mother of early childhood and thereby counterbalance his identification with the castrated one."[204] (But it is not clear here whether "adoption" or "metamorphosis" occurred.)

Or an act of adoption, accompanied by awareness of it, may be a defense against the awareness of having performed another one. "One day," Greenson reports, "the patient had a . . . bowel movement which reminded him of father. This set in motion a growing feeling that he had become like his father. For several weeks he found that he was performing all sorts of activities exactly the way his father did. . . . This awareness of being like his father was absent in only one activity— intercourse. Analysis revealed that . . . he behaved in the sexual act toward his wife exactly as he remembered or fantasied that his father behaved in the sexual act with his mother. He attempted to ward off the memory or the reconstruction of the primal scene by . . . 'hyper'-identification. . . . The . . . 'hyper'-identification with the father was manifested in . . . trivial actions that hid the identification with the father in sexual matters."[205]

60. "The father," reports Annie Reich about a patient presenting "*counter-adoption*" (almost always amalgamated with adoption, to be sure), "was a . . . obstetrician whose office was located in the family home. From early childhood on, the boy had seen many pregnant women. He knew his father operated on them; he heard them scream in his father's hospital. He understood the medical activities of the father as being sexual and sadistic. The father cut and hurt the women. . . . The boy concluded . . . that the mother's illnesses were likewise a reaction to his father's 'brutality.' . . . [As a young man] he . . . could approach girls, but only under special conditions. . . . When they were in need of comfort, help, love, he was able to please them—even with his penis. . . . It was very important to give the woman an orgasm, but he himself had no sensations whatsoever. To quote his own description . . . he had to be 'a knight on a white horse who used his lance only to protect helpless women.' He is identified with his father, but in a negative way. The father, in the child's view, had lacerated women with his penis-scalpel."[206]

61. When "adopts" from a particular other are prominent in me, and if I am highly aware of their being that, one could, for brevity, speak of "*assimilation.*" Instead of a perception of this there may be a prediction, desired or dreaded: "She lived," Greenson observes about a patient, "with an ominous feeling that she might turn out to be like her mother."[207]

62. What I am adopting may be the other's reactions *toward me.*

Reactions that, rather than being current, may belong to the past (as I perceive it), and may be dreaded or desired. "Anna Freud," Pollock recalls, "has described how a child . . . deprived of a mother's care . . . plays 'mother and child' with its own body."[208]

Reactions toward me, and then adopted by me, may consist in conduct that is *not* centered around demands made on me. "Ego identification," as Hendrick points out, "may . . . produce [rather: the word may designate—N.L.] the capacity . . . e.g., to handle a spoon in the way mother handles it."[209]

Or I may start making on myself demands that were hitherto raised against me by others: "*to assume*" such *demands*, if a brief designation of this important class of events were thought to be desirable. (Once more, the obvious label, "to internalize" may have become convenient because of the language habits discussed in Section 1.)

"In Margaret," Ritvo notes about a child, "conscience . . . was being experienced in terms of 'will Mother approve?' rather than 'do I approve?'"[210] That is, I may "*assume an authority*" (any demands it may raise, within certain constraints I may put on it); or, directly, "*assume particular demands*"; to the "superego," then, would correspond "authorities assumed" plus "*demands assumed.*"

Here other movements may be mentioned, for differentiation. I may adopt the *content* of a reaction by an other toward me, without adopting its *application to me*; turning it against him or third parties: still a case of "adoption," but no more one of "assuming"—I may react to myself as I had reacted to another—not a case of "adoption"; e.g., self-reproaches in depression. My former reactions toward the demands made on me by others may be put into the service of the demands I start making on myself—a classical point—or I may react to impositions having become internal as I responded to them when they were external: "The depressed person," observes Greenson, "surrenders his self to the . . . super-ego as he once did to the love-object."[211]

63. There is a current disposition to believe that there is no "adoption of properties" without a "mingling of selves" (a point already discussed in paragraphs 43–45).

To be sure, frequently adoption is thus accompanied. "In the course of therapy," Grinker reports about a patient, "he became aware that he wore the same color in suits and shirts, affected the same mannerisms, enjoyed only the same baseball team, etc., as had his father. But behind this caricature of detailed imitation was the *introjected* patterned relationship with his . . . father . . .":[212] presumably one or another mode of what I have called mingling. "Acceleration of identification [which probably here designates 'adoption'—N.L.] is," according to Hendrick, "commonly accompanied by oral, and especially cannibalistic fantasies":[213] presumably fantasies of inserting the one from whom one adopts into one's self.

Sometimes a good deal of evidence is presented for adoption having occurred, but then the assertion that there is also mingling is quickly made, perhaps with an attempt at demonstration that is puzzling. Thus Lubin develops in detail the point that a woman patient of his "identified" with Moses, with the entire evidence pointing to adoption (for instance, aspects of Moses' relation to Aaron and the Jews being reproduced in the patient's relations to her Rabbi husband and his congregation). But, the author observes, if Moses, as Joseph Solomon has suggested, "is an orally gratifying mother symbol," then "the identification with Moses . . . would represent fusion with a good mother"[214]—only, it seems to me, if it had been established, or could be surmised, that all of us, or those of us resembling the patient, are prone to that fusion.

Adoption may be a factor making for mingling. Jacobson notes the child's "belief that imitating means . . . being or becoming his parents";[215] in fact, the child's imitations of his parents during the first year of life "appear to serve only the one purpose: to bring about the . . . merging of the self with the love objects."[216] When self-consoling thumb-sucking, masturbation, or their derivatives are accompanied by fantasies that the object is sought after, but "unavailable," then, Schecter advances, "the self has been . . . *identified with* the longed-for parent . . . and attempts to *become* that parent. . . ."[217] "Certain psychotic children," observes Mahler, "believe that they *become* [italicized in the text—N.L.] the mother or the sister by wearing their clothes."[218] "A boy of eighteen, in a beginning schizophrenic development," reports Jacobson, "tries, e.g., whenever he is scared and unable to handle a situation, to think of a . . . powerful, admired friend and . . . imitate his appearance, his gestures, behavior, etc. Thus he feels he 'has become his friend. . . .' "[219]

Conversely, when there is mingling between my self and that of an other, I am also apt to adopt properties from him. "It may be," observes Schecter, "that the . . . fusion of self and object images . . . is . . . an early stage of the . . . identification process. . . . 'Before I can become *like* you in this way, I must experience *being* you in this way' ": "a *temporary* blurring . . . of the boundaries of self and object in the service of . . . differentation" [emphases in the text].[220] That is, "the feeling 'at one' with the admired person need not . . . refer to the 'restoring of the unity of the nursing situation,' but may represent a step in the child's . . . 'becoming like' . . . the parent."[221] "The internal father," reports Lois Munro on a patient, "[forced] him to carry out his violent attacks on his mother and her child."[222] Another patient discussed by the same author "felt identified with his mother to such a degree [presumably: had experienced such a metamorphosis of himself into his mother—N.L.] that he had to reproduce her pregnancies and her intercourse with his father. . . ."[223]

But there *are* cases of "mingling" without "adoption." "In the depressions," Greenson notes, "one can observe the introjection of the . . . object without transformations indicative of identification."[224]

Perhaps, in fact, *every* "adoption" in *early* childhood has "mingling" as a condition or consequence. According to Fenichel the infant tends to *imitate* what he perceives (and so as to perceive) on the one hand, and to *swallow* it on the other hand ("in the unconscious all sense organs are perceived as mouth-like")—an assertion of a relationship in *patients* (that insertion and adoption *go together*) that is characteristically shielded and ennobled by becoming the affirmation of an *identity* within an *idea*: "The *concept* of primary identification denotes that . . . 'putting into the mouth' and 'imitation for perception's sake' are *one and the same*"—an allegation that is, however, not meant seriously enough to prevent, a moment later, "one" from being the cause of "the same": "The imitation of the external world *by* oral incorporation. . . ."[225] According to Jacobson, "in the beginning . . .

the child is . . . apt to believe that imitating the mother . . . means being or becoming the mother."[226]

Declaring that "the child . . . imitates whatever attracts his attention momentarily in the object," and affirming that "such imitations express . . . the child's fantasy that he *is the object*" [italicized by the author— N.L.], Annie Reich continues, however: "*or*, later, that he is *like* the object."[227] "With development," Edith Jacobson agrees, "the child's desires to remain part of his love objects, or to make them part of his own self . . . give way to wishes for realistic likeness with them."[228]

It would indeed be surprising if behind *every* act in which a child, after infancy, attains some "realistic likeness" with an adult, there were, for instance, an insertion of that adult into the child, or a metamorphosis of the child's self into that of the adult.

64. So surprising that this affirmation, though often intended, is rarely declared. (*See* paragraphs 43–45.)

An attempt at proving the point (without naming it) may be made, which is apt, on inspection, to depend on the variety in meanings of central words, and to start with a hidden proposition close to (if not identical with) the one that is to be demonstrated. Thus Herman Nunberg (according to Wiggers, reporting on a discussion) "stated that he considered identification 'a tendency to reunite with the mother.' " While, with current habits, the reader is not likely to dwell on this sentence, it may merit attention. Either it *stipulates word usage*: only where there is a tendency to reunite with the mother should we, henceforth, employ the word "identification." This would not eliminate the question at issue, but only renew its wording: Are all acts in which I "adopt" also "identifications"? The doubt that seemed to me appropriate with regard to the earlier formulation could hardly be reduced by this, or any other, change of language. Alternatively, to "consider" every "identification" as a tendency to reunite with the mother could mean to *affirm the law* that such a tendency is present with every event called "identification" according to some implied definition—presumably centering on what I proposed to call adoption. But that law would thus be advanced rather than proved—while the use of the verb "to consider" in the sentence quoted precisely serves to subdue the feeling that all we have so far is an allegation whose fate depends on the conduct of patients. In fact, Nunberg (always in Wiggers' account) in continuing takes the law as established. Then, he merely has to imply that any present tendency to reunite with the mother includes characteristics of the first reunion (which is much more plausible than the preceding assertion), and, moving on ever firmer ground, to recall that "the first reunion is through sucking." One might expect at this point an explicit statement of what I presume to be the belief toward which the author tends: whenever I adopt a property from an other, I suck him. Not so: Nunberg (as paraphrased) concludes that in view of all this identification is "considered" a "psychic derivative" of early orality.[229] Not only is it unclear what the difference might be between identification *being* just that or merely being "considered" it; there is also the fact that the locution "*b* is a psychic derivative of *a*" covers, in established usage, a gamut of relationships between *a* and *b*, some weaker than others. Thus the term might go as far as to designate the constellation of *a* always being present unconsciously when *b* occurs (in which case we would have what I presume to be the belief here approached); or it might merely refer to *b* not occurring unless preceded by *a* in an earlier phase of development—e.g., in the words used by Annie Reich (quoted in paragraph 63) it may be asserted that early desires to remain part of one's love objects, or to make them part of one's own self, are among the necessary conditions for later wishes to be realistically like them—which few might be disposed to dispute, but not many to hail. It is this moderate, safe, and dull meaning of Nunberg's affirmation, however, that shelters its extreme, dubious, and exciting core.

Envisaging "the introjection of the aggressor" on the one hand, and "the . . . identification with the aggressor in the adoption of a particular role" (a "superficial" event) on the other hand, Luquet demands that one "carefully distinguish" between them.[230] However, the major mode of sheltering the affirmation that there is no "adoption" without "mingling" is, as we have already seen in Chapter 3 and as I shall try to show further here, precisely to avoid such pedantry.

In speaking, *unmistakably*, about "adoption," one may use words with a gamut of connotations (and little sustained denotation) that encourage the reader to believe that "mingling" is *also* affirmed, without, however, declaring that this is indeed the case. When a certain type of homosexual "adopts" his mother's property of being a woman, does he *always* undergo, unconsciously, a metamorphosis of himself into his mother? The awkward question is subdued by asserting that "the homosexual man replaces his love for his mother by an identification with her,"[231] the zone of reference of the word ranging, precisely, from superficial "adoption" to deep "mingling." A patient, reports Bychowski, "has an older brother . . . and felt defeated by him. He *incorporated* various elements of his image, among them his 'strong' voice which made him appear so much more manly. While this 'laryngeal' *introjection* was being discussed, . . . [he] felt an obstruction in his throat which he had to clear . . . *as if to get rid of his* fraternal *introject*."[232] The avoidance of *claiming* insertion is even more clearly marked when Grinker discusses a patient with a "pattern within the self" that is "as painful or as pleasurable as the child's early experiences": ". . . the frustrating mother is, *as it were*, what the subject experiences *within* himself, and the self becomes *like* the bad mother":[233] all that is at the end affirmed plainly is "adoption"!

The opposite sequence, a crescendo, is more frequent. At a certain point in the child's development, Fenichel recalls, "prohibitions set up by the parents remain effective even in their absence." In a first reformulation: "A portion of the ego has become an 'inner mother.' " Here the quotation marks still keep predominant the meaning: now a portion of the ego does what mother used to do. That is, "inner mother" may appear largely as a metaphor. Yet, in imagery the mother is already inside. In a second elaboration we learn that "this internalization of the mother"—which still may be taken as: the child is now imposing on himself what the mother used to demand of him—"takes place through an act of introjection": a big step toward suggesting "insertion," in so far as "introjection" as used by this author often, even in declared fashion, means: bringing, in fantasy, another body into one's own. That this is the meaning here, is only confirmed by the third amplification: "Introjection is the first instinctual aim directed towards objects. . . ."[234] Thus the crucial acts of "assuming" by children with regard to their parents are rescued from the superficiality of being merely that; while the going to greater depths does not even entail indicating how the parents are "inserted" by the child, not to speak of giving evidence that they are.

In yet another variant a seemingly good case may be used to support a manifestly weak one. Having affirmed that a depressive patient "in his dreams may show himself filled with . . . *introjects,*" Bychowski starts with a clear (and rare) case of entities outside the body having been, in fantasy, introduced into it, though they happen to be merely connected with people rather than being people themselves: "A female patient dreamt that her vagina was filled with books and phallic symbols as representatives of both her father and her analyst." And then the author proceeds: "Another female patient in her fourth year of age had lost her father, and had *introjected* his legs, which were paralyzed as a result of his illness. . . . [She] experienced pains and weakness in her legs."[235] What is clear in the first case is "insertion," and in the second, "adoption"; what is unmentioned in the first is "adoption"; and (to come to the point) what is suggested to the reader in the second case is "insertion" or, more broadly, "mingling"—what one desires to find everywhere, and in what one helps oneself to believe by the ambiguities I have been describing.

Maintaining a belief in "mingling" beyond the evidence, one may also (in conditions I have not understood) forego it in spite of evidence. "Anna Freud (1936)," recalls Brody, "described a clear-cut instance of identifications in a little girl afraid to cross the hall in the dark because she had a dread of seeing ghosts. One day she said, 'There is no need to be afraid in the hall; you just pretend *you are* the ghost who might meet you.' " A clear-cut instance, I should say, of a low-level metamorphosis-of-self-into-other. But the author concludes to mere adoption: "The child *molds itself after* the frightening object."[236]

65. Finally, the law that who adopts, mingles, may simply be taken as established, and then applied. When a patient of Malin's attributed properties of himself (which he disliked) to the analyst, "the projections were . . . *interpreted* as his need to put bad parts of himself . . . *into* the analyst. . . . He was symbolically *entering* the analyst through these projections, to take control of him by weakening his self-esteem through . . . denigration. . . . He was . . . taking possession, in fantasy, of the analyst *from within.* . . . In his life history there was no precedent for him to assume he could have any relationship with anyone without total control. . . ."[237] That such control can be exercised only "from within" is perhaps too obvious to need establishing.

66. In applying the law in question, one may not only, as we have seen, abstain from "carefully distinguishing" between adoption and mingling (*see* paragraph 64); one may even arrive at both from the same evidence. "[He] was in bed with a man," Bychowski reports about a patient's dream, and "discovered that the other fellow had a vagina. Upon awakening, while doing some exercise in order to relax his aching limbs, he felt as though somebody was moving along him in his bed. We see here adumbrated the externalization [projection—N.L.] of the feminine introject ["mingling"?—N.L.] *and, by the same token,* of the feminine image of the self ["adoption"?—N.L.]."[238] But would not "by the same token" any assertion about the relationship between "introject" and "image" that may be implied here be a tautology?

7 | A Tall Word Without Big Sentences

67. "Early *identifications* with parental qualities which are envied," observes Annie Reich, "may be *represented* by a longing to be like the idealized parent, and may *lead* not at all . . . to a . . . transformation in the desired sense":[239] In characteristic fashion (*see* paragraph 18) the author takes it for granted that there is a type of event called "identification"—about which we do not know more than we would were that word spelled backwards—which is a condition or a common characteristic of a variety of reactions displayed by children toward parents, on the gamut from mere longing to be like them to actually becoming like them. Making the same affirmation in fashionable guise—"using the ideas . . . [of] Wittgenstein"—Koff affirms that "the word identification represents a whole family of concepts, each member of the family bearing only a familiar resemblance to another member," so that "at the extreme ends we may have two members of a family who apparently do not bear any resemblance to each other. . . ."[240] Only one point remains obscure: What determines the location of the "family's" "extreme ends"? In other words, what is the characteristic the presence of which is required for inclusion into the company of "identification*s*"?

68. If the author is silent on this, he has presumably not found it. Nor have I.

I have adumbrated a definition of "adoption" (Chapter 6).

As to "mingling" (Chapter 5), I would already define it with regard to a plurality of reactions: an event shall be called one of "mingling" if it is one or the other of the following:

1. Adding a self onto another (paragraph 52)
2. Inserting a self into another (paragraph 53)
3. Transmuting a self into another (paragraph 54)
4. Putting myself into another's place to a high degree (paragraph 55)
5. Sensing sameness with another to a high degree (paragraph 56)
6. Sensing communion with another to a high degree (paragraph 57)
7. Sensing fusion with another (paragraph 58)

An event that is either "mingling" or "adoption" might be called a *"junction"*: the replacement I would suggest for "identification" in wide meanings.

69. Having herewith concluded my proposals on words, I would like to render explicit a belief that has surely become evident to the reader long ago: When words are used in the ways in which the four which have been my concern in these pages (identification, internalization, introjection, incorporation) are habitually treated, the least bad course to adopt is to discontinue their use.

70. To return to "junctions," one use of the word might be to refer handily to a certain zone of inquiry. One might say about a colleague: He has become increasingly interested in studying junctions.

Another—and this time, capital—employment would be, of course, to appear in propositions on conditions, contexts, and consequences of any "junction," to whatever subclass it may belong. The trouble is that there are not many such propositions; that their body is not rapidly growing; and that those that are have difficulties.

71. Take the famous connection between impairment of object relation (a word I shall here take for granted) and establishment of "junction": the most prominent—if not the only—proposition alleged about "identifications" at large.

According to an extreme, but by no means rare, formulation "the construction of an introject is the sequel to a . . . dissolution of the relationship . . . to an object."[241] This, to me, suggests (and does not declare) that the former event is *always* the sequel to the latter, or at least the latter *always* an antecedent of the former; where "introject," as we have seen, may designate any variant of "junction." Instead of a "dissolution" of the relationship to an object, other, and presumably equivalent, formulations mention its "renunciation" or "relinquishment," or "giving up an object." Observing that "we . . . find identification with a therapist occurring early in treatment," Koff, expressing the penchant to encapsulate a law into a definition (*see* paragraph 22), can then recall that "*according to our definition* this *should be regarded as a defense against an object relationship*"[242]—how free do we remain to "find" that it just isn't?

72. In common sense as well as in clinical practice it is of course taken for granted that nothing is more frequent than for me to have established "identifications" with some other with whom I continue to entertain an object relation. All nonpsychotic children are supposed to do it with their parents. And while "an organ afflicted with a conversion symptom may," as Fenichel recalls, "represent an object that has been introjected," even in this case, "in spite of such an incorporation, the object still remains in the external world, too; hysterical introjection is a partial rather than a total regression from an object relationship to identification."[243]

73. But such is the combined force of definition and theory that what is, to a practitioner, a truism rarely worth mentioning may become a quandary to the same person officiating as a theoretician. "Freud," Edith Jacobson asserts cautiously, "refers to the *probability* of simultaneous object relations and identifications with the love object . . ."; a delicate matter, if "Freud believed that identifications . . . usually [sic] arise from the renunciation of the love object." Still, when we consider "the role of the child's oedipal renunciation in the constitution of superego identifications," "*we must realize that* the child does not actually lose his oedipal love object":[244] as if anybody had ever asserted that in the normal resolution of the Oedipus the child becomes disinterested in his parents, which is presumably what "actually losing the object" means. While nobody did, many may have maintained in isolation a sensible view of what happens to the child's reactions toward his parents with the passing of the Oedipus on the one hand, and the "theoretical" linking of "identification" and "renunciation" on the other hand. If "a 'true' . . . identification is a consequence of a 'true' object relationship, with a renunciation of that object in the external world"—whatever the meaning of such a "true," with or without quotation marks; and above all, whatever the meaning of such an "is": stipulating word usage or affirming an invariant relation between events?—then the fact that "some [sic] individuals . . . both identify with and have object relationships with another person," so far from being obvious (and capital) becomes what it is for Koff: "a phenomenon which needs further discussion"[245]—at some date that has apparently not yet arrived.

74. The contention that *all* "identifications" are "sequels" to *full* "renunciations" of "objects" would be too weird to be prominent were

it not, on the one hand, that *some* among the more striking ones of course are; and on the other hand that *others*, just as clearly, are sequels to *partial* relinquishments of objects.

But is the latter *always* the case when the former is not? According to the very same author whom I just quoted to illustrate the extreme thesis, and on the very same page on which he so vigorously expresses it, "identification in the early stages of treatment may be . . . the only way in which certain individuals can *begin to form* a relationship."[246] Of course, this is just "identification," rather than the same word with the prefix "true" equipped with quotation marks. But then we do not know whether the word thus enriched refers to another class of events—and if so which?—than the term in its bareness, or to a subclass; and if so, which? "Not all infantile identifications," Edith Jacobson goes so far as to observe explicitly, "arise under the influence of the child's . . . conflicts"; some are "developing directly from the child's . . . intimacy with his love objects. . . ."[247] "The identifications of the normal child," the same author asserts more ambiguously "do not arise *in place of* object relations. In fact, the child's object relations and identifications *evolve hand in hand*"[248]—is this a denial of even the moderate variant of the law under discussion? Or perhaps merely an assertion that "normal ego and superego identifications" in childhood soon make up for the damage to object relations to which they, after all, owe their existence: "In the course of the latter [the "identifications" just named —N.L.], the object relations to the parents gain in strength and stability by a decrease of sexual and aggressive components. . . ."[249]

75. We seem left with the contention that some "junctions" follow upon the total relinquishment of objects, others upon their partial renunciation, and yet others do not depend upon impairment of object relations.

The point thus would seem to be to learn more about the conditions making for each of these configurations.

76. Also, if we envisage the intermediate class—"junction" upon partial relinquishment of object—what do we know or conjecture about the conditions that make a particular variant of "identification" toward a particular other follow upon the abandonment of a particular striving?

Envisaging "the theory of identification"—by which he seems to mean the two grand propositions discussed above; which are apparently felt to be one—Koff draws a "consequence" from it: "The boy should also identify with his mother, since she is the main object that is abandoned," and "the girl should have some . . . identification with her father, when she abandons him as an object"; in fact, "clinical observations indicate this does occur regularly."[250] However, the same source of knowledge also shows that the kinds of "identifications" made in these circumstances, as well as their weights, vary widely, making for a manifold of outcomes.

The point, then, would again be to learn more about the conditions making for each of the pertinent configurations, rather than merely preserving the grand theorem.

77. According to a classical point "the principal identification is made with the parent who is felt to give the decisive prohibitions."[251] Is this always true? Has not a single case been observed in which there is a substantial divergence between these two distributions: (1) that, in the child, of his "adoptions" from the one and the other parent; (2) that, among the parents, of contributions to the obstacles put up against the child's penchants? And if the proposition just discussed were taken as true, is that all that can be said about factors influencing a response of "junction" to partial renunciation of relations toward an object?

To close with questions both elementary and unanswered (or so it seems to me) expresses, to be sure, the highly incomplete character of this discussion. But perhaps also a lack of clarity about what we know, and slowness of growth in insight. Both may be related to peculiarities in language and thought that I have attempted to elucidate, and to which I have tried to show alternatives.

Notes to Part One

1. Edith Jacobson, *The Self and the Object World* (New York: International Universities Press, 1964), p. 46.
2. Kenneth Gaarder, "The Internalized Representation of the Object in the Presence and in the Absence of the Object," *International Journal of Psycho-Analysis*, XLVI (1965), 298.
3. Roy R. Grinker, "On Identification," *International Journal of Psycho-Analysis*, XXXVIII (1957), 379.
4. Robert H. Koff, "A Definition of Identification: A Review of the Literature," *International Journal of Psycho-Analysis*, XLII (1961), 362.
5. Peter L. Giovacchini, "Transference, Incorporation, and Synthesis," *International Journal of Psycho-Analysis*, XLVI (1965), 287–296.
6. *Ibid.*, p. 290.

7. *Ibid.*, p. 295.
8. *Ibid.*, p. 291.
9. *Ibid.*, p. 296.
10. Norman Cameron, "Introjection, Reprojection, and Hallucination in the Interaction Between Schizophrenic Patient and Therapist," *International Journal of Psycho-Analysis,* XLII (1961), 86.
11. Edith Jacobson, "On Psychotic Identifications," *International Journal of Psycho-Analysis,* XXXV (1954), 103.
12. Peter L. Giovacchini, "The Frozen Introject," *International Journal of Psycho-Analysis,* XLVIII (1967), 62.
13. George H. Pollock, "On Symbiosis and Symbiotic Neurosis," *International Journal of Psycho-Analysis,* XLV (1964), 20.
14. Robert P. Knight, "Introjection, Projection, and Identification," *Psychiatric Quarterly,* IX (1940), 339–340.
15. Arno Gruen, "Autonomy and Identification: The Paradox of Their Opposition," *International Journal of Psycho-Analysis,* XLIX (1968), 650.
16. Gustav Bychowski, "The Release of Internal Images," *International Journal of Psycho-Analysis,* XXXVII (1956), 331.
17. Knight, *op. cit.*
18. Gustav Bychowski, "The Struggle Against the Introject," *International Journal of Psycho-Analysis,* XXXIX (1958), 185.
19. Bychowski, "The Release of Internal Images," p. 338.
20. Pollock, p. 19.
21. George R. Krupp, "Identification as a Defense Against Anxiety in Coping with Loss," *International Journal of Psycho-Analysis,* XLVI (1965), 303.
22. Giovacchini, "Transference, Incorporation, and Synthesis," p. 292.
23. *Ibid.*, p. 295.
24. Jacobson, *The Self and the Object World,* p. 47.
25. Koff, p. 362.
26. Gustav Bychowski, "General Aspects and Implications of Introjection," *Psychiatric Quarterly,* XXV (1956), 544.
27. *Ibid.*, p. 543.
28. Giovacchini, "Transference, Incorporation, and Synthesis," p. 294.
29. Bychowski, "The Struggle Against the Introject," p. 187.
30. Bychowski, "General Aspects and Implications of Introjection," p. 538.
31. *Ibid.*, p. 535.
32. Krupp, p. 303.
33. Bychowski, "General Aspects and Implications of Introjection," p. 535.

34. *Ibid.*, pp. 532–533.
35. Grinker, p. 386.
36. Morris W. Brody and Vincent P. Mahoney, "Introjection, Identification, and Incorporation," *International Journal of Psycho-Analysis*, XLV (1964), 60.
37. Grinker, p. 387.
38. Bychowski, "The Struggle Against the Introject," p. 182.
39. Giovacchini, "The Frozen Introject," p. 62.
40. Jacobson, *The Self and the Object World*, p. 42.
41. *Ibid.*, p. 50.
42. Grinker, p. 384.
43. *Ibid.*
44. Brody and Mahoney, p. 63.
45. *Ibid.*, p. 58.
46. Pierre Luquet, "Early Identification and Structuration of the Ego," *International Journal of Psycho-Analysis*, XLV (1964), 264.
47. Hans W. Loewald, "Internalization, Separation, Mourning, and the Superego," *Psychiatric Quarterly*, XXI (1962), 489.
48. Martin A. Berezin, "Comments on Dr. Luquet's Paper (*see* under Luquet, note 46 above—N.L.), *International Journal of Psycho-Analysis*, XLV (1964), 270.
49. Grinker, p. 381.
50. Otto Fenichel, *The Psychoanalytic Theory of Neurosis* (New York: W. W. Norton, 1945), p. 149.
51. Arthur Malin and James S. Grotstein, "Projective Identification in the Therapeutic Process," *International Journal of Psycho-Analysis*, XLVII (1966), 26.
52. Koff, p. 59.
53. Knight, p. 334.
54. Herbert A. Wiggers, "Problems of Identification," *Journal of the American Psychoanalytic Association*, I (1953), 548.
55. *Ibid.*, p. 549.
56. David E. Schecter, "Identification and Individuation," *Journal of the American Psychoanalytic Association*, XVI (1968), 52–53.
57. *Ibid.*, p. 52.
58. Grinker, p. 379.
59. Knight, p. 338.
60. Brody and Mahoney, p. 60.
61. Koff, p. 367.
62. *Ibid.*
63. *Ibid.*, p. 369.
64. *Ibid.*, p. 362.
65. Knight, pp. 335, 341.

66. Edith Jacobson, "Contribution to the Metapsychology of Psychotic Identifications," *Journal of the American Psychoanalytic Association*, II (1954), 104.
67. *Ibid.*
68. Koff, p. 365.
69. Brody and Mahoney, p. 61.
70. Ives Hendrick, "Early Development of Ego: Identification in Infancy," *Psychiatric Quarterly*, XX (1951), 57–58.
71. Brody and Mahoney, p. 60.
72. Luquet, p. 265.
73. Berezin, p. 270.
74. Luquet, p. 265.
75. Berezin, p. 270.
76. Knight, p. 338.
77. Schecter, p. 52.
78. Fenichel, p. 344.
79. Bychowski, "The Release of Internal Images," p. 331.
80. Giovacchini, "Transference, Incorporation, and Synthesis," p. 295.
81. Gaarder, p. 301.
82. Giovacchini, "The Frozen Introject," p. 67.
83. Pollock, p. 20.
84. Bychowski, "The Release of Internal Images," p. 331.
85. *Ibid.*
86. Bychowski, "The Ego and the Introjects," pp. 31–32.
87. Malin and Grotstein, pp. 29–30.
88. Jacobson, *The Self and the Object World*, p. 47.
89. Bychowski, "The Struggle Against the Introject," p. 182.
90. Bychowski, "The Release of Internal Images," p. 332.
91. Leon Grinberg, "On a Specific Aspect of Counter-Transference Due to the Patient's Projective Identification," *International Journal of Psycho-Analysis*, XLIII (1962), 436.
92. Bychowski, "The Release of Internal Images," p. 332.
93. *Ibid.*, p. 334.
94. Krupp, p. 312.
95. *Ibid.*, p. 311.
96. Brody and Mahoney, p. 62.
97. Koff, p. 368.
98. Giovacchini, "The Frozen Introject," p. 61.
99. Giovacchini, "Transference, Incorporation, and Synthesis," p. 293.
100. Cameron, p. 87.
101. *Ibid.*, p. 88.
102. *Ibid.*, p. 94.

103. Knight, p. 339.
104. Giovacchini, "The Frozen Introject," p. 63.
105. Cameron, p. 87.
106. Bychowski, "The Release of Internal Images," p. 334.
107. Krupp, p. 310.
108. Knight, p. 336.
109. Bychowski, "General Aspects and Implications of Introjection," p. 537.
110. Giovacchini, "Transference, Incorporation, and Synthesis," p. 295.
111. Brody and Mahoney, p. 59.
112. *Ibid.*, p. 61.
113. *Ibid.*, p. 60.
114. *Ibid.*
115. Knight, p. 338.
116. Malin and Grotstein, p. 28.
117. Jeanne Lampl de Groot, "The Role of Identification in Psycho-Analytic Procedure," *International Journal of Psycho-Analysis*, XXXVII (1957), 456.
118. Samuel Ritvo and Albert J. Solnit, "The Relationship of Early Ego Identifications to Superego Formation," *International Journal of Psycho-Analysis*, XLI (1960), 299.
119. Brody and Mahoney, pp. 60–61.
120. Bychowski, "The Release of Internal Images," p. 335.
121. Grinker, p. 389.
122. *Ibid.*
123. Quoted by Brody and Mahoney, p. 58.
124. Knight, p. 337.
125. Koff, p. 367.
126. Fenichel, p. 438.
127. Brody and Mahoney, p. 61.
128. Ritvo and Solnit, p. 299.
129. Malin and Grotstein, p. 27.
130. Schecter, p. 52.
131. Pollock, p. 20.
132. Malin and Grotstein, p. 31.
133. Bychowski, "The Release of Internal Images," p. 333.
134. Melanie Klein, "On Identification," in *New Directions in Psycho-Analysis*, ed. Melanie Klein *et al.* (London: Tavistock, 1955), p. 344.
135. Grinker, p. 385.
136. Klein, p. 338.
137. *Ibid.*, p. 341.
138. Fenichel, pp. 469–470.
139. *Ibid.*, p. 394.

140. *Ibid.*, p. 408.
141. *Ibid.*, p. 394.
142. *Ibid.*, p. 393.
143. *Ibid.*
144. *Ibid.*, p. 397.
145. *Ibid.*, p. 399.
146. *Ibid.*, p. 398.
147. Gaarder, p. 297.
148. *Ibid.*
149. *Ibid.*
150. *Ibid.*, p. 298.
151. Jacobson, *The Self and the Object World*, p. 48.
152. *Ibid.*, p. 46.
153. Loewald, pp. 488–489.
154. Klein, pp. 326–327.
155. Fenichel, pp. 429–430.
156. Grinberg, pp. 437–438.
157. Bychowski, "The Ego and the Introjects," p. 26.
158. Fenichel, p. 49.
159. Cameron, p. 95.
160. Fenichel, p. 49.
161. Alex Blumstein, "Masochism and Fantasies of Preparing to Be Incorporated," *Journal of the American Psychoanalytic Association*, VII (1959), 295.
162. Lois Munro, "Clinical Notes on Internalization and Identification," *International Journal of Psycho-Analysis*, XXXIII (1952), 139.
163. Blumstein, pp. 292–293.
164. Klein, p. 337.
165. *Ibid.*, pp. 336–337.
166. Hendrick, pp. 57–58.
167. *Ibid.*
168. Brody and Mahoney, p. 63.
169. Bychowski, "The Release of Internal Images," p. 333.
170. *Ibid.*
171. Bruce Ruddick, "Colds and Respiratory Introjection," *International Journal of Psycho-Analysis*, XLIV (1963), 189.
172. Quoted by Pollock, p. 19.
173. Munro, p. 142.
174. Margaret Little, "On Basic Unity," *International Journal of Psycho-Analysis*, XLI (1960), 381.
175. Krupp, p. 304.
176. *Ibid.*, p. 309.
177. Annie Reich, "Early Identifications as Archaic Elements in the

Superego," *Journal of the American Psychoanalytic Association*, II (1954), 233.
178. Pollock, p. 14.
179. *Ibid.*, p. 15.
180. Bychowski, "Struggle Against the Introject," p. 186.
181. Jacobson, *The Self and the Object World*, p. 57.
182. *Ibid.*
183. Quoted by Pollock, p. 26.
184. *Ibid.*, p. 13.
185. *Ibid.*, p. 16.
186. Giovacchini, "Transference, Incorporation, and Synthesis," pp. 291–292.
187. Brody and Mahoney, p. 61.
188. Jacobson, *The Self and the Object World*, p. 39.
189. Krupp, p. 309.
190. Little, p. 377.
191. Malin and Grotstein, p. 37.
192. Little, p. 377.
193. *Ibid.*
194. Fenichel, p. 63.
195. Jacobson.
196. Krupp, p. 305.
197. Hendrick, p. 57.
198. Fenichel, p. 438.
199. Gruen, p. 648.
200. *Ibid.*, p. 652.
201. Reich, p. 223.
202. Jacobson, "Contribution to the Metapsychology of Psychotic Identifications," p. 247.
203. *See* Ralph R. Greenson, "Introduction to a Panel 'Problems of Identification' " and "The Struggle Against Identification," *Journal of the American Psychoanalytic Association*, II (1954), particularly p. 209.
204. Reich, p. 231.
205. Greenson, p. 207.
206. Reich, pp. 224, 228.
207. Greenson, p. 205.
208. Pollock, pp. 26–27.
209. Hendrick, p. 56.
210. Ritvo and Solnit, p. 299.
211. Greenson, p. 199.
212. Grinker, p. 385.
213. Hendrick, p. 57.
214. Albert J. Lubin, "A Feminine Moses: A Bridge Between Child-

hood Identifications and Adult Identity," *International Journal of Psycho-Analysis*, XXXIX (1958), 537.
215. Jacobson, "On Psychotic Identifications," p. 102.
216. Jacobson, "Contribution to the Metapsychology of Psychotic Identifications," p. 242.
217. Schecter, p. 72.
218. Margaret Schoenberger Mahler, "Autism and Symbiosis, Two Extreme Disturbances of Identity," *International Journal of Psycho-Analysis*, XXXIX (1958), 81.
219. Jacobson, "Contribution to the Metapsychology of Psychotic Identifications," p. 240.
220. Schecter, p. 75.
221. *Ibid.*, p. 76.
222. Munro, p. 138.
223. *Ibid.*, p. 136.
224. Greenson, p. 201.
225. Fenichel, p. 37.
226. Jacobson, *The Self and the Object World*, p. 43.
227. Reich, p. 221.
228. Jacobson, *The Self and the Object World*, p. 50.
229. Wiggers, p. 546.
230. Luquet, p. 267.
231. Fenichel, p. 344.
232. Bychowski, "The Release of Internal Images," pp. 332–333.
233. Grinker, p. 388.
234. Fenichel, p. 102.
235. Bychowski, "The Struggle Against the Introject," p. 182.
236. Brody and Mahoney, p. 61.
237. Malin and Grotstein, p. 30.
238. Bychowski, "The Release of Internal Images," p. 335.
239. Reich, pp. 219–220.
240. Koff, p. 369.
241. Brody and Mahoney, p. 59.
242. Koff, p. 369.
243. Fenichel, p. 230.
244. Jacobson, *The Self and the Object World*, p. 115.
245. Koff, p. 369.
246. *Ibid.*
247. Jacobson, *The Self and the Object World*, p. 90.
248. *Ibid.*, p. 65.
249. *Ibid.*, p. 117.
250. Koff, p. 363.
251. Fenichel, p. 506.

Part II
Identity Arrives

SECTION 1: USES OF CONCEPTS

8 | What Identity May Mean

1. "The term identity," announces Kramer at the beginning of a case study, "is used to denote an awareness of one's self as . . . separate . . .":[1] an explicit stipulation of what other words are substitutable for the one that is to be central. In most sciences such a statement will rarely be lacking when it comes to introducing words that possess familiar, but varied connotations from general use and that have, to boot, already received diverse meanings from colleagues. However, for the word at hand—identity—explicit definitions were but rarely proffered when it rose in the fifties and sixties; just as in the case of the classic "identification" (*see* Chapter 1, paragraph 1).

2. What made this omission possible was of course the illusion of understanding created by the word's currency prior to its admission into the upper level of analytic terms. Had *ytitnedi*—"identity" spelled backwards—been proposed for such a place, it might have been difficult to avoid introducing it with a sentence such as "a person shall be said to possess *ytitnedi* if he. . . ."

3. As it is, instead of right away giving a definition, one may first allude to one. "The term 'sense of identity' as used here," announces Harrison, "conforms to my understanding of Jacobson's views as described under 'Identity Formation' "[2]—as if the reader could be expected to have remembered Edith Jacobson's words; and as if these words gave a moderately clear indication of the events in patients to be designated. As a matter of fact, in speaking not of Jacobson's views,

but of his own "understanding" of them, the author seems to admit that this is not the case.

4. When the author thereupon does present other words to be substituted for the Word, they do indeed hardly furnish more indications as to the conditions when it is to be applied. "The sense of identity," he explains, "may be considered" to be "the integration of energies feeding back from all activities of the psyche. . . ."[3]

5. While familiar, "identity" is apt to appear obscure. But that very quality—tied to its nobility—merely strengthens the claim to prominence made on its behalf (see Chapter 2, paragraph 14). A definition—for science, a stipulation of substitutability by other words of clearer meaning—so far from having to be given at the start of the word's career, may seem the consummation of its course, the complete conquest of its many mysteries.

6. In the meantime, it is possible to treat an obscure word as if it were transparent, daring questioners to display their illiteracy by admitting their puzzlement.

Thus Erikson offers at one point his estimates of psychiatric casualties incurred during the last war: "The threat of a . . . loss of ego identity" was experienced by "an untold number"; those who actually "lost and only gradually or partially regained" that part of their psyche were "several hundred thousand" strong; and those who suffered its "acute loss" numbered "thousands."[4] I wonder how large divergences would be if competent readers had to pick members for these three sets from a given population.

7. "Identity" may appear with a variety of adjuncts whose presence perhaps expresses uncertainty about meaning.

"*Inner* identity," declares Erikson suddenly—the quotation marks are his, while the emphasis is mine—is scheduled for completion during intermediate periods between childhood and adulthood:[5] This particular combination of words is never acknowledged as a distinct entity (were it "outer identity" might have to be considered); nor is it ever defined; nor destined to reappear often. Apart from talking about "identity" always, Lichtenstein sometimes speaks of "*fixed* identity",[6] "*behavioral* identity,"[7] "behavioral or *existential* identity,"[8] "*primary* identity (*Uridentität*)":[9] here too, without any definitions nor much recurrence. According to Lomas, a patient's dependence on his father "for identity" threatened to eat up his "real identity."[10] The reader is not expected to be stopped by the adjective and tortured by the question whether it is employed for emphasis or for differentiation. According to Mahler, as paraphrased by Rubinfine, the feeling of "self-identity" hinges on solving the oedipal conflict, while in psychosis the sense of "entity and identity" disintegrates.[11] Neither the producer nor the consumers of such normal phrases seem to query the proliferation of close-by

110

words, the appearance of a variety of which reassures rather than bewilders: It might indeed be the stark repetition of a naked noun such as "identity" that finally would make one demand that rules for its use be indicated.

8. To begin a survey of (usually implicit) definitions conferred upon our word, "sense of identity" might refer to that sense of existing that may be shattered, for instance, in schizophrenics.

Recalling the question "do I exist?" Kenneth Appel, as reported by Rubinfine, affirms that the most massive anxiety occurs when "this sense of identity" is in peril;[12] the same sense that presumably Bak (also paraphrased by Rubinfine) has in mind when he "feels" that the core of anxiety in schizophrenia is the threat of losing "identity."[13]

9. But sense of "identity" may also designate the sense of separateness from others, for example in the usage of Mahler.[14]

10. "In some situations"—which probably means: in some uses—"identity," according to Greenacre, "refers to the unique characteristics of . . . [a] person. . . ."[15]

It is presumably in this sense that according to Lichtenstein the mother "conveys" to the infant "an identity": "The child is the organ . . . for the fulfillment of the mother's . . . needs."[16] The identification of young people with the heroes of cliques and crowds may, according to Erikson, temporarily induce "loss of identity"[17]—presumably not what is designated by this locution when applied to schizophrenics, but merely a relinquishment of idiosyncrasies.

11. However, in another of Lichtenstein's uses "identity" refers to "the capacity to remain the same in the midst of change," and "the sense of identity" to "a consciousness of such."[18]

Announcing that he will be "letting the term identity speak for itself in a number of connotations"—as if behavior proper to the user of a word, say, in poetry, were also conduct befitting here—Erikson foresees that sometimes "it will . . . refer . . . to an unconscious striving for a continuity of . . . character."[19] "Personal identity," he clarifies, refers to "one's self-sameness and continuity in time"[20] (this may be the kind of "and" that makes it possible to avoid both the discomfort apparently induced by a solitary noun and the tedium of obvious pleonasm).—Eissler, in a discussion reported by Rubinfine, "maintained" that the sense of identity was "based on" the ego's capacity to experience itself as a continuum:[21] what is presumably a definition being, characteristically, enunciated in a fashion that makes it easy to mistake it for a statement of causation (*see* Chapter 3, paragraph 37 and Chapter 11, paragraph 54).

12. The word "identity" is also applied, as Greenacre observes, to a person whose parts are "sufficiently well integrated" for the effect to be "oneness."[22]

13. Or the same word may be reserved for what I feel to be my core (if I do sense one in myself), plus all that I experience as expressive of it.

It is perhaps in this meaning that for Shaw, according to Erikson, breaking loose, at a certain moment, meant to avoid the danger of "success without identity";[23] that he did not feel "identical with himself" when he was good.[24] (p. 108).

14. Instead of designating one or the other particular sense of self (*see* Section 2 below)—e.g., one of those that I have just mentioned —the word "identity" may refer (presumably) to an indeterminate fraction of them.

In order to "feel safe in his own identity," Greenacre affirms, even at a mature age one is in need of at least one other person similar to oneself to look at and speak to; this is required if one is to avoid "a diminution of the sense of self and of identity," to escape jeopardy of "one's sense of oneself and of one's own attitudes."[25] (As I noted above, neither writer nor reader are here supposed, or likely, to ponder the meaning of "and": joining synonyms or diverse objects?). When Bak, discussing Greenacre and paraphrased by Rubinfine, notes that it is by fostering one's sense of "uniqueness" that thinking contributes to the sense of "identity,"[26] it is not clear which of the senses of self besides that of uniqueness are designated. Similarly, when Greenacre recalls that the future impostor's intense maternal attachment undermines not only his "sense of a separate self," but also the development of his "identity,"[27] we do not know which other senses of the self besides that of separateness are intended.

15. When the appearance of the word "identity" indicates that the domain of the senses of self is envisaged, but when thereupon a particular sense is named, the latter appellation would seem to be capable of replacing the former; yet the two coexist in apparent comfort (*see* Chapter 8, paragraph 12).

Thus when Bak, as paraphrased by Rubinfine, recalls that "there is frequently some problem of *identity* in the perversions, and a constant attempt through perverse acts to reinforce and repair *the body image*. . . ."[28] Or when Greenacre, reporting on a phase in an analysis, notes that "what is interesting from the angle of *identity* . . . was the . . . emergence of a greater *sense of being somebody*, and a woman at that."[29]

16. When one neither wants to limit the meaning of "identity" to one particular sense of self—as if it were below the richness of this "concept" to be thus restricted—nor desires to let the word hover in indeterminate fashion over the entire domain of the senses of self, one may, momentarily, make it designate a certain subset of them: as when, according to Jacobson (paraphrased by Rubinfine), "the sense

of identity consists of the . . . experience of . . . wholeness, separateness and uniqueness."[30]

17. If the elusive senses of self—usually removed from conscious attention (*see* Chapter 13, paragraph 96)—furnish one zone of referents for implicit definitions of "identity," the individual's often public orientations toward "social" objects supply another.

After having through many pages talked about "identity" in one or the other of the former meanings, Erikson announces that he "shall use the . . . term identity in order to suggest a social function of the ego which. . . ."[31] Attempting to elucidate the phrase "ego identity," he cites "the individual's views, ideals and standards, his behaviour and role in . . . society. . . ."[32] "Identity," for Suslick, "is the . . . apparatus whereby the individual orients himself to others and [sic] to his environment."[33] That there is no feeling of being alive without a sense of ego "identity" is, for Erikson, expressed in the trouble of adolescents who desperately seek for a "sense of belonging."[34]

18. A third group of meanings given to "identity" makes the word refer neither to the innermost nor to the "social" sector of the person, but rather to a vast area of his being that extends into these domains as well as into the sphere between them. What precisely the word's referent then is, may be even more unclear than in the usages already cited. When Erikson refers in passing to the "ego needs and ego functions subsumed under the term identity,"[35] I wonder once more what would happen if a group of qualified readers were asked to list those "ego needs" and "ego functions" that are excluded here. They betray, observes the same author about certain upper-class patients, the violent sense of power, the fury of superiority that makes it hard for them to enter economic competition except on terms of privilege; "and" they often resist cure because it implies a change of "ego identity."[36] Now which modifications induced by analysis in such patients would be *non*-"identity" ones, if the acquisition of a capacity to enter competition without privilege *would* be one in "identity"?

19. Above I quoted Lomas affirming that a patient's dependence on his father threatened to eat up his "real identity." In ideologies, notes Erikson, the superego is apt to regain territory from "identity."[37] The grandsons, he says about an upper-class family, know that they have to break out of the mansion, so to speak, in order to find an "identity."[38] "What the person is—his identity . . ." observes Lomas, who seems to have in mind "a being who is the agent of his own actions."[39] In these cases the definition of "identity" that seems implied—and it better so remain, given the difficulty of rendering it explicit and yet remaining within anaylsis—seems to be something like this: all that of me that springs from within me. Putting this into so many words might raise the question: what about that which I have

113

taken into me? If that is left out, what difference between "identity" and "id" plus endogenous "ego"? Alternatively, would "identity" be a synonym for the highly "ego syntonic," of whatever provenance?

20. Affirming weakness or excess in repudiation to be a consequence of "incomplete *identity*," Erikson explains that whoever is"not sure of his *point of view*" cannot repudiate judiciously.[40] "Identity" may be thus a synonym for: orientations.

21. Or for "ego strength," as when "a gradually accruing ego identity is the only safe-guard against the anarchy of drive as well as the autocracy of conscience."[41]

22. "Identity" may come to designate all that is pertinent to—or good in—growth: "In order to acquire real identity—including sexual potency—the boy," declares Lomas, "must . . .":[42] including sexual potency and excluding what capacity?

23. Finally, "identity" comes to stand for personality, character. "Three identities," observes Erikson about Negroes in America, "are formed: Mammy's oral sensual 'honey child' . . . (2) . . . ."[43] The ego grows in interplay with "the identities of the child's models."[44]

24. Given this manifold of implicit definitions, the stable letters and sounds of the word itself may come to be seen more important than its shifting and uncertain meanings.

"I believe," declares Lichtenstein, enhancing his master concept, "that Freud, in *Beyond the Pleasure Principle*, was aware that he was dealing with problems of identity": Did he not observe that "the repetition, *the rediscovery of identity*, is . . . a source of gratification"?[45] (Author's emphasis.) Never mind that "identity" here is but a synonym for "sameness": The word is there!

25. After all, meaning apart, the choice of a word is supposedly a crucial act, resulting, we are told, from complex calculations, an account of which is usually omitted. Having shown the existence, "before there can be any kind of sense of self," of "a framework, a zero-point," and having recalled that Spiegel names this object "the self," Lichtenstein declares that he "prefers" to call it "primary identity"—"for reasons which I cannot here enumerate."[46]

26. One's discourse gains in elasticity when one can, with little warning or awareness, pass from one meaning of an omnipresent word to another.

Having observed about a patient that "by pursuing a [certain] project, he would be giving *meaning and purpose to life*, i.e., establish an identity," Giovacchini goes on to show that "to some extent a person's identity depends upon how he functions": "If he is," for instance, "for the most part non-functional, this will be reflected in his *self-image*."[47] Where "an assured sense of identity" is missing in adolescence, notes Erikson, friendships and affairs become attempts at

114

"delineating the fuzzy outlines of identity"; but also, "fusion with another becomes identity loss."[48] Only, in the former case, "identity" may (how can we be sure?) designate the persons' beliefs about himself, and in the latter his distinctive traits. Having recalled his "main thesis" of "the correlation between [nonprocreative] sexuality and the emergence and maintenance of identity in man," Lichtenstein continues by showing that in the patient on whom he has reported "the problem of identity . . . was a conscious preoccupation. . . . Again and again she would ask 'Am I a prostitute? They say: a whore is a whore, once a whore always a whore. I do not want to believe it, I know it is not what I really am.' "[49] While in the author's "main thesis" the meanings of "identity" seem to range from regularity of behavior not based on instincts to the sense of permanence of myself through all changes outside of myself and within myself, in the account of his patient the word appears to refer to feelings and beliefs concerning the relationships between certain aspects of oneself and what one feels to be one's core. The referent of "identity" in the theoretician's "main thesis" appears related to what that word designates in the sentence about his patient above all by sameness of letters and sounds.

27. The currency of many implicit definitions for the same word creates a reservoir of pseudo-problems, offering opportunities for exciting riskless and indecisive combat.

"It is my impression," advances Suslick, that . . . 'persons in search of an identity' are not truly without an identity. Rather they have a primitive mode of operating in which they ingest and eject. . . . Nonetheless, this . . . pattern . . . is repeated over and over, and hence represents an . . . identity . . .":[50] Here the author starts out with the word meaning something like "knowing who I am," and ends with its being a synonym for "character."

28. In such considerations one is apt not to distinguish the assignment to a word of a referent, and the discovery of the latter's properties. Having recalled that, "with increasing sophistication of psychoanalytic theory," "the term . . . 'self-representation' is used to indicate one's self"—the word "self" might after all refer to something other than self—and that "the self-representation . . . serves to establish and maintain a sense of identity," Joseph declares: "It is beyond the scope of this paper to discuss in greater detail the *nature* of identity:"[51] presumably both what events the word designates and how they are related among themselves and to others.

29. One may equip a cherished word, which has a rich and vague aura from ordinary language, with a very specific meaning; conduct likely to impress producer and consumers as a creative act (*see* Chapter 3, paragraph 28), while entailing much and mere arbitrariness with regard to current usage.

"Ego identity," declares Erikson, "is"—we encounter a familiar ambiguity: does the verb "to be" here introduce a definition (a convention on the substitutability of words) or an assertion that such and such events go together in the world?—"the awareness of the fact that there is a self-sameness and continuity to the ego's synthesizing methods, and that these methods are effective in safeguarding the sameness and continuity of one's meaning for others."[52] That is, presumably I shall be said to have "ego identity" if the following two conditions are satisfied: (1) I believe, correctly, that I have character; (2) I believe, again correctly, that this fact increases the probability of others having invariant reactions toward me. Of course it is not false—no definition has the capacity to be false—to designate this particular constellation of events by the word "ego identity." But it *is* conferring upon the words involved a highly specific meaning, in contrast to the vague and rich connotations that emanate from "ego" and "identity" as perceived by people who have read a lot. And there are implications to such a step that authors proposing an original definition of this kind are unlikely to have faced. For instance, suppose I do entertain the belief mentioned under (1). But suppose I also note that the various manifestations of my "self-sameness," at any given moment and through time, are so discrepant that my particular "synthesizing methods," so far from "safeguarding," are endangering "the sameness of my meaning for others," while indeed establishing and confirming the "sameness of my meaning" for myself (it would be easy enough to illustrate this configuration). In this case I do *not* have "ego identity" according to the definition as given; which is nothing more, but also nothing less, than awkward. Rendering this possibility explicit, or being confronted with such an actuality would be disagreeable: instead of impressively singular, the definition chosen might appear irritatingly capricious. But how can one be sure one won't run into such trouble if one is going to "apply" the "concept"? The only safety is in abstaining from just that—which can be done easily, and happens frequently: is not the creation of the concept (almost) sufficient unto itself?

9 | What Defining May Mean

30. When a word turns into a "concept," it becomes itself the object of concern, the world receding away from it rather than being designated by it; reserved perhaps for later treatment, once arduous intellectual hurdles have been overcome. When the mastery of a difficult word becomes one's first objective, one may, however, never get to the next.

"Unquestionably," observes Lichtenstein, "in trying to define the concept of identity we face a bewildering complexity of phenomena."[53] One could think of confronting them without the interposition of a central word: naming them in straightforward fashion one by one (there may be many of them, but they are, after all, a finite lot); rejecting difficult words, such as "identity," for their very difficulty, instead of seeing in it dignity and promise. The authors here studied, however, seem to believe that the acquisition of knowledge about what happens in patients presupposes much prior allocation of intellectual energy to pertinent "concepts"—an allocation so massive that it may preclude even examining related, but at the moment less than central words. Thus Lichtenstein, having affirmed that "man is. . . capable of 'infinite' identities," and having "suggested" the word "metamorphosis" for this phenomenon, observes that "it is impossible to discuss even the most basic implications of this concept in this context."[54]

On the other hand, having mentioned several recent studies of shame, the same writer "feels" that he "must postpone a discussion of the problems dealt with by these authors" not, as one might have

117

expected, until more data pertinent to their hypotheses will have been collected, but rather "until a more complete development of the concept of metamorphosis becomes possible"[55]—the mysteries of "developing" a "concept" thus being shrouded in those of the conditions rendering that process "possible." In usual fashion, more than half a decade later nothing of the kind alluded to seems to have happened. Perceiving in Hartmann's "conceptualizations" a certain "ambiguity"—never mind which—and affirming that it is that property of theirs that has "prevented" Hartmann's "distinction between the concept of the ego . . . and the self" to "break" the "conceptual impasse" (no description furnished) of "modern" psychoanalytic theory, the same author goes on to assert (again, flatly) that this "impasse" in turn "prevents" a "successful approach" to—finally the world comes slightly into view—"sublimation, alienation and the self."[56] Is it not evident that we cannot learn more about "the self" without having first "broken" any "impasse" encountered in dealing with its "concept"? A slow growth rate of findings can thus be justified by conceptual torments, and rendered less galling by the prospect of rapid advance as the consequence of a "break-through" in no need of observations or ingenious clinical guesses. Might not "the concept of an identity principle" "permit" us to "integrate" id and ego, and "lead" us to "a new understanding" of ego ideal and superego?[57] The alternative to a slow growth in insights first suggested and then confirmed by the conduct of patients is not a less sluggish increase in knowledge, but a leap forward as a consequence of discoveries made by what is sensed as thinking: "The identity principle," declares Lichtenstein, "includes . . . perhaps . . . even" (that is, in addition to so many other riches) Hartmann's concept of pre-adaptedness![58] Words that have just been coined by oneself or one's colleagues are thus treated as if they were patients as yet badly known.

31. One may then be emphatic even about flagrant differences between definitions of a word, or between clearly distinct meanings of several words.

Having directed attention to "the capacity to remain the same in the midst of change" on the one hand, and to a "consciousness of such sameness" on the other hand; having named the former "identity" and the latter "sense of identity," Lichtenstein can add: "I follow Greenacre who stresses the distinction of the two concepts."[59] It is not required of one to indicate what the alternative to such a posture might be.

32. Conversely, one may be insufficiently aware of the possibility that a divergence in assertions expresses not a discrepancy in expectations about events, but merely a difference in meanings assigned to a given word. "Whether the sense of identity emerges by the age of three-five . . . or . . . in late adolescence . . .," observes Hayman, without raising the question whether such a notable level of apparent

118

disagreement is not due to language rather than observations.[60] "It is often assumed," remarks Lomas, in a similar vein, "that a sense of identity *derives* . . . from the . . . circumstances that are [here] being described as those which *threaten* identity—mainly the allocation of a . . . role in the family. . . ." Then he approaches (no more than that) the solution of this puzzling polarity of assertions: "*But* . . . [a] difference . . . exists between the recognition of the other person as a unique human being and the recognition of him merely in his role."[61]

33. Deciding on the definition of a word may be felt as an operation similar to discovering the properties of a piece of reality; and a divergence on the meanings to be attributed to a given sequence of sounds and letters may be experienced as indistinguishable from a disagreement on points of fact. (*See* Chapter 2, paragraph 23.)

When Kaywin, in Rubinfine's paraphrase, "suggested" that the perception of the self-representation was "synonymous" with the sense of identity, Jacobson "replied" that they "are not the same." And according to Eissler the "mere" development of imagery about the self "does not signify" the establishment of a sense of identity.[62]

10 | A Rich Word is Attractive

34. Comparing a narrow definition of a word—say, "identity" designating the sense of permanence—with a wide one—for instance, the same word referring to all the senses of the self—one may in the present state of analysis presume that the chances of "identity" figuring in novel hypotheses about patients are higher in the first than in the second case. If a producer of "concepts" were seriously expected to

"apply" them in short order so as to prove an often asserted but rarely ascertained "usefulness," they might be disposed to endow their preferred words with severely limited meanings, making them refer to classes of events about whose conditions, contexts, and consequences they are confident of providing novel knowledge.

35. Currently, however, this constraint hardly obtains (*see* Chapter 7). It is usual and proper to elaborate at length on a word (obscuring that it is merely that) without proceeding within a reasonable time to formulate sentences fulfilling these conditions: (1) that they advance new insights; (2) that they contain the word in question; (3) that this word, or a synonym, be needed (a term that, to be sure, requires definition) to express the knowledge gained. The more satisfying the production and consumption of the word by itself, the lower the demand for it to appear in exciting sentences.

36. One may limit oneself to predicting that somebody (no obilgation seems to have been incurred by oneself, when one takes what is allegedly a capital step of sponsoring a certain word) at some time will fulfill the conditions just stated.

"I have," declares Lichtenstein at the end of an article, "arrived at propositions [the reader may find it difficult to state them, while it is easy for him to name the words accented by the author—N.L.] of which I could only give a very abstract presentation. Whether they have any usefulness [not truth; that would be naïve—N.L.] will be decided by their applicability to clinical observation."[63] This suffices for 1965: but it would be odd for these words still to be recalled in 1975, and an effort then to be made to ascertain the degree of usefulness achieved by the concepts in question during the years elapsed; or, in the more probable case, to explain why neither their inventor nor anybody else had proceeded to any significant "application" of them. When Lichtenstein affirms that "from the concept 'possible functions' a theory of psychoanalytic etiology could be derived,"[64] it may at some level short of full consciousness seem likely to all concerned that little effort will be expended on the attempt to realize this potential of the new concept.

37. If one wants to proceed beyond mere claims with regard to a concept one advocates, it is possible to stop at a simple superposition of the new word upon familiar ones, while still provoking the sense not only of having added to insight, but also of having rendered more plausible the prediction of high productivity from yet more "application."

At the end of his monograph centered around "identity," Erikson —in a footnote—proceeds to relate "the components of identity diffusion" to juvenile delinquency.[65] That is, he covers well-known aspects of this type of conduct with the new words—reassuringly familiar in their resonance and excitingly obscure in their significance—

"time diffusion," "identity consciousness," "work paralysis" (an interlude of clarity), "negative identity" (obscurity with a vengeance after such relief), "bisexual diffusion," "locomotorist intoxication" (perhaps a second of incomprehension before one has translated), "intoxication by powerfully moving spectacles," "authority diffusion," and "diffusion of ideals"—such are the "concepts" with which the author would "approach" the "problem" on which he has chosen to illustrate the power of his ideas.

38. When so little is required in the matter of sentences containing the central word in question, the pull toward limiting its referent may be weaker than the push toward expanding it, the latter being nourished from a variety of motives.

39. First, when a word appears to possess high worth, it may seem invidious to limit its scope.

When Lichtenstein calls for the production of a "concept" that will "permit" a "delineation" of "identity" in a manner "appropriate" to "the human condition,"[66] those aspects of man that will finally be left out (not much, I would guess) might thereby be sensed to be declared of lower rank. This may also be the case when Erikson observes that a child resists with the strength encountered in animals who are suddenly forced to defend their lives, when the environment tries to deprive him of the forms of expression permitting him to develop the next step in his "ego identity":[67] What is most valuable in his being is surely included in *that*, and who will be hard enough to judge a particular part of the psyche coming up for (terminological) decision fit for exclusion from it? Thus also when for adults "ego identity acquires its final strength in the meeting of mates whose ego identity is complementary in some essential point":[68] which particular aspect of my being would be easily deemed unaffected by the accrual in strength ensuing upon such a happy event?

40. Second, subsuming a particular and humble event—the affirmation of whose occurrence may be felt to be of a level below "theory"— under a prestigious, rich, ambiguous (and hence tormentingly and gratifyingly difficult) concept might appear by itself as an intellectual accomplishment.

41. Intending a word to *designate* a certain class of events, one may be dismayed by discovering to how many other classes it has already referred in previous usage. But if one desires, usually without full consciousness, a word to be *an entity in its own right*, one may delight in the progressive revelation of its riches. (*See* Chapter 2, paragraph 17.)

"As far as I know," observes Erikson about "identity," "Freud used it only once in a more than incidental way. . . . It was when he tried to formulate his link to the Jewish people that he spoke of 'inner identity' . . . based . . . on a common readiness to live in opposition." In fact, "the term identity . . . connotes both a . . . sameness within oneself . . . and a . . . sharing of some . . . character with others":[69] which makes it richer, as well as more powerful a tool for understanding than if it displayed only one of these two properties. "Identity," Searles maintains, "possesses many and constantly changing faces."[70] Observing that De Levita "develops a concept of identity based on role, defining it as the 'cluster of roles one is enacting . . .,' " and that he has thus "not done justice to that part of life . . . in which one's role is unimportant," Lomas points out that "we still have to find our way to a concept which would *include* uniqueness and mutuality, spontaneity and unpredictability."[71]

42. It tends to be suggested rather than shown that the various classes of events included into the referent of "identity" have something in common (*see* Chapter 2, paragraph 18, and Chapter 7, paragraph 67). Having observed that the hero of Joseph Conrad's *Victory* clarifies his beliefs about himself by a confrontation with his "evil mirror image," and succeeds in "achieving an awareness of himself" through his relationship with a woman, Joseph concludes thus: "In *Victory*, identity is achieved through a medium of object relationships. . . . *Another aspect of* identity is introduced through the mirror image of the hero."[72]

43. From the presence of several classes of events within the range of non-odd *meanings* of an important word one may infer—again, usually without full consciousness—that there is, in *reality*, a link between them. One may even, contemplating that togetherness, conceive a sense of having perceived the relations between these types of events without having gone to the expense of stating them; which is all the more attractive as such statements, with their unavoidable specificities, might be felt as entailing the word's dissolution into its several components. Also, in that case, instead of rejoicing in the plenitude of "identity" as comprising, say, both the sense of permanence and the sense of difference that may thus already seem furnished with a common ground, we might have to deplore the poverty of our knowledge of their relationships; for the discovery of which, once the screen provided by the concept is broken, we are thrown back on the arduous observation or imagining of events, in the place of the reverent contemplation of a word.

44. But, it may be objected, is discovery without inclusive concepts *überhaupt möglich*? Declaring in *The Concept of Identity* that he will call "the feeling of occupying a place of one's own in the community" by the name of "sense of identity," De Levita—not an analyst, but perhaps not different in this regard—offers a justification: "We know no better word for it."[73] He takes it for granted that a "word" is

needed: It seems inconceivable that one could operate with the *eleven* words "the feeling of . . .," while, on the contrary, the *three* words "sense of identity" are felt to be not only of easy use, but even of substantial power. Such properties might, on the other hand, hardly be attributed to, say, the *four* words "feeling of communal place"— manageable perhaps, but also weak, lacking the strength that goes with the richness, obscurity, and elevation of "identity." Similarly, when Erikson chooses the word "ego identity" to designate the growing child's "conviction that the ego is learning . . . steps towards a tangible . . . future,"[74] one might be tempted to replace the two words "ego identity" by the five "sense of adequacy about growth." Again, it might be difficult to prove that this increment of three words would make formulations unmanageable, but easy to show that the sense of possessing a precious verbal entity would be lost: Once more, the five words are all too clear, and much too humble.

Though renouncing "concepts" is apt to entail pronouncing (a few) more words, it is also likely to save energy: Compare, for each of the cases cited, the disquisitions stimulated by a dignified word, and inhibited by a lowly one. But that is just the trouble: Simple terms make it difficult to expend one's ardor on them; they direct it toward the world itself, a less tractable object.

11 | What Concepts May Do for Assertions

45. The cheery response to his mother's adulation that a patient of Suslick's carried over to his other relations, "may," we are told, represent an "identity pattern" that will influence his adult character[75]—

or, avoiding identity pattern, perhaps simply: a pattern which...? It is, observes Erikson about what disturbs young people, primarily the inability to settle on an "occupational identity"[76]—or, simply, an occupation? ("Settling" on it, I am apt to think of myself as one having done so.) I could name more pairs of passages belonging to the class of which the following are members:

> The author's text: "Men whose *ego identity* thrives on military service, sometimes break down after discharge, when it appears that the war provoked them into the usurpation of more ambitious *prototypes* than their more restricted peace-time *identities* could afford to sustain."[77]
> My version: Men who thrive on military service sometimes break down after discharge, when it appears that the war provoked them to higher ambitions than they could sustain in peace-time.

> The author's text: "*Identity* owes its ... significance to the fact that so far ... groups of men, no longer constituting a species ... and not yet ... mankind have needed to feel that they were of some special kind, which promised to each individual the participation in a select *identity*."[78]
> My version: So far, groups of men, no longer constituting a species and not yet mankind, have needed to feel that they were of some special kind.

46. *If* "identity" can be crossed out (as can "identification," etc.: *see* Chapter 3, paragraph 26), it may equally be added, without departing from current style, where it happens, surprisingly, to be absent:

> Author's text: "... young people ... become ... intolerant in their exclusion of others who are 'different' ... often in ... petty aspects ... selected as the signs of an in-grouper and out-grouper."[79]
> My (perverse) version: Young people become intolerant in their exclusion of others whose identities are "different," often in petty aspects, selected as the signs of an in-group and out-group identity.

47. The author's text: "In the *remnants* of the Sioux Indians' *identity* the prehistoric past is a powerful psychological reality. The conquered tribe behaved as if guided by a life plan consisting of passive resistance to the present which does fail to *reintegrate the identity remnants* of the economic past; and of dreams of restoration in which the future would lead back into the past, time

would again become a-historic, space unlimited, activity boundlessly centrifugal, the buffalo supply inexhaustible."[80]

My version: The conquered Sioux engaged in passive resistance to the present, which stood in contrast with the economic
past; and entertained dreams of restoration in which life would
again become changeless, space unlimited, activity boundlessly
centrifugal, and the buffalo supply inexhaustible.

I have eliminated all words that I believe to be unnecessary for the
meaning to be conveyed, and replaced fancy language—particularly
"identity"—by plain terms. While the point made is thus unchanged,
the flavor of the passage is altered: Where "identity theory" seemed to
be applied, ordinary perception is revealed to be reigning (*see* Chapter 3,
paragraph 27). When Erikson remarks that for a psychoanalyst a
cornerstone of his existence may be provided by a particular psychoanalytic "identity"[81]—a word he himself puts between quotation marks,
thus expressing what misgivings?—I would propose substituting, say:
orientation; and the sentence would be harder to pronounce, as its
truth would be distressingly evident (*see* paragraph 49, below).
Similarly:

The author's text: "Individual students of Freud . . . found
their *identity* best suited to certain early theses of his which
promised a particular sense of psychoanalytic *identity*. . . ."[82]

My version: Individual students of Freud found themselves
best suited to certain early theses of his which expressed particular
psychoanalytic orientations.

Actually, the author soon begins to use the word "orientation" himself,
though only partially, when talking about "a professional identity
backed by . . . (a) synthesis of the available (psychoanalytic) orientations."[83] But then, why not:

1. a professional orientation backed by a synthesis of the available
   psychoanalytic identities.
2. a professional identity backed by a synthesis of the available
   psychoanalytic identities.
3. a professional orientation backed by a synthesis of the available
   psychoanalytic orientations?

I would, of course, prefer the last—where, however, again, concep-
tectomy may reduce impressiveness beneath the threshold permitting
enunciation. A patient who is handsome, looks gentile, is (unbeknownst

to most of those around him) of lower class Eastern-Jewish origin, and feels that he has a disgusting Jewish nose which makes him recognizable as a Jew, becomes for Erikson a "case of morbid ego identity."[84] Again the "theoretical" air may perhaps be removed from this passage without impoverishing its meaning: A patient wrongly attributes to himself unfavorable characteristics ascribed to a group to which he belongs. Looking back on a case showing the "pattern . . . 'I want what I want and not what you want, even if what you want is what I want,' "[85] Suslick relates it to "theory": "The 'reactive identity' expressed so succinctly . . . coincides with Erikson's negative . . . identity."[86] Or, Suslick's term "reactive identity" and Erikson's term "negative identity" are synonyms. Suppose they are (I am not sure—but, then, given the absence of sufficiently explicit definitions, it is difficult to be): Once we recognize that we are talking about the "coinciding" of words rather than events (but what would the latter mean? Does "coincide" not seem to make sense in Suslick's formulation because it is experienced as referring *both* to words and their referents? However, what is the meaning of that?), we may be tempted to say—all right; and so what? We might even start deploring the normal scandal of a variety of words being used in a science to designate the same event. In any case, not only is Suslick's "reactive identity" perhaps a synonym for Erikson's "negative identity," it is *surely*, and without our author's awareness, identical in meaning with Spitz's "I-want-what-I-want-and-not-what-you-want-even-if-what-you-want-is-what-I-want," which Suslick used to describe his case in the first place. Why not stick with it? Nineteen words are just unmanageable, the reply in favor of the replacing two ("reactive identity") would probably run. This, I surmise, is (as I have already had occasion to say) only a part of the truth. The other is that Spitz's formula is as definitely not a "concept," whatever that may be, as "reactive identity" emphatically is. Or, for that matter, Erikson's "ego identity"—which makes it possible for him to declare that "lasting ego identity cannot begin to exist without the trust of the first oral stage,"[87] without either having to argue much on behalf of this contention—for it has, by the time he makes it, already been well established under several other nomenclatures—or having to incur the disinterest that may greet the mere repetition of a familiar point; its current disguise is apt to be effective for a time. Having presented his cases, Suslick concludes what he himself observes to have been an examination of "familiar" clinical material. But, he implicitly justifies his enterprise, it was one "from the vantage point" of "a so-called identity process or [sic] apparatus."[88] What he does not seem to have sufficiently considered (though his formulation may betray misgivings) is the possibility—that this "vantage point" offers a view of equivalences between words rather than relationships between events.

48. What is happening in such cases would be more readily recognized if one kept in mind an admission (not consciously felt as such, I suppose) made in passing by Jacobson when she speaks of "the building up of a person's character, of his individual personality, *in short of his identity*.[89] Why, then, the last synonym? Because, still young, it fascinates as the words preceding it did when they had its age; while they are now old, and, hence, merely designative (of a domain, rather than of events about which hypotheses are formulated: In how many statements of analytic characterology does the word "character" need to be present?) "Identity," however, attracts, furnishing a proper object of inquiry: To prepare another article on *The Concept of Identity* is respectable, while to write one more piece on *The Concept of Character* is to look backward or odd.

49. Having shown that a woman patient experienced an identification with Moses, Lubin advances that "this . . . identification could not form *a complete identity* . . .": In other words, there were respects in which she could not resemble Moses, much as she managed to become like him in others. After all, as the author points out, "a woman . . . cannot be a man any more than a modern mortal can be a figure from the remote past."[90] "Action," Angel maintains, "has *identity* value because it creates physical separation from the mother . . ."[91] It is thus that it makes me feel a being separate from her. Having further advanced that "action has *identity* value . . . because of the gratification of the action itself," the author furnishes, on the same page, what I would surmise to be a translation: "The gratification of action leads to the experiencing of the self as . . . autonomous . . . ."[92] "An *identity fragment* in her . . . young life," explains Erikson about Dora, "was that of the woman intellectual"—that is, she felt herself to be one, aspired to being one. But "the *negative identity* of the 'déclassée' woman so prominent in her era, she tried to ward off with her sickness": Becoming a déclassée woman, a fate so prominent in her era, she thus attempted to avoid. "Her mother's 'housewife's psychosis' . . . Dora blended with her own then fully acquired *patient identity*": with her feeling herself very much a patient. "To be a famous, if uncured patient had become for this woman [three decades later when she was seen by Felix Deutsch—N.L.] one lasting *positive identity element*," one lasting and precious quality of herself. "We know today that if patient-hood is permitted to become a young patient's most meaningful circumstance, his *identity formation* may seize on it as a central and lasting *theme*": He may seize on it.[93] "Much of the spontaneous polarization of tastes, opinions and slogans . . . of young people," observes Erikson, "and much of the sudden impulse to join in destructive behavior, are *loose ends of identity formation waiting to be tied*

together by some ideology."[94] In other words, a "polarization" that is "spontaneous" may—or may not—be subsequently replaced by an "ideological one": important but also evident. "Greenacre's observations," Lichtenstein recalls, "show clearly"—presumably, then, elucidating something obscure—"that even where there is *a stable core concerning the sense of identity*, it changes during life, following the stages of body maturation and psychological growth":[95] Would not the only finding worth communicating be that the sense of identity (whatever it be) is unaffected by maturation and development? While man, according to the same author "does not have 'an' identity," "his identity is an artefract"[96]—which I take to mean: Regularity in human behavior is due to postnatal influences (so that "loss of identity is a specifically human danger"):[97] a simpler text which the author might have found it difficult to present both as his "assumption" and his "basic proposition," a double status he can easily accord to his own difficult formulation. "You would expect," Lichtenstein further affirms, "that man, whose instinctual drives are no more than 'innate dispositions to act in a certain manner,' but no longer automatisms, must find means to 'acquire' an identity."[98] Disregarding the attractive but puzzling quotation marks around "acquire," and guessing from the context that "identity" here stands for "regularity of conduct," the sentence may be thus translated: Man is acting in fairly regular fashion, because he would perish if he were not—a point that seems much less acceptable or interesting than when it puts on "identity" dress. When the same author insists that "the mother imprints upon the infant not an identity, but an 'identity theme' [a new and, as usual, undefined enrichment of the central word—N.L.] . . . capable of variations,"[99] he seems merely to be saying that the mother contributes importantly to determine adult behavior, but does not do more than that. More specifically, the child, having developed certain traits (a character) in his relation with the mother, will often still have before him a variety of possibilities—some pathological, others not—of acting in ways compatible with these traits. The truism that the post-infant can often still "choose" either illness or normalcy or supernormalcy may then be expressed in the following way: The "identity theme" imprinted by the mother upon the infant is often "capable of variations that spell the difference between human creativity and a 'destiny neurosis' [why not also any other kind of neurosis or psychosis, or their absence?—N.L.]."[100] According to the author, not only does "the animal's *Umwelt*" make "certain identities" "recognizable" to him, such as "the identity of the animal's preys, its equals, its foes," that *Umwelt* also "delineates the animal's identity."[101] Suppose now I were to agree with the author on the *Umwelt* rendering the identity of the animal's preys, etc., recognizable, but to disagree on the *Umwelt* also delineating the animal's own identity—what kind of evidence might he adduce to confute me? All he could—and needed to—do, if he were constrained to enter such a discussion, would be to translate his impressive assertion into a truism, such as: It is by confronting its preys, its equals, its foes that the animal becomes aware of itself. Finally, when in his "main thesis" the author affirms that there is a "correlation" between "(nonprocreative) sexuality and the emergence and maintenance of identity in man,"[102] the sense of novelty that this combination of words no doubt inspires seems to depend on the inclusion of one unnecessary word and the nontechnical use of another one, which does have a prominent technical meaning. As to the first, all human sexuality is, in the author's usage, "nonprocreative." As to the second, "correlation" is not employed in the meaning given it in statistics. The sentence, which—mainly because of the associations with research thus provoked—seems bold, therefore seems merely to affirm that there are relations, not saying which, between sexuality and "identity"; which—whatever the last word may mean, as long as it means much—is all too true (*see* Chapter 3, paragraph 30).

50. A sentence might be conceived and received with little awareness of the fact that it might with equal ease be viewed as true (or false) by virtue of its components' *meanings*, or as depending for its fate upon observations of what happens in *patients*. Such an indetermination is emotionally as attractive as it is undesirable intellectually: The first possibility furnishes a sense of certainty, the second one of richness; and thus one avoids the dismaying recognition of the trade-off usually prevailing between these two characteristics.

When, according to Lichtenstein and in an often-heard locution, Spitz and Eissler "equate" the sense of identity and the sense of self,[103] this may mean either that these authors have decided to use the two terms cited as synonyms, or have observed that they are thus employed by others; or it may signify that there is, in patients, between the distinct referents of both terms a relationship called "equation" (whatever that is); or both of these meanings may, on condition of not being distinguished, be present. Similarly, when, according to Erikson, ego identity "could be said to be characterized" by "the sense of the reality of the self,"[104] one may wonder whether the author here enunciates, in part at least, what he has resolved to mean by the words "ego identity," or whether he advances a finding about what in reality goes together with "ego identity," a term already defined (how?). The first meaning—where the sentence just quoted turns out to be part of a definition—becomes plausible when the author goes on to talk about the words "ego ideal," which "could be said to represent" a set of to be striven for, but never quite attainable ideal goals for the self,[105] which is close to the ordinary meaning of these words. When for Lichtenstein identity in man "requires" a repetitive doing in order to "safeguard" the sameness within change which this author "believes" to be "a fundamental aspect" of "identity in man,"[106] we know from previous passages that this sentence merely restates his definition of "identity" (or rather one of them); but the expression chosen—look at the words I put between quotation marks—suggests his having discovered a capital property of (an otherwise defined) "identity."

51. Other sentences present mainly the appearance of assertions about reality—while inspection raises doubts whether they are that.

An overly facile tendency to identify with another person in a transient and superficial manner may, Schecter advances, "indicate" a weak (between quotation marks), unstable sense of identity":[107] Is that trait not one of those that the term "weak, unstable sense of identity" is itself supposed to designate? Recognition of self-boundaries is, Hayman holds, "at least a part of the basic prelude" to the achievement of identity:[108] Would we *say* that the latter has been achieved if the former has not been recognized? Having implicitly made the word "identity" refer (also) to secrecy—perceiving "identity diffusion" in a patient with "feelings of having little that is . . . secret," "a poor sense of identity"—Margolis can then say about that patient that "reexamining his secrets . . . he is . . . *of course*, reexamining that on which his identity is based (and, *therefore*, his identity as well)."[109] Having remarked that a person's self-realization and social definition may "fall out of synchrony," Tabachnik advances that "at this time symptoms of distress in the self occur":[110] Would we still speak of such a "falling-out" if they did not? That, according to Lichtenstein, "the maintenance of identity is tantamount to the maintenance of life itself"[111] seems to be true not by virtue of observations on the respective occurrences of "identity" and "life," but rather by virtue of the (implicit) definition of "(biological) identity": a property an organism shall be said to have as long as it has life. However—how can one be sure without explicit definitions?—the sentence may be as much as a familiar point in fancy dress (*see* paragraph 47 above), rather than as little as a tautology, in this interpretation: As Cannon has shown (he is quoted by the author in this context), as long as an organism has life, there is much "constancy" in its reactions. Now, if "identity" be a synonym of "constancy," then one can also say: As long as an organism is alive, it has "identity," which would then be a paraphrase of Cannon's law, extended from physiology to all human reactions. When, according to Lichtenstein, "the comparative lack of behavioral identity" in noninstinctual man as distinct from instinctual animal "removes" from man much of the instinctual rigidity of the animal,[112] the verb chosen creates the impression that a relationship between two aspects of reality is affirmed; however, the situation called "comparative lack of behavioral identity in man as against animal" appears to be the

130

same as that named "the lesser instinctual rigidity of man in comparison with the animal." "The oedipal conflict and the incest barrier," affirms Sarlin, "are possible only when the identities of mother, father and self are . . . established"[113]—to be sure, as, on the one hand, the definition of "oedipal conflict" contains words such as "mother," "father," and "self"; and as, on the other hand, "the establishment of the identity" of another for me seems implicitly defined as the emergence of his existence for me, when "the identities of self and object become crystallised."[114] Erikson refers in passing to "that certainty which comes from . . . an . . . increased identity":[115] Naturally, as "identity" here appears to refer to my beliefs about myself, the more of them I have and the more strongly I entertain them, the more "certain" I am. Greenacre, asserts Lichtenstein, makes "the important point [which recalls the one by Sarlin just discussed] that hostile aggression" does "imply" a sufficient degree of individuation for there to be a sense of self and the others against whom acts are directed. The "significance" of the "question" raised by Greenacre, explains her commentator, lies in the fact that it points "clearly" to a "correlation" between aggression (as destruction) and the process of individuation, i.e. the problem of identity; a "correlation" which is "decisive."[116] But perhaps the "significance" of the entire passage "points clearly" and merely to the implicit definition of "hostile aggression (as destruction)": strivings for the destruction of the self, or of a nonself entity. That is, where there is no "individuation," there, by arbitrary (and perhaps convenient) stipulation, *we just don't call* penchants to destroy "hostile aggression." It would be another, and more serious, matter to affirm that prior to "individuation," in early infancy, *there are no* dispositions to destroy: a statement that is too vulnerable to be made overtly, but whose hidden presence may lend force to the passage quoted.

52. A sentence—instances may already be found among those inspected in the preceding paragraph—may be proffered and received all the more eagerly when it seems difficult to conceive that it be false: What is a sign of vacuity is then taken for a token of health.

When Erikson maintains that "there is no feeling of being alive without a sense of ego identity,"[117] this, right away, seems all too true. Yet, for the sentence to state a relationship among events rather than words it must be possible to indicate what it would look like to have, for instance, a *low* feeling of being alive together with a *high* sense of ego identity, or a *high* feeling of being alive together with a *low* sense of ego identity (*see* Chapter 3, paragraph 33). Similarly, when the same author observes that "it is only after a reasonable sense of identity has been established that real intimacy with . . . any other person, or even with oneself, . . . is possible,"[118] I suspect that as long as I have but little "sense of identity," no *conceivable* reaction of mine toward

131

myself or another would, by implicit definition, be *called* "intimacy"—in which case the sentence in question would turn out to be true by words alone. That this may be the case is suggested by the context. "The surer," observes the author, "he [a youth] becomes of himself"—and hence presumably of his "identity"—"the more he seeks it [intimacy] in the form of friendship, combat, leadership, love and inspiration."[119] But what about the youths mentioned three pages earlier, who "to keep themselves together . . . temporarily over-identify . . . with the heroes of cliques and crowds"?[120] That just isn't "intimacy," the presumable answer would be—which suggests that by definition "intimacy" involves "identity."

53. A sentence may right away appear as evidently false—unless it be construed as a tautology (*see* Chapter 3, paragraph 36).

"Man," declares Erikson, "to take his place in society, must acquire a 'conflict free' habitual use of a dominant faculty to be elaborated in an occupation."[121] Suppose we take the locution "to take one's place in society" in its ordinary meaning. Then, as even a non-analytic clinician knows, the sentence is grossly false: nothing more usual than the man who has taken his place in society by an occupation, and whose exercise of that occupation is not "conflict free." The rejoinder may of course be that if it isn't "conflict free," he hasn't really taken his place in society; in which case the sentence turns out, by an implicit redefinition of "to take one's place in society" to be true by virtue of a common locution being discreetly given an unusual meaning. "Where this is . . . missing," observes the same author about "firm self-delineation" in adolescence, "the young individual, when seeking tentative forms of playful intimacy . . . is apt to experience a peculiar strain" [122] which, I would surmise, will be taken to mean that where this is not missing, there will be little strain. However, if the "firm self-delineation" is, say, compulsive? Of course one could say that there is no real "self-delineation" then—which would, again, make the statement in question true by virtue of the referents assigned to the words composing it.

54. Renaming a more or less plainly described event by a "concept" may give the impression of having explained it (*see* Chapter 3, paragraph 37).

Making the word identity designate the integration of energies feeding back from all activities of the psyche, Harrison asserts that it is the relative constancy of this dynamic equilibrium that "accounts for" the capacity to remain the same in the midst of change:[123] but is it not precisely when that capacity is present that we *say* of the equilibrium in question that it is "relatively constant"? Observing that impostors may emerge from "crude" atmospheres, and in their imposture combine "skill" with "stupidity," Greenacre adds that "this may be described as a struggle between two . . . identities."[124] Precisely, it may be thus *described*, that is renamed, the "identities" in question being defined by the various stances indicated. In a patient who senses his masculine and feminine penchants as being of the lower orders and of his own upper-class milieu respectively, Erikson discerns an "identity diffusion as projected on segments of society"[125]—all right, on the condition that we do not yield to the temptation of believing that we have entered etiology by thus renaming the patient's state. Similarly, when we hear that it is the same "diffusion of identity," which, in young patients, "reverses their gears" toward oedipal competitiveness and sibling rivalry.[126] When young adults engage in genital activity without intimacy or, on the contrary, underplay the genital element, it is, Erikson discerns, "bisexual diffusion" which may "lead" them to such conduct.[127] But is it not precisely when one or the other of these events occurs that he has decided to say that "bisexual diffusion" is taking place? With the grandfather's death, observes the same author, the patient's affects went dead, "because" they were "part of an abortive ego identity formation"[128]—but when we say that these affects were that, do we not designate, among other events, the fact that they went dead with the grandfather? Quoting Mahler about the type of child unable to decide whether inanimate objects in his environments are himself or not, Lichtenstein, rather than looking for the conditions, contexts, and consequences of such a reaction, goes on to observe that Mahler speaks in this regard of "dissociation of identity" which is "characterized" by "the loss of the . . . faculty of discrimination between animate and inanimate";[129] which suggests explaining an inability by "the loss of the faculty" of doing what one can't.

55. An assertion that would appear as unexcitingly true if it referred to *some* members of the class of persons envisaged, and as evidently false if it made its claim for *all* of them, can become interesting when this choice is obscured.

"Out of the infinite potentialities within the human infant," affirms Lichtenstein, "the specific stimulus combination emanating from the individual mother 'releases' one . . . way of being . . . [an] instrument [for her]."[130] If this means that *some* mothers *succeed* in fashioning their children according to their unconscious needs, it is hardly worth repeating; if it affirms that *all* mothers arrive at such a result, it is clearly false—unless the implicit definition of "instrument" be such that no infant could conceivably not be it. "While submitting sexually to a man," notes the same author, "the prostitute permits the man to treat her as an extension of himself, negating . . . her . . . separateness":[131] could this still be advanced if the "the" preceding "prostitute" were

133

replaced by "every"? (Unless, again, the meanings of "separateness," or rather of its "negation," and of "extension" be suitably extended.) Envisaging at one point a "partnership" in which each partner experiences himself as uniquely capable of serving as the instrument of the other's sensory gratification, Erikson adds that such a partnership "can be called" a partnership of "sensual involvement," and declares his "belief" that this type of relationship is, in the adult, established in "the" sexual involvement of two individuals. But does analysis really oppose the common belief that such is the case in *some* relations of this kind, rather than in all of them? (Here the pertinent words—"uniquely capable . . . sensory gratification"—are of a clarity that would make it more difficult than in the preceding cases to assure truth by inflections of meaning.)

56. Tabachnik asks us to "consider the following hypothesis: 'Identity problems arise when . . . [there is] a disequilibrium between the . . . social definition and self-realization aspects of the self.'"[132] To be sure, whenever *that* disequilibrium occurs, we will presumably want to *say* that there is an "identity problem"; i.e., would we still *say* that social definition and self-realization are in "disequilibrium" if there were no such problem? Still, does it occur *only* then, as the author's formulation suggests? That is, may there not be an "identity problem" *without* there being a disequilibrium between social definition and self-realization? We can't say for sure, as "identity problem" is not defined; but if we follow the current usage with which we have become acquainted, the answer is, of course, yes. It is, however, precisely the implicit denial of what the reader presumes to be the case and what perhaps nobody would want to query out aloud that renders the hypothesis exciting. "Where self-realization and social definition go hand in hand," the author declares a bit later, "a relatively stable identity results."[133] Again, would we still desire to say that identity is "stable" if they did not? But they might, and still there could be an "identity problem" with regard to aspects of the self unaffected by what is "social." It is the implicit exclusion of this obvious possibility, an act rendered easy by the kind of language I am examining, that makes the assertion quoted feasible and interesting.

57. Sentences with implications that are bizarre may be protected by their not being drawn.

Seven factors (it is I who have counted and numbered them) enter according to Erikson into "the process of identity formation": (1) constitutional givens, (2) idiosyncratic libidinal needs, (3) favored capacities, (4) significant identifications, (5) effective defenses, (6) successful sublimations, (7) consistent roles.[134] Does the author mean to exclude an eighth factor, (2a) idiosyncratic aggressive needs? We shall probably never know. In the meantime, its absence—among others—enhances the attractiveness of the selective series presented. "When a child," the same author asserts, "begins to feel that it is the color of his skin, the background of his parents or the cost of his clothes rather than his wish and his will to learn which will decide his social worth, lasting harm may ensue for his sense of identity."[135] Erikson fails to infer that *most* children at *most* times and in *most* places have had a permanently damaged sense of identity; whatever this means. (What is the alleged difference, clinically, between otherwise comparable children in contemporary New England whose "sense of identity" will not have been thus "harmed" and children in Spain where it will have?)

58. Fancy dress may hide not only familiarity (*see* paragraph 47 above), but also weakness.

That according to Erikson "the synthesizing function of the ego" constantly works on "subsuming" in fewer and fewer "images and personified gestalten" the "fragments and loose ends of . . . infantile identifications"[136] would seem to mean that there is a negative correlation between one's age and the number of highly charged conceptions, personified or not, with which one feels oneself connected—a text more vulnerable (less likely to be advanced) than the author's.

59. The danger of disconfirmation is also reduced if, instead of asserting *such-and-such* relationships between certain factors, one limits oneself to affirming that *there are* relationships between them, without indicating which (*see* Chapter 3, paragraph 30).

Having spoken of the "self" as a framework, a zero point, an organizing principle preceding all other mental development, Lichtenstein, impressively—and merely—affirms that it has a "close and demonstrable relationship" to the development of the sense of personal identity:[137] without proceeding to indicate in what precisely that "close" relationship consists, and how its existence can be "demonstrated"; nor, I would guess, incurring much surprise for his failure to do so.

60. When a situation alleged to obtain in patients is described under the guise of a relationship between words, or, even more so, intellectual operations, the resulting sentence may, again, gain in plausibility.

If, Lichtenstein advances, human individuation is "understood as" a process of identification, the danger of losing identity "cannot come into view"[138]—an assertion less easy to attack than its presumable patient-oriented equivalent: If individuation were the result of identifications, human beings would not feel threatened by loss of identity. What would human beings look like, the latter text might make one ask, if their "individuation" *were* the result of "identifications"? When the same author believes he "must insist on postulating" that "identity" is not "inherent" in "the concept of the ego,"[139] does he do more than recall that in his language the words "identity" and "ego" are not synonyms? (A strange speech if they were.) Does he perhaps want to affirm that there are or might be (whatever such a "might" may mean) human beings who have identity but not ego, or, slightly less implausibly, ego and yet no identity? Any such formulation speaking about patients directly rather than through concepts darkly seems more difficult to enunciate than its "meta-psychological" counterpart.

61. A formulation that is as attractive as it is debatable may of course be shielded by ambiguity; as when Lichtenstein, having asserted that the *outline* of a *primary identity* becomes *delineated* through the processes stimulated by the maternal libidinal cathexis of the child, adds that the mother *reflects back* to the child a *configuration* of its own presence.[140] Whatever observations anybody might think would disconfirm this truth could easily lose that power if one were to develop in appropriate fashion the meaning of one or more of the words I italicized.

62. One of the meanings of an ambiguous word may allow for an exciting, but fragile, assertion, protected by another such meaning, which furnishes a claim less attractive but safer (*see* Chapter 3, paragraphs 41, 42). When I experience myself independently of others, but *not too intensely*, I am capable at the same time—is that not the normal state?—of experiencing myself as related to (among other things, reacted to) by others—presumably what Erikson has in mind when he remarks that "the conscious feeling of having a personal identity is based on two simultaneous observations: the immediate perception of one's self-sameness and continuity in time; and the simultaneous perception of the fact that others recognize one's sameness and continuity." However, when my experience of myself as unrelated to others goes *beyond a certain intensity*, I cease also to feel myself related to them—which may be what Erikson means when proposing that "...'the identity of knowing transcendence'... can only be discovered by man when the possibility for any social definition of identity is shattered beyond any restoration." Quoting the first passage unfavorably, and the second with assent, Lichtenstein asserts a "dilemma of human identity": "the ... experience of the 'actuality of being' " and "self-objectivation" are "mutually exclusive":[141] right, but unsurprising if "actuality of being" designates exclusively what comes to view in an experience usually called mystical; wrong, if "actuality of being" is less narrowly defined; and controversially attractive if no decision between the two meanings is made—which, I would guess, is the actuality of the sentence.

63. A patient *desiring* to remain such appears to Erikson as "choosing the ... role of a patient as the basis of his ... identity." And instead of this desire being related to the position of a patient seeming more *gratifying* and *reassuring* than other options, it will be said that this "role" proves "more *meaningful* than any potential

identity experienced before."[142] The *desire*, on the part of Lichtenstein's woman patient, to become a penis so as to ward off the *wish* to be devoured by her mother, is turned into the "phallic *variation* of Anna's *identity theme*" being a "defense against the . . . threatening *implications* of . . . devouring phantasies."[143] When a man combats penchants sensed by him as feminine because he wants to avoid feeling castrated, it is, for Erikson, a "dominant prototype of masculinity" which "forced . . . [him] to exclude from his ego identity all that which characterizes . . . [the] image of the lesser sex, the castrate."[144] "The analyst and the analysand," Shevin observes, "may become . . . mother and child . . . engaging in a mutual seduction, repeating the examination of each other's genitals." Then, "despite the apparent innocence of the intellectual processes of dream interpretation, . . . [there is] an unconscious acting out with the patient of . . . childhood scenes and encouraging him to maintain this ancient identity formation,"[145] rather than this ancient pleasure. A woman patient in whose life the fact of being a rabbi's wife played a great role conceived unfavorable feelings toward her husband and was attracted to another man: Her "identity" being thus "threatened", Lubin explains, "anxiety . . . became manifest . . . [which] resulted from the threat to her identity . . ."[146] rather than from that to her established gratifications and defenses.

64. Such turns of speech seem to express the unformulated contention that *every* psychic event of some cathexis produces a belief about oneself "I am the one in whom X has occurred (is happening)"; a belief that our authors may then call an element of "identity." Also, any ascription of characteristics to oneself by others tends to be thus transformed.

"The child may come to develop, in the use of voice and word, a particular combination of whining or singing, judging or arguing": this, for Erikson, is a "part" of an "element" of an "identity," "namely [of] the element 'one who speaks and is spoken to in such-and-such-a-way.' "[147] When a mother combats her child's penchants toward separateness, she, for Lichtenstein, "excludes from the child any identity theme that is compatible with separateness."[148] When she provokes in the child the desire to be drunk by her, she "imprints on the child the identity to be someone's 'drink of blood.' "[149] "All through his childhood," Erikson narrates, "Shaw seems to have been exposed to an . . . assault of music making. . . . Finally . . . he taught himself the piano . . . with . . . noisiness. . . . He may have learned the piano in order to get even with his musical tormentors. . . . He compromised by becoming . . . a music critic, that is, one who writes about the noise made by others. As a critic, he chose the *nom de plume* Corno di Bassetto . . . the name of an instrument which nobody knew and which is so meek in tone that 'not even the devil could make it sparkle.'

137

Yet Bassetto became a sparkling critic. . . ." All this, however, seems to be told mainly to establish one "element" in Shaw's "identity formation," the element of the "noise-maker."[150]

65. Desires and fears having produced identity elements, it is with these that the person henceforth has to deal; it is between them that conflicts arise.

Erikson speaks about "psychoneurotic casualties" in America whose ego, rather than fighting against and fleeing from desires to cry like a baby, to bleed like a woman, to submit like a nigger, fights and flees "an . . . identity which includes elements of the crying baby, the bleeding woman, the submissive nigger. . . ."[151] Instead of the desire on the part of Lichtenstein's patient to be drunk by her mother being incompatible with her wish to be separate, there is incompatibility between "Anna's identity theme" and a high degree of separateness.[152] In a patient Erikson discerns "the danger to identity emanating from the association of her sexual conflicts with . . . [a] pair of historical prototypes, an ideal prototype (German, tall, phallic) and an evil prototype (Jewish, dwarfish, castrated, female)"; "the patient's ego identity had attempted to subsume this dangerous alternative in the role of the radically modern dancer."[153] It becomes difficult to perceive behind this array of essences the desires and fears between which the patient attempts a compromise; with which desires satisfied in what fashion, which fears reduced in what manner? Another patient's father was an Eastern European Jew whom the mild and meek grandparents had taken as a five-year-old to the New York East Side, where he could survive only by "superimposing on his childhood identity that of a guy who hits first." This rule "he built into our patient's identity"[154]—rather than: a father who, leaning over backwards within himself, requires of himself that he hit first and thinks of himself as one who does that, renders his son similar to himself in these respects.

66. The main trouble with not satisfying a desire is that I may then be unable to preserve my identity element of being one-satisfying-that-desire.

That the wish of Lichtenstein's patient to be separate is impeded by entailing the relinquishment of her desire to be drunk by her mother then becomes: "Separateness means loss of her identity [theme]." On the other hand, her moves toward satisfying this desire in homosexual relations are "efforts to implement her identity theme through a homosexual symbiosis";[156] just as her prostituting herself is "a . . . form of maintenance of . . . [her] identity theme";[157] or as, generally, "destructive orality" is—a strong assertion hidden beneath a sophisticated "may be seen as"—"a form of implementation of an identity theme of 'being somebody's part' [not also of somebody being a part of myself? —N.L.]."[158] As to prostitution, again, it is not simply the case that homosexuality plays an "important part" in it; it is rather the "interpretation" of prostitution "in terms of" a certain "imprinted" type of "identity" that "makes understandable" the part played by homosexuality.[159]

67. For the "task of identity maintenance"[160] is supreme. "The maintenance of the identity theme"—the single one allegedly "imprinted" by mother upon infant—"is claimed to have priority over all other needs—those emanating from drives as well as . . . ego interests":[161] after all—as Spitz is affirmed to have shown, perhaps to his surprise— "infants may die when . . . reinforcement of their identity theme is lacking. . . ."[162]

68. It is only if a desire also serves "identity" that it can muster a cathexis sufficient for obtaining satisfaction.

"The 'wish to die,' " declares Erikson, "is only in those . . . cases a . . . suicidal wish where 'to be a suicide' becomes an . . . identity."[163] (Would the author not *call* me "one with the identity of a suicide" if I *were* to kill myself?)

69. Desire merely masks belief.

"In Anna," Lichtenstein admits about his patient, "the emphasis is on her being the *feast* of another one, but the oral language serves . . . the *thought* of . . . being the '*essence*' of the other one."[164] It was only "on superficial examination," Angel observes about a patient, that his acting out "appeared . . . to be merely the acting out of an Oedipal fantasy," while "further study revealed its real function—that of defense against loss of identity."[165]

12 | The Product of Identity Theory

70. An author may, at the outset of his work, declare that he is going to contribute to "identity theory," while an inspection of his piece will show that even the word "identity" plays but a minor role in what he is doing.

"In recent years psychoanalysts have paid increasing attention to the fascinating problem of identity," notes Jacobson in her "Introduction" to *The Self and the Object World*. "In the context of several studies published during the past decade . . . I have discussed different aspects of . . . identity. . . . Comparing my ideas with those expressed in recent papers and books on this subject, I have discovered considerable differences of opinion, which have stimulated my own thinking and caused me to expand and reorganize my earlier papers . . . into this volume."[166] However, in the book thus prefaced the word "identity"— an aspect on which I am constrained to fasten because, as I already often had occasion to suggest and shall repeat in a moment, I have not found much more than the exaltation of the word in present-day "identity theory"—occurs rarely. Also, a large fraction of its uses is in a chapter called "Review of Recent Literature on the Problem of Identity"—where the mention of "identity" derives from its previous employment by others—and in a last chapter, dealing with post-adolescence, where "social" matters may stimulate recourse to the word. Similarly, in Sarlin's article "identity" dominates the title—"Feminine Identity"—is prominent in introductory paragraphs, and then subsides.

71. In fact, then, "identity" is often a word designating a domain

for inquiry—the domain of what I propose to call the senses of self—rather than a variable to which hypotheses on this domain have reference.

72. I would call the "gross product" of "identity's" rise to prominence during recent years the totality of hypotheses that (1) contain the word, (2) refer to clinically observable events, (3) were, when first appearing, novel in content, and not only in wording, (4) do not seem probably false (as those reported in paragraphs 63–69 above would appear to me).

In my guess this gross product—which I have not attempted to aggregate here—is low.

73. I would call the "net product" of "identity" theory that part of its gross product that could not without notable loss of convenience be reformulated in available language *minus* "identity."

I believe that to be zero.

13 | A Rough Scheme

74. While the merit of analysts interested in the word "identity" has been to increase awareness of the fact that the senses of self had been considered more by "phenomenologists" and "existentialists" than by analysts, the untoward effect of their orientation, as described in the preceding pages, has been to obstruct progress in the very area of their interest.

We do not even have a statement of what analysts, studying widely varying patients and employing sharply differing sets of words, have already learned or guessed about the senses of self.

It is not my present purpose to produce such a statement. I shall merely set down an elementary outline—yet one going beyond what I have seen in the writings examined above—and note within it points that our authors have made (or repeated), as well as a few that occurred to me; for the sole purpose of recalling types of relationships about which very much more could be said if an inventory of literature were made and clinical experience consulted. In developing this outline, I shall propose a nomenclature (indicated by italics and quotation marks), not with any expectation of having it accepted, but rather for the purpose of illustrating how language could be both standardized and simple.

75. As I implied above, the knowledge about "*the sense of existing*" derived from the study of psychotic and borderline states (where its acuteness is of course related to the prominence enjoyed by "*the sense of losing one's self*") has not yet been sufficiently related to points about other senses of self.

When, as is "frequently" the case, according to Jacobson, "in the

143

course of successful actions, intense . . . feelings of identity are . . . experienced,"[167] one might want to say that *"the level of the sense of existing"* is heightened, as it might be said to be reduced in certain states of depression.

76. *"The sense of separateness"* is, as we have seen (Chapter 8, paragraph 9), often a part or even the whole of the referent of "identity" as used by our authors.

77. To mention one hypothesis about unconscious concerns for the sense of separateness: According to Greenacre a type of impostor, "having been . . . incorporated by his mother," gains from his impostures a heightening of his feelings of integrity."[168] Perhaps, by possessing more than the ordinary single autobiography and by acquiring a history in which his mother does not figure, he makes sure that he is no more one with her.

78. A high sense of separateness does not always go with a low *"sense of permeability."* "When she speaks," Hayman reports about a patient, "she feels as if she excretes or gives away or in some other way gets rid of those things which she feels I acquire by listening." In fact, "she was afraid to tell me how awful she was feeling, in case it made me as ill as she was. In the same way, she implores me not to use the word 'ill' in making an interpretation, as that would put illness into her."[169]

79. Jacobson, after Eissler, may be referring to *"the sense of an ineffable quality of one's being,"* when, according to her, about the age of two or two and a half, the child (paraphrased by a philosopher?) has the "startling . . . experience 'I am I.' "[170]

80. As to *"the specifiable sense of distinction from others,"* one may desire to heighten it so as to safeguard one's sense of separateness. This, according to Bak as paraphrased by Rubinfine, "highlighting in a bizarre way unique qualities of the individual" may "serve in part the purpose of demarcation of self from non-self."[171]

On the other hand, the wish to reduce one's sense of distinction may aim at diminishing dismay about separateness.

81. A *"sense of not knowing oneself"* (often accompanied by a sense of loss of self) is characteristic of several situations. According to Bell, as paraphrased by Rubinfine, prepubertal body changes normally produce a burst of "who am I?," "what am I?" feelings.[172]

82. When one's sense of knowing oneself is low, there is apt to be a *"sense of the self's inaccessibility."* Exemplifying a reduction of this sense, a patient of Suslick "became aware . . . that in contrast to always using an external frame of reference for 'what is a me,' she had a feeling of 'I am me.' " In one type of case, as Margolis points out, "the person knows that there are . . . truths about himself which he has greater access to than any one else"; in another he "[believes] that others know

better than he . . . what he is. . . ."[174] Of course he may also hold that nobody has that knowledge, least of all he himself: "There is a girl in here who doesn't even know her own name," said a weeping schizophrenic to Searles.[175]

83. "Having returned to an old object," tells Jacobson of patients illustrating a type of low "*sense of permanence*," "they could hardly 'remember' their past feeling . . . and not even empathize with their recent enthusiasm about the new object and their former . . . rejection of the old one. They felt . . . estranged from whole periods of their past life, when they had been involved with persons and activities that they had later relinquished. They looked back to such past periods as though they had been experienced by a different person."[176]

84. In a rare illustration of the obvious capacity of the different senses of self to combine in *several* ways, Kramer (as paraphrased by Rubinfine), having "defined the sense of identity as a person's awareness of being an entity separate . . . from all others," goes on to "cite clinical observations in which the feeling of continuity was interrupted, while the sense of identity remained intact."[177]

85. Patients of course differ as to the kinds and degrees of change in themselves and in their environment they tolerate without their sense of permanence being affected; and in their capacity to avoid a sense of loss of self despite an impairment in the sense of permanence. "Earlier," Searles reports about a schizophrenic, "she was . . . afraid to let me see how malevolent she feels herself to be; but whenever I now react to her as being the increasingly warm and friendly person I find her becoming, she shows equally great fear, for . . . to her, still, to lose the malevolent creature in her would be tantamount to losing her real self. . . . One of my patients, looking back over her years of profound illness and the many subsequent months of increasing health, expressed her relief that 'I am still myself.' " "Until late in his recovery," the same author observes about a type of psychotic, "the spurts of progress which he manifests seem *either* to occur during the psychotherapy sessions *or* during his daily life outside the therapist's office, but seldom in both these areas concurrently. . . . It is as though he has to maintain . . . one . . . set of relationships . . . *in statu quo* while he is branching out a bit in other areas of his living, in order not to suffer the loss of . . . identity which a . . . forward move on all fronts would . . . inflict upon him"[178] (emphases in the text). "She had played much tennis," the same author reports about another patient, "but never thought of herself as even potentially top-ranking." Hence, "describing a time when she had made a . . . winning shot during a match with a top-ranking player, she made clear that she had suffered thereupon a transitory loss of identity on the tennis court. When she had progressed . . . and I suggested that she learn to drive an automobile—

something that . . . apparently she had never dared even to consider —she . . . said, 'Why, I wouldn't even know myself, driving a car.' "[179] "A woman told her therapist," the author recalls, "in explanation of why it was so urgent to her that he sit still, 'When you move, *everything* moves' "[180] (emphasis in the text). "When an ashtray was missing from its usual place on my table," Hayman notes about a patient, "*she* felt changed"[181] (emphasis in the text).

86. As to factors affecting "the feeling of self-sameness in spite of continuous changes," according to Jacobson the "differentiation" between the "child's wishful self-images"—here, in contrast to other uses of this term by the author, not what the child fancies himself to be, but rather what he would like to become—and "his representations of his actual self" "must" "strengthen" that feeling.[182] (No evidence for this contention is furnished.)

87. There is "*the sense of unity*," as against that of "*being frag-mented*" into several entities.

88. A person may feel that he has a "*core*": my real self, what is really me, what I really am.

He may believe that this core resides in a certain part of his body; or is that part.

"I used to keep my secret self inside my mouth," confided Lomas' patient, "it was my tonsils."[183]

As with other senses of self, that of core has a "*level.*"

"I am a nothing," declares a patient of Suslick, exemplifying a low level of this sense, "less than a nothing, a cipher, a zero. . . . I am not-a-person. . . . I feel as if something is missing in me." That is, "not attached-to-me-missing, but in-me-missing."[184] I may sense my core to comprise certain properties, e.g., being a woman or a man ("*core properties*"); my belief in possessing them may in varying degrees depend on events in my life (cf. paragraph 93 below).

89. I may feel qualities and happenings that do not belong to my core as (1) expressing it (and perhaps enriching it), (2) neutral toward it, (3) at variance with it, and, perhaps, (4) impinging on it, if not (5) altering it.

"Sometimes," declares a patient of Suslick, exemplifying (4), "I feel like a five layer cake, and the fifth layer, which is me, is all squished into a corner."[185] "She could," says Lichtenstein about his patient's feelings about her prostituting herself—presumably illustrating (3) and obscuring it by his preferred word—"not arrive at an integrated sense of identity, because the identity experience based on her actions did in no way correspond to the . . . experience of her 'real' self."[186] A patient of Greenacre's experiences a transition from (3) to (1): "Since the age of five this young woman had had a feeling: 'I really am somebody else just living in my body and looking out of my eyes. . . . Later [having acquired the capacity for genital pleasure —N.L.] she said: 'That is what rushed me into myself.' "[187]

The types of acts sensed as expressing core differ and vary. "Neither can thoughts be used to help these patients feel that they are themselves," Angel observes about certain cases; "the only thing that makes them feel themselves is action."[188]

90. Any expression of one's core, it may be believed, will cause unacceptable damage: withdrawal of another on whom one depends, or destruction of what has been expressed: "You cannot touch me if I am as you wish," a patient declared to Gruen. "This . . . became the cornerstone of . . . [his] development—not to strive for authenticity . . . but to remain invulnerable." "A schizoid woman patient . . . explained to me," the same author reports, "that she could now see that all her life she had tried to be completely empty—except for some peanut shells in her pocket—so that in case someone held her up (that is, made a demand of her), 'I could turn my pockets inside out and say, 'You see, I have nothing worthwhile taking!' "[189] In such cases, abstention from expressing one's core in the present may be accompanied by hope for the future: ". . . denuding oneself . . . one maintains the possibility of someday having a self of one's own making."[190]

91. One obvious variant of sensing that I am *not* expressing my core is to believe that I am complying with somebody else. In a certain type of patient, Angel notes, "the identity problem [sic] . . . manifests itself by such statements as: '. . . I never know whether I am really giving you my thoughts or whether I am repeating what I heard or read some place.' "[191]

However, the opposite may be the case: thy will be done, not mine! It is when submitting that one may feel supremely oneself: a possibility that may be overlooked—of course one could only be sure if one knew the meanings of the key words I shall italicize—when Lomas asserts that "the only way in which a . . . *sense of identity* can be established is not by an *identification* in which the child feels he exists only by or through his parent . . . , but by the *assimilation* onto *the original self-schema* of the environmental features (primarily the parents) which are suitable. . . ."[192]

92. Events that have happened to me or in me I may feel to be outside of myself altogether—for an obvious purpose of defense.

"The . . . spontaneous behavior of which he was terrified," observes Lomas about his patient, "would sometimes break through, following analysis of his control, in . . . a . . . fit. During these episodes his head would shake from side to side, he would sweat and groan and say such things as . . . 'I am not here. There's no me.' "[193]

147

93. Events happening to or within the self may affect beliefs about the self—its core properties or the rest of it—in varying degrees.

Thus for "normal" persons anything that happens to belief about relations with others of their own sex seem to have a belief about their gender less conditional upon their feelings and conduct than those who dread such relations. In fact, while many "normal" *males* begin to doubt whether they are *men* when they become aware of desiring sexual contact with other males, some homosexuals apparently confirm and reinforce their sense of being men precisely by the conduct that threatens that conviction in others. (They may of course thus be opposing a deeper reaction of the latter kind). Having made this point, Greenson adds that the "gender identity" of a "pervert" may even be unaffected by "the enactment of fantasies of being of a different sex."[194]

On the one hand, as Robert Stoller has pointed out in *Sex and Gender*, the more firmly fixed the belief in my gender, the *greater* the threat created by homosexual penchants: the less do I have an alternative belief about my gender to fall back upon. But also, as we have just seen, the more firmly fixed the belief in my gender, the *smaller* the threat in question: the less is that belief affected by my other feelings, thoughts, actions.

94. Changes in beliefs about myself may affect some or all senses of self in differing degrees; they may do so through having an impact on what I feel to be my core properties, or otherwise.

Thus, for "normal" persons anything that happens to belief about gender is apt to have noticeable repercussions upon the senses of self; e.g., altering the sense of the self's quality, impairing that of its permanence.

95. Changes in senses of self are, to be sure, apt to be accompanied by dysphoria, even panic. But perhaps not always to the same extent. If it be true that women, at least in the contemporary West, seem to react in a less psychotic manner to homosexual strivings, is it because their beliefs on gender are less conditional? Their senses of self less sensitive? Their proneness to panic smaller? and if "abandonment of identity sometimes produces . . . anguish," "it can," Lichtenstein reminds us, "also be experienced . . . as ecstasy."[195]

96. "Most adults," Greenacre observes, about what I call the senses of self, "seem to accept their own identities . . . without much contemplation, except under . . . unusual circumstances," such as "coming out of an anesthetic, being alone in a foreign country . . . having some experience which . . . seems . . . completely new." Otherwise only "young children, philosophers, artists and certain sick individuals concern themselves constantly with questions of their own identities"[196] —worth remembering, as the authors who talk much about "identity"

are apt to give the impression that at least contemporary man is much preoccupied with such questions as "who or what am I in relationship to what is man or human?"

14 | Identity Revisited

Coming back once more to our authors' style, one may note that they are apt to talk about "identity problems" without permitting the reader to know—and without encouraging him to know that he does not know—precisely what senses of the self they have in mind (*see* Chapter 8, paragraph 14.) When Lichtenstein advances that shame is a compromise formation between the temptation to "abandon identity" and the fear of doing so; that this temptation is fostered by the fear of being abandoned by others; that "blushing, warmth, palpitation betray the urge to yield to it [abandoning identity], and indicate the lustful anticipation of one's "identity's" death[198]—does he really have in mind to an equal degree all the senses of self that I have tried to enumerate (to be sure, incompletely)? When Erikson recalls that he was able to observe profound "identity problems" in patients with latent or manifest homosexual conflicts,[199] I would guess that competent readers, if asked to name the clinical syndromes that come to their minds with regard to this, will vary widely in their understanding of what the author has seen. Speaking about a patient's exhibitionistic fantasies and maneuvers toward a woman to whom he was close, Lomas tells us that she was the one who "evaluated" him, in fact "bestowed identity" on him—which allows for a number of plausible happenings in the patient; a number only slightly reduced by the information that he was concerned with "appearance and performance," though more substantially diminished by the disclosure that he dreaded being "small and helpless."[200]

If, according to Erikson, the legal classification of a juvenile delinquent's deed may "seal his negative identity as a criminal once and for all,"[201] this formulation, though leaving open a smaller range of possibilities than the ones previously quoted, still admits, for instance, of these two: The young delinquent may gain the conviction that he is a criminal in his core; or he may merely say to himself: If I have the name, I might as well play the game—a difference unlikely to be irrelevant for judge or therapist. Of course one might adopt an explicitly formulated linguistic convention to say "sealing of negative identity" whenever either one or the other of these two reactions occurs, or any one of a larger number which would have been enumerated. In current practice however, the immediate laying on of "identity" is apt to divert attention from interesting differences between numerous events designated by this blanketing word.

From other passages it becomes clear that the same author applies the same variant of his central word, "negative identity," to each of the following events:

(1) If I have a fortunate rival who is marked by a characteristic which is consciously undesirable, I may yet unconsciously aspire to that characteristic, wishing to acquire with and by it his good fortune too: "A mother whose first born son died and who . . . has never been able to attach to her later surviving children the same amount of . . . devotion that she bestows on the memory of her dead child, may well arouse in one of her sons the conviction that to be sick or dead is a better assurance of being 'recognized' than to be healthy and about."[202]

(2) I may endeavor to resemble a negative figure presented to me as such by parents, etc.

Whatever the usefulness of coining the word "negative identity" to refer *explicitly* to each of these reactions, the current mode of its employment involves the damage I noted above: Once the exalted word can be applied to a certain event—such as (1) or (2) above—less care is bestowed on indicating what that event is like: The no doubt elementary formulations that I just gave for (1) and (2) belong to a class of sentences rarely encountered in our authors' writings.

Where firm self-delineation is still missing, observes Erikson—to present another example of the same case—the young individual, when seeking tentative forms of playful intimacy, is apt to experience a peculiar strain, as if such tentative engagement might turn into an

150

interpersonal fusion amounting to "a loss of identity."[203] This, as far as I understand, may mean at least one or both of the following events: (1) the loss of my sense of being separate from others—an extreme reaction; (2) the loss of my ability to prevent the replacement of what I presently take to be my distinctive characteristics by those of another to whom I become attached—a less severe occurrence.

Likewise, speaking of the tendency of latency children to form groups consisting of members of one sex and similar ages only, the author affirms that "the experience of belonging to the same age and sex group . . . reinforces the sense of personal identity"[204]—which may mean that it (1) reinforces the *sense of membership* in one's sex, gender, and age, which is plausible enough, and surely unrelated to analytic theory; (2) augments the *sense of one's difference* not in relation to outsiders (which is apt to go with [1]), but rather with regard to one's very peers of age, sex, and gender: which is equally unrelated to analysis, less onvious, but also less probable. My assertion here is not that we may be in the presence of a familiar point in fancy dress or of a dubious point sheltered by a "concept," but rather that it is difficult to know whether one, the other, or a third contention is intended; for between us and the author's meaning (if not also between himself and his own claim) is the opaque screen of "identity."

Notes to Part Two

1. Paul Kramer, "On Discovering One's Identity," in R. S. Eissler et al., *The Psychoanalytic Study of the Child* (New York: International Universities Press), Vol. 10, p. 47.
2. Irving B. Harrison, "A Reconsideration of Freud's 'A Disturbance of Memory on the Acropolis in Relation to Identity Disturbance,' " *Journal of the American Psychoanalytic Association*, XIV (1966), 522; Edith Jacobson, *The Self and the Object World* (New York: International Universities Press, 1964).
3. Harrison, *loc. cit.*
4. Erik H. Erikson, *Identity and the Life Cycle* (New York: International Universities Press, 1959), p. 43.
5. *Ibid.*, p. 111.
6. Heinz Lichtenstein, "Identity and Sexuality," *Journal of the American Psychoanalytic Association*, IX (1961), 184.
7. *Ibid.*
8. *Ibid.*, p. 185.
9. *Ibid.*, p. 189.

10. Peter Lomas, "Passivity and Failure of Identity Development," *International Journal of Psycho-Analysis*, XLVI (1965), 543.
11. David Lawrence Rubinfine, "Report on a Panel on Problems of Identity," *Journal of the American Psychoanalytic Association*, VI (1958), 138.
12. *Ibid.*, p. 141.
13. *Ibid.*, p. 140.
14. *Ibid.*, p. 137.
15. Phyllis Greenacre, "Early Physical Determinants in the Development of the Sense of Identity," *Journal of the American Psychoanalytic Association*, VI (1958), 612.
16. Lichtenstein, p. 208.
17. Erikson, p. 92.
18. Lichtenstein, p. 193.
19. Erikson, p. 102.
20. *Ibid.*, p. 23.
21. Rubinfine, p. 131.
22. Greenacre, p. 612.
23. Erikson, p. 103.
24. *Ibid.*, p. 108.
25. Greenacre, p. 618.
26. Rubinfine, p. 136.
27. Phyllis Greenacre, "The Impostor," *Psychoanalytic Quarterly*, XXVII (1958), 369.
28. Rubinfine, p. 136.
29. Greenacre, "Early Physical Determinants in the Development of the Sense of Identity," p. 624.
30. Rubinfine, p. 141.
31. Erikson, p. 150.
32. *Ibid.*, p. 197.
33. Alvin Suslick, "Pathology of Identity as Related to the Borderline Ego," *Archives of General Psychiatry* (1963), p. 253.
34. Erikson, p. 90.
35. *Ibid.*, p. 146.
36. *Ibid.*, p. 34.
37. *Ibid.*, p. 158.
38. *Ibid.*, p. 33.
39. Lomas, p. 452.
40. Erikson, p. 125.
41. *Ibid.*, p. 93.
42. Lomas, p. 451.
43. Erikson, p. 38.
44. *Ibid.*, p. 113.
45. Lichtenstein, p. 235.

46. Heinz Lichtenstein, "The Role of Narcissism in the Emergence and Maintenance of a Primary Identity," *International Journal of Psycho-Analysis*, XLV (1964), 54.
47. Peter L. Giovacchini, "The Frozen Introject," *International Journal of Psycho-Analysis*, XLVIII (1967), 66.
48. Erikson, p. 125.
49. Lichtenstein, "Identity and Sexuality," p. 216.
50. Suslick, p. 260.
51. Edward D. Joseph, "Identity and Joseph Conrad," *Psychiatric Quarterly*, XXXII (1963), 450.
52. Erikson, p. 23.
53. Lichtenstein, "Identity and Sexuality," p. 185.
54. *Ibid.*, p. 227.
55. *Ibid.*, p. 228.
56. *Ibid.*, p. 245.
57. *Ibid.*, p. 252.
58. *Ibid.*, p. 250.
59. *Ibid.*, p. 193.
60. Anne Hayman, "Verbalization and Identity," *International Journal of Psycho-Analysis*, XLVI (1965), 455.
61. Peter Lomas, "Family Role and Identity Formation," *International Journal of Psycho-Analysis*, XLII (1961), 379.
62. Rubinfine, p. 141.
63. Heinz Lichtenstein, "Towards a Metapsychological Definition of the Concept of the Self," *International Journal of Psycho-Analysis*, XLVI (1965), 127.
64. *Ibid.*, p. 126.
65. Erikson, pp. 162–163.
66. Lichtenstein, "Identity and Sexuality," p. 201.
67. Erikson, p. 90.
68. *Ibid.*, p. 40.
69. *Ibid.*, pp. 101–102.
70. Harold F. Searles, "Review of Edith Jacobson's *The Self and the Object World*," *International Journal of Psycho-Analysis*, XLVI (1965), 531.
71. Peter Lomas, "Review of David J. deLevita's *The Concept of Identity*," *International Journal of Psycho-Analysis*, XLVIII (1967), 124.
72. Joseph, p. 565.
73. Lomas, "Review of David J. deLevita's *The Concept of Identity*," p. 151.
74. Erikson, p. 89.
75. Suslick, p. 255.
76. Erikson, p. 92.

77. *Ibid.*, p. 43.
78. Erik H. Erikson, "Reality and Actuality," *Journal of the American Psychoanalytic Association*, X (1962), 462.
79. Erikson, *Identity and the Life Cycle*, p. 92.
80. *Ibid.*, pp. 21–22.
81. *Ibid.*, p. 152.
82. *Ibid.*, p. 153.
83. *Ibid.*
84. *Ibid.*, p. 32.
85. Suslick, p. 259.
86. *Ibid.*, p. 260.
87. *Ibid.*, p. 91.
88. *Ibid.*, p. 259.
89. Jacobson, p. 97.
90. Albert J. Lubin, "A Feminine Moses: A Bridge Between Childhood Identifications and Adult Identity," *International Journal of Psycho-Analysis*, XXXIX (1958), 545.
91. Klaus Angel, "Loss of Identity and Acting Out," *Journal of the American Psychoanalytic Association*, XIII (1965), 82.
92. *Ibid.*
93. Erikson, "Reality and Actuality," pp. 459–460.
94. Erikson, *Identity and the Life Cycle*, p. 161.
95. Lichtenstein, "Identity and Sexuality," p. 190.
96. *Ibid.*, p. 207.
97. *Ibid.*
98. *Ibid.*, p. 189.
99. *Ibid.*, p. 208.
100. *Ibid.*
101. *Ibid.*, p. 201.
102. *Ibid.*, p. 216.
103. *Ibid.*, p. 192.
104. Erikson, *Identity and the Life Cycle*, p. 149.
105. *Ibid.*
106. Lichtenstein, "Identity and Sexuality," p. 235.
107. David E. Schecter, "Identification and Individuation," *Journal of the American Psychoanalytic Association*, XVI (1968), 52.
108. Hayman, p. 462.
109. Gerard J. Margolis, "Secrecy and Identity," *International Journal of Psycho-Analysis*, XLVII (1966), 520–521.
110. Norman Tabachnik, "Self-Realization and Social Definition, Two Aspects of Identity Formation," *International Journal of Psycho-Analysis*, XLVIII (1967), 75.
111. Lichtenstein, "Identity and Sexuality," pp. 188–189.
112. *Ibid.*, p. 184.

113. Charles N. Sarlin, "Feminine Identity," *Journal of the American Psychoanalytic Association*, XI (1963), 796.
114. *Ibid.*, p. 795.
115. Erikson, *Identity and the Life Cycle*, p. 143.
116. Lichtenstein, "Identity and Sexuality," p. 242.
117. Erikson, *Identity and the Life Cycle*, p. 90.
118. *Ibid.*, p. 95.
119. *Ibid.*
120. *Ibid.*, p. 92.
121. *Ibid.*, p. 110.
122. *Ibid.*, pp. 124–125.
123. Harrison, pp. 522–523.
124. Greenacre, "The Impostor," p. 364.
125. Erikson, *Identity and the Life Cycle*, p. 130.
126. *Ibid.*, p. 128.
127. *Ibid.*, p. 145.
128. *Ibid.*, p. 36.
129. Lichtenstein, "Identity and Sexuality," p. 228.
130. *Ibid.*, p. 208.
131. *Ibid.*, p. 225.
132. Tabachnik, p. 72.
133. *Ibid.*, p. 75.
134. Erikson, *Identity and the Life Cycle*, p. 116.
135. *Ibid.*, p. 88.
136. *Ibid.*, p. 31.
137. Lichtenstein, "The Role of Identification in Psycho-Analytic Procedure," p. 54.
138. Lichtenstein, "Identity and Sexuality," p. 207.
139. *Ibid.*, p. 232.
140. Lichtenstein, "The Role of Identification in Psycho-Analytic Procedure," p. 54.
141. Heinz Lichtenstein, "The Dilemma of Human Identity," *Journal of the American Psychoanalytic Association*, XI (1963), 193.
142. Erikson, *Identity and the Life Cycle*, p. 139.
143. Lichtenstein, "Identity and Sexuality," p. 224.
144. Erikson, *Identity and the Life Cycle*, p. 31.
145. Frederick F. Shevin, "Countertransference and Identity Phenomena Manifested in the Analysis of a Case of 'Phallus Girl' Identity," *Journal of the American Psychoanalytic Association*, XI (1963), 337–338.
146. Lubin, p. 546.
147. Erikson, *Identity and the Life Cycle*, p. 115.
148. Lichtenstein, "Identity and Sexuality," p. 220.
149. *Ibid.*

150. Erikson, *Identity and the Life Cycle*, pp. 107–108.
151. *Ibid.*, p. 43.
152. Lichtenstein, "Identity and Sexuality," p. 221.
153. Erikson, *Identity and the Life Cycle*, p. 30.
154. *Ibid.*, p. 28.
155. Lichtenstein, "Identity and Sexuality," p. 282.
156. *Ibid.*, p. 225.
157. *Ibid.*, p. 228.
158. *Ibid.*, p. 230.
159. *Ibid.*, p. 223.
160. *Ibid.*, p. 249.
161. *Ibid.*, p. 230.
162. *Ibid.*, p. 248.
163. Erikson, *Identity and the Life Cycle*, p. 127.
164. Lichtenstein, "Identity and Sexuality," p. 221.
165. Angel, p. 81.
166. Edith Jacobson, *The Self and the Object World* (New York: International Universities Press, 1964), pp. xi–xii.
167. *Ibid.*, p. 83.
168. Greenacre, "The Impostor," p. 371.
169. Hayman, p. 462.
170. Jacobson, p. 59.
171. Rubinfine, p. 140.
172. *Ibid.*, p. 136.
173. Suslick, p. 256.
174. Margolis, pp. 519–520.
175. Harold F. Searles, "Anxiety Concerning Change, as Seen in the Psychotherapy of Schizophrenic Patients, with Particular Reference to the Sense of Personal Identity," *International Journal of Psycho-Analysis*, XLII (1961), 79.
176. Jacobson, pp. 206–207.
177. Rubinfine, p. 133.
178. Searles, pp. 82–83.
179. *Ibid.*, p. 79.
180. *Ibid.*, p. 80.
181. Hayman, p. 462.
182. Jacobson, p. 51.
183. Lomas, "Passivity and Failure of Identity Development," p. 443.
184. Suslick, p. 255.
185. *Ibid.*, p. 256.
186. Lichtenstein, "Identity and Sexuality," p. 217.
187. Greenacre, "Early Physical Determinants in the Development of the Sense of Identity," p. 625.
188. Angel, p. 83.

189. Arno Gruen, "Autonomy and Identification: The Paradox of Their Opposition," *International Journal of Psycho-Analysis,* XLIX (1968), 650.
190. *Ibid.,* p. 652.
191. Angel, p. 81.
192. Lomas, "Family Role and Identity Formation," pp. 378–379.
193. Lomas, "Passivity and Failure of Identity Development," p. 441.
194. Ralph R. Greenson, "On Homosexuality and Gender Identity," *International Journal of Psycho-Analysis,* XLV (1964), 218.
195. Lichtenstein, "The Dilemma of Human Identity," p. 213.
196. Greenacre, "Early Physical Determinants in the Development of the Sense of Identity," pp. 612–613.
197. Suslick, p. 252.
198. Lichtenstein, "The Dilemma of Human Identity," p. 214.
199. Erikson, *Identity and the Life Cycle,* p. 73.
200. Lomas, "Passivity and Failure of Identity Development," p. 444.
201. Erikson, *Identity and the Life Cycle,* p. 163.
202. *Ibid.,* p. 131.
203. *Ibid.,* pp. 124–125.
204. *Ibid.,* p. 138.

Part III
The New Ego

15 | Considering the Analyzing Mind
     | Rather than the Analyzed Events

1. Having affirmed that in infancy the localization of unpleasure outside the body invites the cathexis of the source of unpleasure with aggression, and that this, in turn, channelizes aggression away from the self and thus protects it, Hartmann, Kris, and Loewenstein (whom I shall call "the authors") add that "this view is . . . valid only under conditions of . . ."[1]—rather than saying: this event occurs only when. . . . Calling "the dependability of morality vis-á-vis reality and opposing pressures from within" its "autonomy," Hartmann observes that, in relation to the secondary autonomy of the ego, the superego's autonomy is "comparable in its definition"[2]—not in its shape. One of the controversies that, the authors recall, has been important in recent years "concerns the role of instinctual drives in psychoanalytic theory,"[3] rather than in life. Having recalled that to the extent to which indulgence prevails, comprehension of the breast as part of the self is dominant, while to the extent to which deprivation is experienced, or indulgence delayed, distinction (between the infants' self and his mother's breast) becomes possible, the authors surmise that "the . . . term 'distinction' may be preceded by . . . a number of . . . experiences," which may range from expectation of, or longing for gratification to feelings of disappointment and even rage against the source of frustration[4]—rather than the distinction itself being thus preceded. "Two groups of hypotheses," the authors announce, "will be discussed: some dealing with dynamic and some dealing with genetic propositions"[5] —rather than: relationships.

2. The penchant to replace talk about patients by references to operations or products of the mind that studies them (*see* Chapter II, paragraph 60), may express itself more conspicuously than that. "However *clinically important the assumptions concerning* the internalization of aggression are, *we cannot, in establishing the general hypotheses on* the vicissitudes of aggression, *be satisfied with the dichotomy of* self-destructive and externalized aggression":[6]—or, aggression is sometimes neutralized. Recalling that narcissism is ("strictly defined") libidinal cathexis of the self, Hartmann notes that "a *description from the angle of* narcissism *does not account for* . . . the differences . . . between the cathexis of the self image . . . and of ego functions—*a distinction . . . relevant . . . in . . .* psychoses":[7] In other words—perhaps —for a given degree of narcissism, the ratio between the cathexis of the self-image and that of ego functions—a ratio influential in psychoses —may vary. Because mental phenomena are no less "real" than the outer world, "it might," Hartmann surmises, "prove useful to *broaden the concept* of reality testing to include testing of the inner world":[8] That is, as events over which my control is incomplete may be mental, acts similar to what has until now been called reality testing occur with regard to my inner world. However, if this formulation were adopted, two questions might arise: Would it not, on balance, be inconvenient to change the accepted meaning of a term, as famous as "reality testing"? Second—never mind terms—what are the similarities—and differences —between my taking account of inner as against outer happenings? Referring to "regression in the service of the ego," Hartmann observes that "these phenomena . . . *must be looked at from the viewpoint* that to achieve optimal adaptation more primitive functions may be needed to supplement the highly differentiated ones"[9]—rather than merely recalling that the term in question has been coined to *designate* optimal adaptation thus achieved.

3. Drawn toward talk about the analyst's mind rather than about patients, one may conclude with the former even when one has begun with the latter. Observing that id tendencies are more estranged from reality than animal instincts, Hartmann infers that "the *description* of drives *in terms of* instincts has . . . *delayed the progress of psychology.*"[10] In the twenties, the author recalls, when Freud tried to account for the phenomena of life by the interplay of the two primordial drives, he also accentuated the relative independence of the non-instinctual forces of the ego: "Obviously," he concludes, "we are confronted here" with two sets of events related in a fashion now to be shown. No, "with two different levels of theory formation."[11] As "the development of object representation . . . creates an 'inner' representation of the outside world," "*we want to emphasize,*" the authors declare, "that object representations . . . *must be described . . .* as

162

parts of the 'inner world.' "[12] If "the manifold activities of the ego . . . [belonging to] the 'conflict-free sphere' . . . often do exert an influence on . . . conflicts," as Hartmann shows, "*this means*" "that *our attempt to explain* . . . conflict will often have to *consider* also the nonconflictual elements."[13]

4. The importance of *events* may thus be that they determine the shape of *assertions*; about themselves, as in the cases just mentioned, or about something going beyond them. In the earliest stages of development, Hartmann reminds us, the dependence of perception upon drives is obvious: "In these stages, *then*, perception *must be described* . . . also as to the ways it is used by sexual and aggressive tendencies."[14] The processes of energy transformation, rather than having such and such consequences for the ego, "*establish a link between the two chapters of psychoanalytic theory* dealing with instinctual drives and ego psychology."[15] "The knowledge of the . . . ego," rather than being an end in itself (therapy apart) "[leads] to a neater definition . . . of the psychoanalytic approach. . . ."[16] While the importance of the aims and objects of drives soon outdistanced, in the development of psychoanalysis, that of their sources, the latter remain "*relevant*" also because insight into them "may be helpful in *classifying* the drives."[17]

5. More particularly, the discovery of relations between classes of events may, rather than being acknowledged as desirable for its own sake, be enjoyed for the reassuring and pleasurable movement of abolishing lack of connection. When "the concept of libido was viewed in physiological terms," it was supposed to "*establish the link* to physiological processes."[18] And Freud's "concept of sexual drives" served "to *integrate* phenomena that had previously been *pigeonholed in isolated chapters* of psychology and psychopathology."[19] Considering his new points on schizophrenia, Hartmann perceives "an *attempt to breach at least one of the gaps between* the instinctual and the ego aspects of schizophrenia"[20]—rather than an effort to increase insight into the relationships between instinctual and ego phenomena in that illness.

6. What patients are like in a certain respect is not unimportant, as the status of important propositions may depend on it. One of the major controversies of recent years, the authors recall, is "concerned with the role of past experiences, *i.e.*, the importance of genetic propositions."[21] The endeavor to validate psychoanalytic hypotheses, Hartmann observes, is "welcome in analysis," "as it might help"—the ascertainment of truth? Rather, "toward a clarification of . . . theories."

163

16 | It's the Context as Much as the Content

7. The connections between a given statement and other assertions may appear to be as relevant as its relationship to the events that it affirms to occur (*see* Part I, paragraph 19). "If we refer to alternative views as not, or less, meaningful," the authors note about "dissent" in psychoanalysis, "we often refer to the disregard of the hierarchy of propositions, and not merely to the contradictions to some."[23] In fact, "quoting Freud is . . . meaningful only if it is a part of a . . . attempt to gain insight into the position of the quoted passage within the development of Freud's thought."[24] If this contention sounds excessive, it is perhaps due to the fact that I omitted, through my first dots, a qualification: it is only "as a rule" that an inquiry into the relation between what Freud says and what patients do is not "meaningful." But then we are told nothing about the unusual cases in which a confrontation between sentence and event would be crucial, after all.

8. Does not the very meaning of any sentence depend on the meanings of sentences in its neighborhood (however delimited)? An "individual" quotation from Freud "lends itself to distortions";[25] we are not told at what size a quotation ceases to be "individual." Quoting Freud, as we already know, "has sense only if the hierarchy of [Freud's] propositions is kept in mind."[26] The authors working in the field of culture and personality violate this postulate when they select out of the manifold of psychoanalytic propositions just some, "without concern for their interrelations with other . . . propositions," though these are "essential."[27]

164

9. They are "essential," in the words following this adjective in that passage "in psychoanalysis as a . . . system";[28] for that is what the "set of propositions" to which the designation "psychoanalysis" refers constitutes.[29] This the authors affirm often, in many (presumably synonymous) ways. They allude to "how the various parts of the . . . system with which psychoanalysis operates hang together."[30] The designation "psychoanalysis" refers to a set of propositions that is "internally cohesive";[31] the authors speak of a "system" in view of "the cohesion and interlocking" of propositions.[32] (Could these conceivably cohere without interlocking, or interlock without cohering? Or are the two words synonyms?) When recalling the cohesiveness of psychoanalytic propositions, the authors inform us, they refer to their "interrelatedness or integration";[33] an "or" which raises the question I asked about an "and" and a moment ago.

Whatever "systematization" is, it "confers dignity . . . on a concept."[34]

10. Increasingly so, as time passes: "progress" in psychoanalytic theory has led to "a better integration, an ever clearer connection" of its parts:[35] a point repeatedly asserted, but not proved, not even illustrated.

11. That analysis is a "system" may be adduced as a reason against changes. At an early moment when Hartmann, in contrast to later usage, denies that analysis is a "system"—it is rather a "cohesive organisation" of propositions—he can already warn that "any attempt to isolate" parts of it "invalidates its parts."[36] The authors disapprove of the inclination to look upon Freud's work as a collection of statements that can "freely" be "combined or interchanged."[37] (Again, might one advocate combination while rejecting interchange, and vice versa? Or does the "or" join synonyms?) The preference for the earlier phase of Freud's work on the part of some who are out of sympathy with his later revision of theory is, the authors claim, an instance of "disregard" for analysis as a "coherent" set of statements.[38]

12. But that analysis is a "system" is, on the other hand, no reason for not making changes. To be sure, "the theories of psychoanalysis follow principles of systematisation." Yet a "considerable part" of analysis is "tentative"; "reformulations"—less than changes in what is asserted about patients?—of "various aspects"—less than parts?—of theory have repeatedly become necessary. In short, though analysis be a "system," it is "far from being a closed [one]";[39] it is, the authors remind the reader, not "rigid," but rather "open to modification arising out of a validation or invalidation of its parts."[40] How does this situation differ from one in which analysis would not be a "system"? The question is not put, and thus does not need to be answered.

13. While the authors assign much importance to analysis being a system, they do little to show that certain relationships (which precisely?) in fact exist between analytic propositions even where at first sight they do not seem to obtain.

14. It is rare for them to "raise the question" (without answering it) why no "systematic" presentation of psychoanalytic theory has ever been "compiled"[41]—a participle whose connotations stand in contrast to the "dignity" that, as we have seen, systematization confers on its objects. And instead of observing that a "systematic presentation" of analysis, when accomplished, will finally render evident its possession of a precious quality, they merely note that "such a presentation could help to take the place which the reading of Freud's work in historical sequence at present occupies in the education of psychoanalysts."[42] On another occasion a "higher degree of systematization" will be in the service not of truth, to be sure, but rather of intellectual activity—it would "facilitate . . . discussing psychoanalysis as a . . . theory"—and of status: It would "clarify the standing of analysis as a scientific discipline."[43] Perhaps the protracted work of discovering varied relations—or their absence?—between particular propositions of analysis seems less attractive than the single and powerful act of affirming that analysis is a whole. In 1958 Hartmann, writing on *Scientific Aspects of Psychoanalysis*, observes that "the level of systematization [of analysis] is . . . low, in spite of efforts to remedy this state of affairs."[44] The following year, discussing *Psychoanalysis as a Scientific Theory*, he notes that a work by Rapaport published in 1958 "comes close" to being a "systematical outline" of analysis "from the angle" of showing the "hierarchy" of hypotheses as to their "closeness to observation," their "generality" and—to close the list—"the degree to which they have been confirmed." But far from this sudden and radical change in the common subject of both articles providing the central topic for the later one, it is mentioned only in passing; and the author does not indicate those characteristics of Rapaport's achievement that make him say that it merely "comes close" to "performing" the "task" in question, rather than accomplishing it.[45]

17 | No Major Statement Lacks a Theoretical Basis

15. Apart from being but an element of a vast "system," a statement is apt to be credited with a more circumscribed "theoretical basis."

The authors may observe that attention to theoretical bases is insufficient: "The . . . theoretical basis of this distinction," they say about that between conscious and unconscious ego functions, "has been neglected"; "the theoretical foundation," they note about the distinction between unconscious and preconscious awareness, "upon which this distinction rests, found little attention."[46] But they themselves, as far as I can see, do not—with a single exception (*see* Chapter 39, paragraph 270)—furnish any exposition of a particular "theoretical basis" that would constitute a deductive chain of some complexity.

16. One may present as a *significant inference* what is the consequence of a statement being combined with an (implicit) *truism*. The "assumption" that countercathexes against drives are "mostly" fed by "neutralized" aggression "would *imply*," Hartmann advances, that countercathexis "may" be a "*general*" way of utilising aggression "in one of its neutralized forms":[47] to be sure, if countercathexes are pervasive within the psyche. (Had the text carried an "is" instead of the excessively modest "may be," this might have been more visible.)

17. A law may be presented as a "reason" for a case conforming to it. Declaring that for healthy behavior to occur the demands of all [three] psychic systems will have to be considered by the ego's organizing function under which all psychic tendencies will have to be subordinated,

167

Hartmann concludes: *"These considerations . . . make it clear why* the many attempts to plan human existence . . . based on an appeal to a certain group of ego interests . . . lead to unforeseen conflicts."[48] There are, Hartmann recalls, situations in which the ego itself induces a temporary discarding of some of its most highly differentiated functions. Now, to do this, not only without impairment of normal function, but even to its benefit, is an achievement that has to be learned; the child, up to a certain age, is not capable of using this mechanism, or feels threatened by its attempted use. "I think," the author adds, "that this is probably *one reason why* the child fails vis-á-vis the demand for free association . . ."[49] rather than that failure being *one instance* of the law enunciated. (Again, had this been presented as a "reason" *surely* rather than "probably," it might have been easier to conceive doubts as to whether it is one).

18. For a statement that appears, at first sight, grounded in observation, one may affirm—without showing—a complex derivation from "theory." What is it that "precludes the functional equation" of animal instinct and human drive? In other words (presumably), what demonstrates the falsity of the assertion that there are no relevant differences between them? It is not observations, but rather "multidimensional structural considerations" that "allow the understanding of. . . [this] significant distinction between man and lower animals."[50] Having decided to call the degree of the ego's "resistivity" to impulse its degree of "secondary autonomy," Hartmann affirms—and does not prove—that it is two "assumptions"—first, that a process similar to that of sublimation of libido exists for aggression, and second, that this transformation of energy "might be designated as" neutralisation— which "permit" the "introduction" of "the concept of secondary autonomy."[51]

19. Similar claims may be made with regard to seemingly obvious procedures. The direct observation of child development by analysts, declares Hartmann without any proof, "presupposes" "a theory of adaptation"; it even does so "clearly":[52] a contention that it may be difficult to maintain unless lack of such a theory were to deprive one of the quality of "analyst," or unless the verb "to presuppose" here refers to the (not logical, but psychological) impact that accepting such a theory may have on analysts, drawing them from the consulting room to the one-way screen. What about the combination of longitudinal observation from early childhood on with the reconstructive data furnished by analysis? Capital, but producing theory rather than presupposing it? No, for it "has been made possible only as a consequence of . . . structural psychology . . . which provided us with the indispensable frame of reference and [sic] with the necessary tools for a fruitful collaboration"[53]—a claim soon reduced: A few pages later it is merely

for "a more systematic correlation" of the two procedures that "the new level of ego psychology" has "proved decisive."

20. The ease with which the existence of "theoretical bases" can be asserted becomes more intelligible when one considers some inferences that the authors find it worthwhile to oppose. Having rejected the affirmation that the fact of object representations being part of the inner world is the *result* of introjection or identification, the authors declare it "hardly necessary to stress" that "this distinction [sic] . . . *does not imply* that . . . object representations do not *influence* . . . identifications. . . ."[55] Having mentioned what he calls ego interests—for instance, those concerned with social status, influence, professional success, wealth, comfort and so forth—Hartmann observes that "their prevalence in an individual *does not warrant the assumption* that the drives are harmoniously included in the ego, or that the superego demands have been integrated into it."[56] "You will remember," he appeals to his listeners, "how . . . on the basis of the correct insight into the role of defense in neurosis, *it was deduced* . . . that every defense leads necessarily to pathology."[57] "The fact that we attribute internal perception to the ego *certainly does not imply*," the authors find it appropriate to point out, "that internal perception could not come under the influence of superego functions":[58] an inference that has presumably been made by some without enunciating a premise such as that no "function" of one "system" influences any of the other—a belief that can, of course, be entertained only as long as it is not stated.

18 | Fruits of Focusing on the Mind's Activity

21. When one starts out with talking about intellectual operations, and only afterward proceeds to speak about events, the latter may seem less unsurprising than might otherwise have been the case. "Some of the pertinent questions of structural psychology," affirms Hartmann, "can be viewed from the angle of what, borrowing a term from biology, I called 'change of function.' . . . It is part of what I now call 'secondary autonomy.' It . . . invites marking off more clearly the functional aspect from the genetic one." With this preparation, events themselves become speakable: "in some cases," "functions of the ego" are "irreversible" in "everyday" circumstances; though "even in many of these instances reversibility . . . [occurs] in dreams, in neuroses and psychoses, and in analysis"[59]—a pronouncement that might have seemed all too true had it not confronted us as the result of "viewing" a "pertinent question of structural psychology" from the "angle" of "change of function."

22. Focusing on intellectual operations may help in reducing one's awareness of not yet having formulated a hypothesis. "Only the choice of appropriate means to a given goal may be called rational," Hartmann first affirms, but then shows that "our considerations have forced us to broaden the concept of 'rationality,' so that it becomes equivalent to the organizing function." For "this broader concept of rational behavior is a . . . better measuring rod of biologically and socially purposive behavior than the narrower concept we discussed first."[60]—expressions that may detract attention from a question concerning not

"concepts" but events: Just what relationship between which properties of the "organising function" on the one hand and the level of "purposiveness" on the other hand is asserted?

23. "The biological *approach . . . indicates a framework* within which the fact that man is a social animal becomes *meaningful*":[61] Had the authors affirmed instead that social factors operate within limits set by biological ones, they themselves, as well as readers, might have been less convinced of the need to issue this pronouncement, and more inclined to reserve words for enunciating new knowledge about the interactions in question. "It is advisable to distinguish . . . the cathexes of contents [of ego and superego] from the cathexes of [their] functions":[62] Or, presumably, we surmise that several combinations of content cathexis and function cathexis occur. While the expression chosen by the authors imposes only an easy obligation to *"distinguish,"* the formulation oriented on the clinic rather than the concept burdens one with the heavy duty of *discovering* relationships between the classes of events "distinguished."

24. "The . . . *theory* of neurosis . . . *viewed as* a process . . .":[63] But had the authors affirmed in passing that neurosis *is* a process, they could have aroused the question what it might look like were it not. If "the differential [as against which other kind?—N.L.] study of the ego," instead of rendering it *"meaningful to speak* of 'structures in the ego' and of 'structures in the superego,' "[64] had proved that structures *exist* in these places, the query might again have been raised what the "systems" in question would look like if they did not possess structures. "If a 'tension between superego and ego' results in the ego's submitting to . . . the superego, this," the authors remind us, "is in itself not a phenomenon *to be classified as* 'masochism,' as has . . . been suggested. . . ."[65] Had they instead affirmed that there are cases of the ego's submitting to the superego without masochism, they might have been impelled to say more about them, as well as to indicate in greater detail what their opponents in the matter had affirmed; and thus to elucidate the grounds of the disagreement—possibly, a difference in referents assigned to the word "masochism." "One could try to describe the impairment of ego functions [in schizophrenia] . . . by reference to narcissistic regression, but such a description is . . . incomplete":[66] If Hartmann had instead asserted that ego impairment in schizophrenia consists not only in narcissistic regression, he might have found it difficult to avoid an informative and arduous "but also . . .," which a style focusing on intellectual operations rather than clinical events makes it easier to omit.

25. The advantage of formulations centered on the mind's activities rather than the inquiry's objects may not only, as in the preceding paragraph, be that they impede, rather than foster, demands—perhaps

difficult to meet—for *details*; they may also hinder, rather than provoke, requests for the discovery of *conditions*. Close to a passage quoted above, the authors observe that *"we will often have to classify* the need for punishment as masochistic":[67] Had they noted that the need for punishment often *is* masochism, they might have inspired a question as hard to reject as it might be to answer: Precisely in what conditions is it that?

26. "The distinction of primary and secondary processes," the authors declare, "becomes fruitful only if we supplement it by that of . . . energy into 'states,' bound and mobile":[68] Or, presumably, there are (and will be) no interesting hypotheses about relationships between events referred to by the former pair of words, which do not also refer to relationships between events designated by the latter one—which suddenly seems more dubious than the expression the authors chose. "I cannot follow Fenichel," Hartmann observes, "when he *simply equates* sublimation with successful defense."[69] You may be for or against "simply equating" A with B; you will in any case be less vulnerable than if you assert that whenever there is A, there is B—vulnerable either to the discovery of a single case in which there is the one without the other, or to the revelation that your contention follows from the words' meanings.

27. "One might wonder *whether or not we can speak of* inherited traits of the superego . . .":[70] It may be more feasible to maintain a state of indecision (also with regard to what is required for a decision) about this than if the question were: *Are* there such traits or not?

28. Having defined "maturation" as events depending upon inheritance and having affirmed that present knowledge does not provide us with any cogent reason to speak of inheritance in the case of the superego, the authors merely *"think it advisable not to use the term* maturation with respect to the superego"[71]—while their premises would enable them to surmise that *there is no* maturation of it: a trenchant expression that would have sacrificed urbanity as well as heightened commitment. "It is conceivable," the authors observe about the anthropologists' classes of "preliterate" or "primitive" societies on the one hand and those that are not on the other hand, "that the differences to which these expressions refer . . . could in part . . . be *viewed in terms of ego psychology.* One might say that the increase in autonomy of the ego or . . . superego . . . *would lend themselves for the description* of such differences."[72] What seems to be approached here is the contention, to put it in middlebrow words, that civilization's advance is related to a reduction in the power of both the environment and the impulses over man's conscience and reason; a hypothesis that appears not only less worn, but to which one also becomes less wedded, if, apart from open expressions of detachment ("it is conceivable,"

"one might say"), one talks about maneuvers of the mind rather than affirming a correlation between events.

29. What Freud says about the splitting of the ego in the process of defense, or Richard Sterba about its splitting in analysis, observes Hartmann, are "examples of intrasystemic *thinking*,"[73] rather than *findings* about what goes on within the ego. And thinking may seem more attractive than observing, even if one is capable of perceiving the unsuspected.

30. "Growth, *as we generally describe it*," the authors remind us, "is not limited to the . . . zones of predominant erotogeneity; it includes. . . ."[74] Had they simply stated that growth *is* not thus limited, not only might the pronouncing of this sentence seem less worthwhile (possible blindness of some pioneers apart, who could maintain that it is? Unless of course the meaning of "growth" were implicitly diverted from usage); in addition, a precious sense of freedom would be lost. As the formulation stands, it is not just a matter of what growth *is*, it is a question of how we *choose* to describe it; and even if we mostly do so in one way, we are still enjoying the privilege of rejecting others. "Contrary to Freud," the authors explain, "*we do not find it necessary to stress* as much as he the hereditary elements in . . .":[75] There is more of the analyst's *doing* in this than in case of a mere *recognition*, by more data and better reasoning, that the elements in question just happen to be less important than Freud affirmed. "*To us*," the authors declare, "*it seems reasonable to view* . . . the ego ideal . . . in close relation to . . . other developments which originate in the oedipal conflict . . .":[76] As the data and logic that might command such a decision are not presented, it bathes in freedom. "Freud's theory," the authors maintain, "*allows us to include* among the genetic determinants of 'conscience' also . . . the pre-oedipal vicissitudes of aggression":[77] Freud has expanded the range of acts *open to us*, rather making us see that the pre-oedipal vicissitudes of aggression *do have* certain consequences for conscience. "Earliest stages of ego development," Hartmann advances, "*can be described from several angles*: as a process of differentiation . . .; *as* a process that leads from the pleasure to the reality ego; *as* the development of the reality principle; *as* the way leading from primary narcissism to object relationships; *from the point of view of* the sequence of danger situations; *as* the development of the secondary process, *etc.*":[78] A more exciting range for the exercise of the mind's agility is here provided than if we had been reminded that all these (well-known) developments are occurring; that all of them are important (in the ordinary meaning of this word); hence that all of them (given the ordinary meaning of "science") must (not can) be described. Instead of angles being chosen, domains for study would have been imposed.

31. The discreet exaltation of intellectual liberty frequently takes

off from the obvious freedom for any analyst (if not for the profession) to choose his subject of inquiry. Tensions between ego and superego, the authors claim, *"can also be considered"* in relation to cultural systems:[79] There presumably *are* relationships between such tensions and such systems, a subject that any analyst may choose to make his own or not. "We said," the authors recall, "that the formation of a lasting object relationship depends on a partial neutralization of libido. *From the viewpoint* of the present discussion we added that . . . similar requirements exist . . . [for] aggression":[80] The "viewpoint" is the subject chosen by the authors, namely aggression. Having indicated what he properly calls an "object of research"—the antagonistic and synergistic relationships between ego functions—Hartmann, in a concluding parenthesis, returns from the constraint of facts to the sovereignty of spirit: "Intrasystemic approach," he adds.[81] "At one point," he declares about intellectual and motor development in childhood, "we may be interested in . . . [their] genetic relationship to . . . disturbances, and at another point in . . . [their] adaptative value." So far, so evident. But now the twist of freedom through the turn to the activity of the mind: *"Our vantage point determines"* which aspect of the process will assume importance [to be sure, as the word "vantage point" here presumably refers to the same events as does "importance assumed by aspects of process"—N.L.]: The two relationships pertain to two different *points of view,"*[82] rather than being merely two different objects of inquiry. That there is nothing more to it than that is a contention (surely judged epistemologically naïve) that Hartmann explicitly opposes at another point: Having recalled that a measure that is successful in relation to defensive needs may be a failure from the standpoint of achievement, and vice versa, he points out that "we are . . . concerned here with two . . . approaches to . . . the same fact, and not with two . . . sets of facts"[83] —without indicating what the situation would have to look like for the latter to be the case.

32. Freedom conduces to powerful activity. "The instinctual drives [are] *conceived* in psychoanalysis *in sharp distinction* from instincts, at least in lower animals"[84]—rather than: Instinctual drives are much different from instincts, at least of lower animals (but, then, who would object? And who could then stress?). If one recognizes, Hartmann declares, that "one cannot describe cross sections of development in terms of . . . the sexual drives only," that "it is important to describe them also in terms of . . . the aggressive drives," "this already constitutes a . . . broadening and differentiation of the . . . frame of reference we use"[85]—a momentous act, whose counterpart, if one chooses to talk about patients directly, seems to be the assertion that aggressive drives are of nonnegligible impact.

19 | Truth Has Become Awkward

33. "We consider *misleading*, and will therefore reject, any theory which . . ."[86] Hartmann does not—he rarely does—use the adjective "false," as little as he is given to claim that the points he advances are "true."

34. Instead of an affirmation of falsity, there may be an imputation of incompleteness. "It is a one-sided approach to consider only the genetic relations between animal instinct and human drive; it means an *overlooking* of the no less important relations between animal instinct and human ego functions"; in fact, this is a "mistake" that is "suggested" by "formulations which stress [rather than: affirm—N.L.] the identity of instincts and drives."[87] What seems both approached and avoided here is a flat declaration that it is false to affirm animal instincts and human drives to be identical (which would raise the question: in which respects? A single affirmation would have to give way to a manifold of queries).

35. Or a statement may be rejected on the ground that the intellectual operations leading to it are improper, with regard to a code that is apt to remain unformulated. To "discuss" drives toward self-preservation on the one hand and sexual and aggressive ones on the other hand "on one plane," in "juxtaposition," Hartmann advances, "may well be," again, "misleading"; for one "cannot"—we are not told by virtue of what axiom—"put them one beside the other" if they "reflect" what are "different principles of classification."[88]

175

36. In approval, "meaningful" (undefined) may replace "true." The preferred adjective may appear even if its omission were to leave the assertion in question intact. Not even the simplest clinical observation in psychoanalysis, Hartmann observes, "would be meaningful without assuming" unconscious processes;[89] each such observation assumes them.

37. If one merely questions the "meaningfulness" of a statement one eschews the rudeness of calling it false. Mechanisms, Hartmann recalls, developmental stages, modes of reaction with which we have become familiar for the part they play in neuroses, are by some analysts automatically relegated to the realm of the pathological, and health is characterized as a condition in which these elements are absent. But, he pursues, the contrast thus established between health and neurosis "can have no meaning so long as we fail to appreciate" how much of these mechanisms, developmental stages, and modes of reaction is active in healthy individuals[90]—rather than: the affirmation (for instance) that only neurotics regress is false.

Similarly, being favorable merely to the extent of judging an intellectual product "meaningful" serves both prudence and modesty. "The genetic propositions of psychoanalysis," the authors admit, "seem to us . . . to facilitate *meaningful* predictions"—a restraint, with regard to the alternative of "true," that allows assertiveness within its confines: "We feel that the clinical material at our disposal is in this respect unambiguous."[91] If it is, in contrast, assurance that is expressed first, moderation may follow: Having affirmed that psychoanalysis allows for predictions of human behavior that no other set of propositions has made possible, the authors note that they "refer to alternative views as *not, or less, meaningful,*"[92] abstaining from a declaration of their inferiority with regard to truth, which might be sensed not only as rude, but also naïve.

38. Even more useful than "meaningful" is "useful." "To emphasize . . . one partial concept of the ego, at the expense of other aspects may be a question" of what goes on in certain clinical syndromes rather than others? No, "of *expediency* vis-à-vis specific problems."[93] Recalling that Freud's hypotheses on the dream were formulated before the end of the last century, the authors claim that they have since that time "lost nothing of their . . ."—truth? No, "usefulness."[94]

39. "Useful" for what? Usually unstated. The question may appear uncouth, as it is "an essential insight" of the twentieth century, positivism having been overcome, that "hypotheses are primarily tools": "[The] understanding of hypotheses as tools [is] a principle widely accepted in every science"; in the case at hand being a tool is to possess "fruitfulness in . . . psychoanalytic work"[95] (the context does not suggest that the "work" is therapy). Are hypotheses tools for the production of more and better hypotheses, which will in their turn,

austerely, be tools again? Or is the present a tool for consummation of truth in the future?

40. For the moment at least even what others might call truth is a tool. "A theory of adaptation will be *more useful for our purposes* [unstated—N.L.]," explains Hartmann, "*the more clearly it shows* the interplay between adaptive functions and the . . . organizing . . . functions."[96]

41. Speaking about usefulness rather than truth allows one, once more, to remain polite toward opponents, and gentle toward one's own. Dealing with dissenting views of psychoanalysts the authors suggest that in each of them theory is simplified "at the price of its usefulness."[97] Recalling that Freud "speaks," with regard to infancy, of a gradual differentiation of the ego from the id, this, the authors observe, implies that the infant's equipment at birth is part of the id. Now, in the sense generally accepted for the word id, the innate apparatuses and reflexes "cannot all" be part of the id. That is, I would continue, they are not all part of the id. Hence, Freud's (implicit) *assertion* is *false*. According to the authors the situation is less stark: "Freud's *formulation* has . . . *disadvantages*";[98] a moderation that permits vigor: Where I put dots, the authors have "obvious." Freud's *error* is indeed obvious; not calling it that, allows not asking oneself what he could possibly have had in mind when committing it—did he forget, for the moment, that the neonate possesses innate apparatuses and reflexes, or did he temporarily lose sight of what he usually designated with a word that he happens to have created himself?

20 | We Must Distinguish

42. If one is still concerned with statements, it may be more difficult to avoid the question whether they are true or false than if one is absorbed with other products of the mind, such as "distinctions."

43. One may be for or against "distinctions" as one used to be for or against contentions. "There is," the authors declare when dealing with a study by Piers and Singer, "no reason to object to a . . . distinction between 'guilt' and 'shame.' "[99]

44. One can be, once again, polite about declining a "distinction" where one might have to be peremptory in asserting the falsity of what is, through it, affirmed about events. Considering Piers and Singer's "assumption" that one "can" "distinguish" between shame and guilt "in terms of" outer and inner sanction, the authors observe that "it seems *unlikely* to us that one can [do that]"[100]—whereas they might not have been able to avoid pronouncing *plainly* false the assertion that shame is never related to inner sanction, and guilt never to outer.

45. One may treat as a respectable mistake the nondistinction (there is usually no indication as to what this means) between classes of events that to common sense seem noticeably, if not vastly, different from each other. There is, according to the authors, a "frequent confusion or [sic] equation" between self-perception and self-condemnation.[101] "The distinction between 'being a function of' [superego or ego] and 'being accessible to the influence of' [one or the other] has," the authors observe, "not always been clearly made. . . ."[102] Illustrating "the difficulties with which the study of psychoanalytic theory is fraught,"

showing how "the complexity of psychoanalytic theory fosters misunderstandings," the authors affirm the existence of a "widespread misapprehension" among analysts, namely a nondistinction between two meanings of the word "ego," designating at times "parts of . . .[the] personality," and at times "the total personality." In fact, "the lack of distinction between the ego as an organization and the self" (something, it would seem to me, on the order of a "lack of distinction" between Washington, D.C., and the United States) is nothing less than "the theoretical basis" of an entire body of thought within psychoanalysis, namely Federn's ego psychology, the "merits" of which have despite this peculiar foundation managed to be "considerable." And when the authors "insisted on a sharper definition of 'self' in constrast to 'ego,'" affirming that the cathexis of the self "is by no means identical with or [sic] limited to" the cathexis of the system ego, were their clarifications greeted as superfluous, or as liberating from a mistake difficult to comprehend in hindsight? Not entirely, for "some objections were voiced."[103]

46. Effort seems in fact required for "distinguishing" what it may at first sight seem difficult not to set apart. The function of a behavior, Hartmann shows, "should be distinguished," "often" and "even," "from its genesis." For instance, he explains, the question: What is the adaptive achievement of expressive movements? "must be distinguished from" another question: How do such movements come about?[104] Directing the reader's attention to the fact that we have "self-images," that we enjoy "ego functions, as thought and action," which "may be object directed as well as self-directed," and that we bestow "cathexis" on each of these parts of our selves, the author points out that it is "clinically and theoretically important" to "make a difference between" the cathexes of the former and of the latter.

47. To distinguish between what at first sight seems unconfoundable is "useful." "We . . . deem it expedient to distinguish between" the state of being adapted and the process by which it is achieved.[105] "The concept of secondary autonomy"—the ego's degree of "resistivity" toward environment and drives—is "a direct outcome" of "stressing the difference" between "the functional and the genetic approach,"[106] i.e., between the fact that the "resistivity" in question is negligible in infancy, and the fact that it may be substantial later. (Note how the approach through "approach" renders the sentence more speakable: cf. paragraph 21 above.) As to the "distinction in theory" between the total personality (called "self") and a certain part of it (called "ego"), "there is little doubt"—so little that it need not be dispelled by a demonstration, which, in fact, might not be easy—that it is this that "permits us to formulate more specific hypotheses, e.g., in distinguish-

ing psychotic from non-psychotic behavior or psychotic and psychosomatic reactions. . . ."[107]

48. Distinguishing the radically diverse being difficult, it is apt to require, as any advanced production, tools; only that here the producer's good may resemble the product. "It appears to me desirable," observes Hartmann, "to note clearly the difference between" the case in which the vulnerability specific to a phase of development is mainly determined by what happened prior to that phase, and the case in which that vulnerability is mainly determined by what happens during it. Noting clearly this difference "may help us" to "distinguish more clearly" two classes of events that are by implication affirmed to be different from the first pair: on the one hand "the specific features of a given phase," and on the other hand "its genetic determinants."[108]

SECTION 2: WHAT CLINICAL EVIDENCE
COULD REFUTE THIS CLAIM?

21 | Taking a Position on a Statement While Leaving Obscure the Evidence for Doing So

49. As to "early . . . identifications . . . in the superego which 'stand apart,'" "we *prefer*," the authors declare, "to regard [them] . . . as genetic determinants without classifying them as 'early forms' of the superego."[109] To this pronouncement the authors limit themselves— though implying that other analysts disagree, and though the analyst-reader, in my surmise, will find it difficult to indicate the divergences in definitions of "superego" implied or in clinical evidence acquired that account for such disagreement. While, the authors observe, "object representation . . . [is] an 'inner' representation of the outside world," "still . . . one cannot say, as is sometimes implied . . ., that this character of the object representations of being part of the inner world effaces their distinction from the self-representations."[110] Again, no clue is furnished as to what divergences in the definition of "to efface" or in clinical evidence require others to say just that. "I do not think," pronounces Hartmann—this time we are not told whether others do— that the "dependence of aggressive ego defense on the . . . superego [the *aggressive* superego pressure on the ego resulting in the ego's utilizing *aggressive* energy in its dealings with the id—N.L.] applies to all of its [presumably: aggressive ego defense—N.L.] forms":[111] while once again, the analyst-reader, presented with any such form, might not find it easy to name the evidence he should request in order to discover whether the dependence in question does apply or not; he is told nothing more. "It might," the authors affirm less strongly, "not be" an "unjustified extrapolation" from "analytic material" to assume that "self-destructive" tendencies exist even at an early age;[112] but we

are told nothing, either by text or reference to literature, about (1) what events are designated as "self-destructive" in contrast to "indiscriminate discharges of aggression" against oneself, (2) under what conditions extrapolation is justified, and (3) what the kinds of analytic material are that go far (but not the whole way, it seems) toward meeting these conditions.

50. What is affirmed in such fashion may be a mere probability rather than a certainty; which does not reduce obscurity. "It is not unlikely," the authors declare, "that the *protracted* development of the superego serves humanization . . .":[113] nothing is added about the kinds of evidence that would render the truth of this statement more, or less, likely.

51. Or judgment may be suspended; and, again, no reasons given for one's present hesitations, nor procedures sketched for resolving it. "The question that often arises," the authors observe, "whether the submission of the ego to the superego has to be attributed to its strength or to the 'masochism of the ego' is *not always easy to decide.*"[114] If they put quotation marks around "masochism of the ego"—a term less their own than "ego strength," exempted from such treatment—it is perhaps to indicate their awareness that this locution is neither always used in the same sense nor always well-defined; but might this not be one—or the—source of the difficulty noted? Whether object libido must be transformed into narcissistic libido before it can be neutralized is for Hartmann "a question *not easy to decide*":[115] Nor does it seem to him pertinent or feasible (to judge from his silence) to decide merely on procedures of rectifying language and enriching evidence that would make the question easier to decide.

52. The question, judges Hartmann, whether the first counter-cathectic structures are cathected with neutralized aggression "cannot be answered *so far*":[116] But nothing is said about what it is that is "so far" lacking in logical analysis or evidence. "*At the present stage of our knowledge,*" the authors admit, "we are unable to decide whether . . . [during the undifferentiated phase in infancy] acts of . . . self-destruction occur. . .":[117] no indication as to the contours of the difference between the present and a future that would permit the decision. That it is indeterminacy in the meaning of words rather than insufficiency of observations that renders it difficult is made plausible by the authors' asking themselves, in the full text, whether "acts of *actual or 'true'* self-destruction" occur in the conditions indicated: both adjectives are highly ambiguous, which is, presumably, acknowledged for one of them by quotation marks; and they are, here, probably synonyms. "At the present stage of our knowledge," likewise, "we are unable to decide whether . . . the observed destructive actions of the infant—such as self-infliction of damage . . . by scratching—can be explained by assuming

that the distinction between self and external world is not yet possible . . .":[118] once again, the reader is given no information about the kinds of advance in knowledge that would notably reduce or enhance the capacity to "explain" enjoyed by the "assumption" mentioned.

53. Such a stance may be maintained even when it is difficult to avoid the suspicion that a few and common words in a statement are in part responsible for one's quandary about it. Asking himself about the relation of automatisms to the pleasure principle and the repetition compulsion, Hartmann merely deems it "possible" that the latter two only "trigger" the former, but do not "regulate their subsequent course."[119] The point seems to make sense, as the words I put within quotes have, in most uses, a fairly definite meaning; a fact that confers an aura of clarity on their present employment; which in turn, may make one overlook that one might be hard put to sketch the clinical pictures of two patients, in one of whom the principles in question merely "trigger" automatisms, while in the other they also "regulate their course." "In terms of psychoanalytic theory," the authors observe, "we are reluctant to overemphasize" the "*separateness*" of the ego ideal from the other parts of the superego."[120] As most sentences in which we talk about more or less separateness are rather clear—that is, as we usually would have little difficulty in sketching how the world would have to look like for any such statement to be false—we may overlook that the situation is different for the degree of "separateness" between ego ideal and superego; and overlook this all the more readily as the statement is made "in terms" not of patients, but of "theory," and as it contains one component we will hardly doubt: Who would not be reluctant to overemphasize whatever it is he is stressing? We may enable ourselves to use words beyond their ordinary reach by the very approach to an admission that it is that which we are doing: as when the authors, in a passage already cited, themselves use quotation marks when talking about identifications in the superego "which 'stand apart.' "[121]

54. Instead of being common words applied outside of their familiar boundaries, the vocabulary whose (unrecognized) obscurity renders a statement undecidable may mix ordinary speech with technical parlance. Take words about origins. The authors consider the question whether the vicissitude of drives known as "turning upon the self" is a "*forerunner*" of the superego's turning aggression against oneself. It "*looks very much like a potential*" one, they hold; this is a "*possibility.*" Now if a weak meaning is given to the crucial word, this is too little: one of the two events envisaged occurring earlier than the other, and having a nonnegligible similarity to it, is then *surely* its "forerunner." By claiming this to be merely *probable*, the authors convey that they have a stronger meaning of "forerunner" in mind. They do not say which; and it is not easy to imagine one with precision. But, again, the

183

aura of clarity that the word possesses by virtue of its customary uses assures us, without our having to think about it, that there is such a meaning, the exacting nature of which renders the uncertainty attributed to the statement appropriate. *"We think it could well be* one of the cases," the authors declare (still with regard to the relationship between a turning upon the self of drives in early childhood and a later turning of superego aggression against oneself) in which a characteristic of drives is "a *prototype"* of noninstinctual functions. However, *"we do not know much about it clinically,"* and, in addition, "would . . . *not* assume a *simple and* [sic] *direct* correlation":[122] That the relationship in question is complicated (that is all we learn about it) apart from being uncertain reinforces the suggestion that the definition of "prototype" (never given) goes beyond what-goes-before-and-resembles. Given the rapid oscillation from manifestations of positive to manifestations of negative attitudes toward an other in infant *and* child, *"one might assume,"* according to the authors, that the intermittent changes between projection and introjection, which were concomitants of the infant's trials to establish a distinction between the self and the environment, *"survive"* as a tendency toward and away from the human object.[123] In the same vein Hartmann asserts about primitive functions of the autonomous ego merely that *"we may consider"* them "the *first elements"* of what later will be used in defense;[124] about the early apparatus serving postponement of discharge merely that they *"probably"* are *"precursors"* of later defense mechanisms;[125] about early processes in the autonomous area merely that *"it may be"* that they are, *"genetically speaking, precursors"* of such mechanisms;[126] about the same processes, at another moment, merely that *"it is . . . tempting to consider"* them *"forestages"* of later defense, that they *"may be"* *"transitional steps"* to it, that they *"impress us"* like *"models"* of it.[127]

But when it comes (as it rarely does) to giving examples, it is a weak meaning—which has been furnishing a solid basis for larger claims all along—that may become manifest. Having stated the *"hypothesis"* that the features of defense against instinctual drives are *"modeled after"* defense in situations of danger from without, Hartmann illustrates: "withdrawal of cathexis *would correspond* to flight, and countercathexis to fight"[128]—that is: One may, within the current usage of this verb, "fight" not only enemies, but also drives; and one may, within the ordinary employment of that verb, not only "withdraw" from enemies, but also "withdraw" one's emotional charges from a target within or outside oneself.

55. The word of uncertain meaning that renders difficult a decision on a statement containing it needs of course not be close to common language, as was the case in most of the instances mentioned. At the other extreme with regard to ordinary speech stands a new word for

which a definition may never have been given, but which repetition is soon rendering familiar. "One expression of the coordinating tendency [in a person]," recalls Hartmann, "is *known to us as* the synthetic function":[129] which is indeed known to us, at this point in the text, by a certain number of the word's appearances on prior pages, but *about which* nothing is known, except that it synthesizes.

56. As for a word, one may exaggerate for a statement what "is known to us." That psychic events can act upon the superego though they are *"hidden from the ego"* is, the authors affirm, *"clearly demonstrable clinically."*[130] If "ego" here means "unconscious ego"—otherwise the statement would be but an affirmation of the occurrence of unconscious events—where is that demonstration furnished?

57. Apart from underestimating available knowledge (cf. paragraph 54) or exaggerating it, one may rapidly vary one's evaluation of it. According to one paragraph of the authors deprivation is *"probably"* an *"essential"* condition for the infant's ability to distinguish between the self and the object; according to the next deprivation, *"we have said,"* *"is"* a *"necessary but clearly not a sufficient"* condition for that capacity.[131]

22 | Decisions on Constructs

58. As unconscious processes "cannot be observed," the authors recall; every statement of psychoanalysis goes beyond observation, and includes "explanatory concepts" apart from "descriptive" ones,[132] that is, contains "constructs."[133] Perhaps even mainly or only them, as may be implied when Hartmann notes "the explanatory nature of . . . [the]

185

concepts [of psychoanalysis]."[134] When two competing statements are envisaged between which the reader may presume that observations could and should decide, it may be taken for granted that this view is a naïve error. Both for the formulation of hypotheses and for "the process of fact-finding," Hartmann declares, "it makes a decisive difference" whether "the concept of drives" chosen is such that they are affirmed to have the levels of "plasticity and variety" possessed by sexuality, or only "that lesser plasticity and . . . variety . . . we find, for instance, . . . in the case of respiration":[135] Clearly you can't just *"assume"* them to have those levels of plasticity and variety that observations *show* them to have! Once you have made an unfortunate "assumption," you are apparently bound to it until its negative consequences have reached a critical level. In fact, you may never be able to free yourself, as the very "process of fact-finding" is determined by your initial step.

59. While "constructs," Hartmann recalls, "cannot be . . . defined in terms of observational data," "inferences from . . . constructs can be tested by observation";[136] and it is, the authors remind us, by the validation or refutation of "propositions derived from them" that "constructs can be shown to be useful or useless."[137] In the case of the constructs adopted by the authors we are, however, given but few instances of such "deriving"; and some of the examples furnished do not seem pertinent. That there are different conditions of energy and that they may be transformed into each other, observes Hartmann (alluding to some of his own constructs) "has proved helpful"—for discoveries about patients? No, "in describing the energic aspect of the psychic systems":[138] Construct services construct.

60. Having recalled that every analytic case report, "however 'factual,' " is "replete with *inferences* based upon theoretical *assumptions*," the authors proceed to what "best illustrates" this point. They remind us that the *choice* of events in their patients to which analysts are *attentive* will in part be *caused* by what they believe to be the invariant relationships that obtain in the psyche (relationships between aspects of the psyche, which, I would want to add, may well be observable); and that analysts—the authors seem to take this, implicitly, for granted—have a well-developed capacity to find what confirms their beliefs; all of which they imply (wrongly, it would appear to me) to be pertinent to the omnipresence, in analytic statements, of "inferences" from "assumptions":

> . . . changes in *the focus of attention* in clinical work are frequently *dependent upon* changes in psychoanalytic *theory*. . . .
> In the case history of Little Hans few data on the personality of the parents are given, particularly on the personality of the mother,

who had been Freud's patient. If the same case history were reported today, this problem would . . . be given . . . prominence. This difference . . . *reflects* a change in *theoretical assumptions*; i.e., the importance of environmental factors on earliest stages of development in general and the role of pre-oedipal experiences specifically. But even today there is . . . *disagreement* on the role of these factors; *consequently* case reports by members of the British school of psychoanalysis *differ* . . . from those currently presented in this country, *because* the etiological relevance of environmental factors is *evaluated* differently. . . .[139]

Nothing said here seems to bear on the respective deductive powers of competing constructs; in fact, the particular "theoretical" "change" and "disagreement" that is envisaged is formulated—to me, commendably— without any reference to such entities.

61. In the rare case where what is presented when illustrating a construct's productivity is in fact a (brief) chain of sentences, it may by one of doubtful validity. To assume an *un*differentiated (as between ego and id) phase at the beginning of life, as the authors do, rather than a gradual differentiation of the ego *from* the id, as Freud did, "permits a better explanation" of—indeed, "accounts for"— the "impression that many manifestations of the id are further removed from reality than any comparable behavior of animals."[140] Why so? Whatever the degree of the id's removal from reality, in the classic "assumption" it would be precisely the gradual differentiation of the ego from it that would bring about a gradual increase in the young human's capacity to secure his survival in the face of his "unrealistic" id.

62. Where there is no discontinuity in deduction, it may be incomplete. In working on patients' resistances, Hartmann recalls, one meets resistance against the uncovering of resistances; negative transference may come to predominate. "Is it not *possible*," he asks, that part of the cathexis of this transference is the reaggressivized energy of the resistances being uncovered? They, in his "assumption," are cathected with neutralized aggression. Thus clinical events and this particular construct "agree."[141] To be sure, but might this not be the case for any number of other "assumptions" too? For instance, as defense is under the influence of other processes in the ego and intervenes in a variety of them—according to Hartmann himself in the same article —we could (let us not follow the author in his "we must") "assume that this interdependence has also an energic aspect";[142] that the ego, threatened in its resistances, is free to draw upon a vast sector for energy to meet the threat. To arrive at the conclusion desired by Hartmann in his argument quoted at the beginning of this paragraph an additional premise has to be introduced: Reactions related to a

187

certain part of the person (such as his resistances) are likely to draw on energy already within that part—a sentence awkward to *formulate* (also because it seems to be in contradiction with the point on "energic interdependence" just cited), but which does seem *implied* in another demonstration attempted by the authors. They recall, on the one hand, the frequently noted fact that any interruption of activity, at least in the child, is likely to evoke an aggressive response; and, on the other hand, their "assumption" that it is neutralized aggression that supplies the ego with essential parts of its energy discharged in action. In these conditions *"we find it easily understandable"* that act interruption is likely to mobilize aggression;[143] that is, the mobilization of act-alien (if I may coin a term) energy would be *difficultly* understandable: the additional premise that I formulated above. (Even if that premise is introduced, Hartmann's reasoning remains incomplete: *Then*—a point not made by the authors—*the interruption of an activity (largely) cathected with neutralized libido* (if there still be any such) *should evoke less of an aggressive response than occurs in the authors' case.* Here we might have a hypothesis, derivable from the authors' constructs, which is both testable and new.)

63. While I have found no case satisfying these conditions in the text examined here, I have noted just one where an extant clinical finding can be derived from a construct advocated by the authors, while it cannot be from the one they reject. According to Freud's "assumptions" the avenues available for transforming aggressive energy are more restricted—or at least not wider—than those open to libido; according to Hartmann they *are* wider: Aggressive energy is assumed to be the cathexis of choice for countercathexes as well as ego functions. Now—points not stated by the authors, but, it would seem to me, implied—the more avenues for the transformation of a certain kind of energy, the less repression; the less repression, the less pathology. Hence, *from the "assumptions" made it follows that aggression should be responsible for less pathology than libido*—and this is what clinical experience supposedly shows. Thus Hartmann can say about one of his "assumptions" (at this occasion called "hypothesis")—"the use, in countercathexis, of energy withdrawn from the drives is more general if they are of an aggressive than if they are of a libidinal nature"—that it "might be helpful . . . towards explaining the etiological predominance of sexual over aggressive factors in neurosis."[144]

64. Usually, however, the authors abstain from proving while often claiming, the superiority of one construct over another; where proving —if one of the "criteria" for the "value" of a "theory" be its "ability to supply . . . fruitful hypotheses"[145]—would mean to establish the sets of hypotheses that can be derived from the two constructs, respectively, and then calculate the aggregate worths of these sets,

applying whatever rules would seem appropriate. This, however, the authors hardly envisage. Having recalled that maturational changes proceeding during the second half of the first year give the child further control of his own body and enable him partly to master the inanimate objects in his life space, they merely add, in a footnote: "*We do not, however, follow Hendrick . . . in assuming* the existence of an 'instinct to master.' "[146] "*It seems,*" they note, "*that* from the vantage point of the assumptions we here pursue [such as "the assumption of an independent primary aggression" in contrast to "aggression . . . as a consequence of . . . deprivational experiences" on the one hand and to "the theory of the death instinct" on the other hand—N.L.] *new light can be shed* on the relation of deprivation and aggression":[147] That is all we hear.

65. When the superiority of a certain construct is curtly claimed, it may not be easy to imagine with regard to what other "assumption" it is affirmed to possess an advantage. Having observed about the superego that "its definition rests on its functions (e.g., conscience, self-criticism, . . . holding up ideals)," the authors declare that "such a definition of the substructures of personality in terms of their functions . . . appears to be the most adequate way of accounting for some essential problems of a structure psychology"[148]—as against what other types of definition?

66. It may not even be clear whether it is the superiority of one construct over another that one is claiming, or rather a certain construct's monopoly. Envisaging (in this sequence) psychic structure and the interrelations of its parts, psychic energy, degrees of neutralization, mobile and bound energies, primary and secondary processes—"no complete enumeration is here intended"—the authors observe that psychoanalysis does supply "*the best or, more precisely* [sic], *the only*" set of assumptions that at present explain (no, "permit an explanatory approach") to mental functioning.[149]

67. Where two competing constructs arouse sharply diverging *sentiments*—and thus may indeed have diverging *impacts* on analytic *activity* (*see* paragraph 60)—it may be taken for granted that *the hypotheses derivable* from them will greatly differ. Thus the authors regard it as otiose to elucidate the nature, though not to celebrate the magnitude, of the "advantages" offered by the "assumption" (here called "concept") that aggression is "an independent . . . drive" rather than "one of the partial instincts of sexuality," or "an instinctual equipment of the ego." "The analyst trained in the 1950s"—"who can hardly visualize any clinical impression in which aggression . . . or defenses against it do not play an important part"—also "can scarcely imagine *the theoretical dilemma* [not described—N.L.] which arose at a time when aggression was one of the partial instincts of sexuality,

and the scarcely less intense *discomfort* [a fleeting irruption of what I suspect is the truth: It is for feelings that the two formulations do make much difference—N.L.] of the . . . period in Freud's thinking when aggression was viewed as an instinctual equipment of the ego. . . . The *cleavage* between these and the current view seems very great indeed." Specifically, once aggression was "assumed" to be an "independent drive," a number of "areas" and "phenomena" "became *accessible*," "*entered the orbit* of psychoanalytic thinking," and discoveries in them "became *possible*." This was the case for: the relation of aggression to unconscious guilt feelings, the dynamic functions of the superego, the negative therapeutic reaction, self-destruction, the part internalized aggression plays in the origin of physical illness.[150] The contention seems plausible, as it may well be that *faith* in aggression being an "independent drive" fostered the *production* of hypotheses on the various matters enumerated—from which it does not follow that these hypotheses follow from premises of which the "assumption" in question is one. Nor does it follow that it is impossible to arrive at these hypotheses as consequences by starting from one or the other of the two earlier "assumptions" on aggression recalled by the authors; though their persistence might have reduced the likelihood of the "discoveries" in question being made. Sometimes the authors themselves choose words that perhaps express a concern not with what can be *deduced* from constructs, but to what they *inspire*. More useful concepts, they say in passing, are those that "suggest" better hypotheses.[151] In some respects, Hartmann admits, equating instinct and drive has proved "stimulating."[152]

68. Short of claiming that a certain construct *is* the best, one may, as in the case of nonconstructs (*see* paragraph 50 above), merely affirm such a *possibility*. Considering the degrees (1) to which the instinctual character of a given energy has been transformed, and (2) to which, in the acts cathected by it, the primary process has been replaced by the secondary cne, Hartmann contents himself with observing that the two "may" coincide;[153] it is "not unlikely" that positions on these two dimensions "go mostly parallel."[154] Envisaging the levels of (1) the ego's capacity to neutralize instinctual energy, and (2) its strength, he simply notes that the former "may well be" an "indication" of the latter.[155]

69. Or one may express an attitude avoiding both acceptance and rejection, a stance perhaps recommended by requirements of propriety in public speech. "I am not convinced," observes Hartmann about Hendrick's "instinct to master," that its introduction is "really unavoidable."[156] Federn, he recalls, came to modify the concept of the ego in a way "which seems to me not altogether convincing." In fact, "I would prefer" to integrate Freud's early formulations on narcissism

into his later views on mental structure, rather than changing any of the main aspects of the latter.[157]

70. Finally, one may—as with nonconstructs (*see* paragraph 51 above)—declare one's indecision: without indicating to what it is due, hence what would render decision possible. When Hartmann, discussing in a passage quoted above one of his "assumptions" ("the use, in countercathexis, of energy withdrawn from the drives is more general if they are of an aggressive than if they are of a libidinal nature"), declares that "I would not dare to decide whether or not it will prove to be correct." One may add that he does not even dare to decide *how* one should decide that question.

71. One may—as with nonconstructs (*see* paragraph 52)—declare that it is impossible to answer a certain question *for the time being*, without even a partial indication of what kinds of intellectual events will have to occur for that situation to be changed. Affirming that the question whether all energy at the disposal of the ego originates in drives is one "hard to decide" at the present state both of "factual insight" and of "conceptual tools,"[159] Hartmann abstains from disclosing any details on the lacunae thus alluded to. The "possibility" that part of the energy at the ego's disposal belongs to it from the very start, he repeats elsewhere, "cannot today be proved," which is "equally true" of the "hypothesis" that none does: "we can hardly estimate" "how much or how little does"—a matter that "leads . . . back to physiology."[160] No indication of what the pertinent physiological evidence might be.

72. One may juxtapose polite indecision and loyal choice. "*We do not decide,*" begin the authors, when recalling that Balint and others assume an object relation in the neonate, "how far this assumption is warranted"; after which they proceed to note that Freud's theory of primary narcissism "*seems still best to account*" for facts observable immediately after birth.[161]

23 | Treating Constructs as if They Were Words with Referents that Are Observable

73. If the acceptance or rejection of constructs is not, actually, based on a measure of productivity, it is tempting to treat them as if they referred to observable events after all; thus following a penchant that Hartmann perceives in others when he observes that in current writing "constructs . . . are . . . reported . . . as data of observation," "described as findings."[162]

In this vein one may use about constructs words concerning probability; that is, words mostly employed in sentences about which it is ordinarily believed that observable events will, directly, have to decide upon their fate. When it is the superego that stimulates repression, there is, declares Hartmann, *"possibly"* a shift of aggressive cathexis (presumably from the superego to the ego—N.L.) combined with an increase in its neutralization.[163] *"It is not unlikely"* that already the primordial forms of postponement and inhibition of discharge are fed by energy that is partly neutralized;[164] and *"it is likely"* that part of the energy that the ego uses belongs to it from the very first.[165] *"Probably"* neutralization takes place already through the autonomous forestages of the ego;[166] and *"probably"* it is a continuous process.[167] *"Most likely"* the defenses of the ego are fed with neutralized aggressive energy;[168] and *"certainly"* action uses energies of the ego.[169] The language of probability may even appear in an elementary inference: Having recalled Freud's "assumption" that as long as all needs are gratified the infant tends to experience the source of satisfaction as part of the self, the authors conclude that partial deprivation *"thus"* is *"probably"* an essential condition for the infant's ability to distinguish between the self and the object.[170]

74. Or one may affirm an "assumption" only for a *fraction* of a certain class of events. It is *"often"* that the willing acceptance of superego demands by the ego can be traced to the latter's synthetic function (and to what when not?);[171] it is *"habitually"* that the ego uses a mode of energy different from that used by the drives (what does it look like when it behaves unusually in this regard?).[172]

75. One may combine the two modes I just discussed, presenting an affirmation about a construct as both less than certain and referring to less than the entire population of events considered: The energy used in countercathexis is *"probably as a rule"* neutralized aggression.[173]

76. One may also use about constructs the customary language of research. Enlarging Freud's idea of desexualized energy to include neutralization of aggressive energy *"does not seem too hazardous"* to Hartmann,[174] while *"it seems hazardous at present to venture a hypothesis"* about the nature of the drive energies whose mode is being changed in the process of the formation of countercathexis.[175] *"What we know"* about the energic aspects of ego interests *"is too small a basis for any definite conclusion"* concerning their efficacy.[176] As to assumptions concerning the differentiation responsible for the relation of the id to the ego and the tension between these two systems, "what these assumptions *describe"* is relatively independent of environmental conditions; they aim at *"describing"* the equipment of man,[177] while "the concept of instinctual drive . . . is . . . a construct . . . designed to *describe* . . . phenomena of conflict in man."[178] They have said that libidinal energy has been transformed into aim-inhibited libidinal energy, the authors recall about a certain process, when *"studying"* this process with respect to the distribution of psychic energy."[179]

77. Words usually employed about observations may, in talking about constructs, appear side by side with others that indicate that it is not observations one is considering. Having noted that the source of the neutralized energy with which ego interests operate *"seems"* not to be confined to the energy of those instinctual strivings out of which or against which they have developed, but that other neutralized energy *"may"* be at their disposal, Hartmann goes on to remark that this is *"implied in thinking"* of the ego as an energetically partly independent system.[180]

78. Finally, words that one expects to hear about constructs may be applied to sentences about observable events. The *"assumption"* that early in childhood the interruption of activity rather than its prevention may be a crucial experience "leads us," the authors explain, to the *"proposition"* that interruption of practice is likely to upset the balance in psychic energy.[181] One way or the other, constructs are

merged in a whole that is benefiting from the presence in it of statements sensed to be secure by observations.

24 | Deriving Constructs from Realities

79. Instead of justifying constructs by their deductive power (the authors' manifest choice) or their suggestive impact, and instead of assimilating them to observations, one may, finally, ground them in implicitly asserted patterns of being or of the mind: The "assumptions" themselves then appear *derived* in compelling fashion, rather than as creative acts justified by what one can *derive from* them. It is this that may be expressed when Hartmann affirms it to be desirable that if there is construction, we indicate "how it has been *arrived at*";[182] when to the authors "it seems *unavoidable* to assume" something;[183] or when for Hartmann something is "*clearly* to be postulated" (e.g., neutralization of energy, from the time at which the ego evolves as a more or less demarcated substructure of personality).[184] Alluding to patterns of the mind rather than of its objects, it may "seem *reasonable*" to replace one construct (the ego works with desexualized energy) by another (the ego also works with neutralized aggression);[185] certain "phenomena seem *easier to understand* if one accepts the hypothesis [here standing for: assumption—N.L.] that . . ." (e.g., "some counter-cathectic energy distributions [which] probably arise in infancy" seem easier to understand if one accepts the assumption of "gradation of neutralization");[186] or certain "assumptions" (e.g., those concerning deinstinctualized energy) in contrast to others (e.g., that of independent

194

ego drives), "permit *a particularly clear presentation*" of certain phenomena (e.g., some of the ego functions).[187]

80. Observing what constructs the authors seem to derive from what nonconstructs, one may attempt to make explicit the laws that permit "to arrive" at "assumptions," and regard for which apparently puts the mind at ease—at least as long as they are not formulated.

81. First law: The effect resembles the cause. This seems to be the implicit premise behind Hartmann's "*it might well be*" that "the *aggressive* superego pressure on the ego . . . results in the ego's utilizing *aggressive* energy in its dealings with the id," "turning one aggressive intersystemic relation (superego-ego) into another (ego-id) [rather: adding one onto the other—N.L.]"; from which "we may develop the assumption" that "the ego's countercathexes against the drives are mostly fed by neutralized aggression."[188]

82. Second law: The greater the difference in nature between an energy and a function, the smaller the contribution of that energy to that function's cathexis.

83. Third law: Whether an energy does or does not belong to the area upon which a function operates does not, Freud to the contrary, affect the probability of its becoming part of that function's cathexis.

The second and third laws seem presupposed by the authors' conviction that countercathexes are largely fed by neutralized *aggression* rather than by the neutralized energy of *whatever* drive they oppose. "We assume [rather: observe—N.L.]," the authors explain, "that there is an affinity between inner conflict and aggression, and think [rather: assume, if that verb is to be used at all—N.L.]" that the defenses of the ego are most likely fed by neutralized aggression.[189] In other words, in countercathexis "at least one feature of the aggressive drive, that is, 'fight,' is . . . demonstrable";[190] hence—in view of what I called the second law, which remains, however, implicit: a form in which it may be easier to accept—"countercathexis widely uses one of those conditions of . . . neutralized aggressive energy . . . which still retain some characteristics of the original drive (fight, in this case)."[191] (Compare this derivation with one presented by Hartmann, which, I believe, is incorrect—I shall leave it to the reader to form his judgment on this—but has the advantage of not requiring sentences as awkward as the one I called the second law. The assumption that the ego's countercathexes against the drives are mostly fed by neutralized aggression is, Hartmann claims, one which "we may develop" "on the basis of . . . two hypotheses": [1] free aggression may be a factor in the disposition to conflict, [2] defense against drives is modeled after defense against external danger).[192]

84. Fourth law: The smaller the difference between two functions, the higher the probability that one will draw on the other's energy.

Hence "it is *likely*" that when the ego appeals to the id for energic support, the appeal is "mostly" made to those forces in the id which are "precursors" of the ego activity in question.[193]

85. Fifth law: The area from which a function's cathexis is drawn coincides with that to which the function is related (though—see the third law—not with that upon which it operates). As, Hartmann recalls, defense is under the influence of other processes in the ego on the one hand, and, on the other hand, intervenes in a variety of them, and as "*we must assume* that this interdependence has . . . an energic aspect"—an unusually explicit formulation, disclosing that there is an "assumption" *behind* that to be derived—the "*conclusion*" is that for countercathexis energy withdrawn from the warded-off drive itself is not (as Freud had it) the only source.[194]

86. Sixth law: The energy of any "independent" drive goes everywhere. Hence the "formulation" that countercathexis consists "as a rule" of desexualized libido "belongs to a period of analytic theory formation" in which aggression was not affirmed to be "independent," while "today we would assume" that countercathexis "may equally well" consist of neutralized aggressive energy.[195]

87. Seventh law: Each type of event is caused by its very own principle. Considering differentiation and integration in the child's early phases of development, and apparently desiring to affirm that when they occur in certain ratios there will be normalcy and otherwise pathology, the authors feel "*compelled to assume a principle regluating their interaction.*" Recalling that premature ego development is one of the factors predisposing to obsessional neurosis, they repeat that "*the regulation of this interaction can* [no compulsion this time—N.L.] *be attributed to a principle of balance . . . that regulates . . .* development."[196] Wanting to explain "unusual sensitivities of children," Bergman and Escalona, notes Hartmann with seeming approval, "used the concept of a 'thin' protective barrier against stimuli" in "accounting for" them.[197] Recalling certain observations—effects of interpretation in analysis frequently transcend the drive-defense set-up commented upon—and "trying to account for" them, Hartmann introduces a "principle of multiple appeal": "we assume that the process set in motion by a stimulus (interpretation being only one instance in question) produces not only, so to speak, 'local' reactions. It goes beyond the stimulated 'area' . . . affecting a variety of aspects of the . . . system. . . . Its appeal often reaches from one system into the others, and its unconscious side-effects may transcend the barriers of countercathexis":[198] The fit seems perfect. Having recalled that incorporation is a genetic precursor of identification and that we often find incorporation fantasies connected with identification, the authors declare that it "may" be "*through a kind of appeal*" to their genetic

forerunners that identification processes reactivate such fantasies.[199]

88. Eighth law: What is assumed should resemble what has been observed. Declaring that countercathexis widely uses neutralized aggressive energy, even when the warded-off drive is not of an aggressive nature, Hartmann argues as follows: To *assume* that the ego uses for defense only energy withdrawn from the drives against which it defends itself *"does not agree too well with what we know today* about the high degree of . . . plasticity characteristic of the ego. . . ."[200]

SECTION 3: DISCOVERING RELATIONSHIPS OR ELUCIDATING WORDS?

25 | Defining

89. While there is much talk about definitions, they themselves are rare (*see* Chapter 1, paragraph 1, and Chapter 8, paragraph 1). "I stress again," says Hartmann, "that no satisfactory definition of the concept of ego strength and ego weakness is feasible without taking into account . . . ego apparatuses. . . ."[201] But nowhere in the study from which this passage is taken and for which that "concept" is central is its definition *presented*; at no point does there appear a sentence close to the following: when in this study the words "ego strength" occur, the following (presumably longer and clearer) string of words may be substituted: ". . . ." The author makes a point of observing that certain "factors"—"of ability, character, will, etc. [sic]"—are "empirical," but not "theoretical" "correlates" of " 'strong' or 'weak' egos."[202] But though the quotation marks presumably convey that the referents of the words thus surrounded may not be known to the readers, they are never going to be indicated, nor are the definitions of the two classes of "correlates" mentioned ever going to be enunciated. As, according to the authors, in the course of the relationship between ego and superego a "*workable equilibrium*" is apt to be established between them, but as "this conception may easily be misinterpreted," "we want to add" perhaps a definition of the new term? No, merely "a few . . . remarks" that should be "clarifying" and run thus:

> Of course we do not mean that the tension between the two
> systems tends to become constant, or that these tensions are

abolished. We rather assume that the scope of these tensions tends to become a characteristic of the individual—as long as the individual does not get involved in neurotic or psychotic disease. This factor of greater or lesser habitual tensions can also be considered in relation to . . . cultural systems. What matters above all is the degree to which the two agencies can collaborate, while at the same time preserving the optimum tension between them. This optimum can be defined in several respects: in relation to mental health, to social adjustment, to realistic and to moral behavior, and so on.[203]

From this the reader will perhaps gather that whenever a person is not neurotic or psychotic, he also shall be said to possess a "workable equilibrium" between ego and superego. If the reader, however, were to deem it unlikely that the authors wished to engage in so advanced a discussion merely to create a synonym for nonpathology, he might be at a loss to know which persons "not involved in neurotic or psychotic disease" have an "equilibrium" between ego and superego that is "workable" and which don't (then, by the way, having one that is not, or none?). The "concept 'reality principle,' " Hartmann indicates, "is meant to cover" a rich set of "processes and . . . problems":[204] nowhere exhaustively enumerated.

90. ". . . whether we are *justified in speaking* of earliest self-destructive tendencies . . . or whether we *assume* that in an earliest phase *we are faced with* indiscriminate . . . aggression . . .," declare the authors, and proceed, without ever defining "self-destructive act" and "indiscriminate aggression" against the self.[205] Had they avoided the focusing on intellectual operations through the words I italicized (cf. Chapter 15) and asked whether at the beginning of life infants already commit self-destructive acts or whether they merely aggress themselves in indiscriminate fashion, it might have been more difficult to abstain from indicating precisely what events are to be designated by these two terms respectively.

91. In the rare case when a definition is given, it may consist in replacing a word by a nobler synonym (*see* Chapter 8, paragraph 4). Observing that, with development, "the ego aspect . . . partly can become *independent* from the drive in a secondary way," Hartmann adds: "*That is what I mean* by the . . . [term] secondary *autonomy* in ego development."[206]

92. Advocating a (never given) definition of the term "ego ideal" that excludes "early idealizations," while affirming the latter to be among the "genetic" factors behind the former, the authors convey how unusual it is to be acutely aware of just what events are, and which are not, included in the referent of a crucial word: "We meet here

again," they observe, "an issue . . . ubiquitous in psychoanalysis," the "distinction" between "genetic continuity"—the conditions of the configuration designated by an important word—and "functional characterization,"[207] presumably: that configuration itself. To overlook that "distinction" is, apparently, a respectable error; to make it, a notable achievement.

93. Similarly, one may note that the referents of two words are close to each other, without indicating just what the small difference between them is. "The term neutralized energy as used here," affirms Hartmann about one of his major words, "is *not fully synonymous* with the term 'indifferente Energie' . . . which Freud used in a passage . . .":[208] the individuality of the preferred word thus established, we are not told what precisely makes it unique.

94. Even when it is rather clear how a word is implicitly defined, that definition may be disregarded. While the authors do not enunciate a definition for the term "undifferentiated phase of psychic structure" when asserting that it is with such a phase that life begins, it seems plausible that the word designates two undifferentiations: that between libido and aggression, and that between self and nonself.[209] But then we hear that "during the undifferentiated phase one might assume *aggression* (*and libido*) to be centered *in the self.*"[210]

95. It may be taken for granted, with regard to a word's meaning, that previous usage will prevail over precise stipulation (and yet one won't decide to abandon such a word: the intellectual loss would be too great). "There is still the fact," the authors note, "that the meaning of the psychoanalytic concept of 'instinctual drive' is overshadowed by that of the word 'instinct' ":[211] the "concept" is not less indispensable for that.

96. The very requirement of precision in defining may be abandoned. A definition may be desired that, while still "unequivocal," is also "flexible."[212] "Used in one sense," Hartmann observes about "the term reality principle"—to which "in our literature two meanings are currently attached"—"it indicates a tendency to . . ."; "but in another . . . sense, we refer *primarily* to . . . a tendency to wrest our activities from the immediate need for discharge . . .":[213] nothing about what the term then means nonprimarily, nor about what it means to mean in one of these ways against the other. When we speak of self-preservation, Hartmann explains in this vein, it is the ego functions that we consider "*mainly.*"[214]

97. How much does it really matter what a word means precisely? Having recalled about "sublimation" that the "terminological possibilities" are "several"—we may choose to speak about it only when libido is involved; or so as to designate the disinstinctualization of both aggression and libido; or reserve the term for changes of aim; or use it

for nondefensive ego functions—Hartmann concludes that "for the purposes of my presentation, a decision between these alternatives does not seem necessary."[215]

98. "It is difficult," observes Hartmann, "to ascertain when neutralization starts in the child."[216] He does not go on to consider to what extent the difficulty is due to characteristics of the word's definition—after all, this particular word presumably refers to a construct—in contrast to obstacles against acquiring the observations (which?) required by that definition; the reader, I would guess, will sense only the latter source of difficulty, and may, in this, be wrong. In the earliest postnatal stage, Hartmann observes in the same vein, it is "difficult to disentangle" the nuclei of functions that will later serve the ego from those which we attribute to the id.[217] Again, is it difficult to disentangle these two because our vision is not sharp enough, or also (if not only) because we have not decided what it is we are looking for? When the authors begin a lengthy discussion by posing the question "What is . . . the relationship between 'ego ideal' and 'superego'?"[218] they seem to take it for granted that the two classical words have been well enough defined for the only remaining tasks to be deducing and observing—though their treatment shows them shifting back and forth between a variety of (always implicit) definitions of these famous terms;[219] just as Hartmann may fluctuate between a *wide* implicit meaning of "defense" (anything that reduces the unmodified expression of drive) and a *narrow* and equally implicit one (anything that does so through countercathexis), and in the process utter sentences false for both meanings: ". . . there is a defensive [wide—N.L.] aspect to neutralization. . . . Sublimation . . . represents one of the most efficient means to deal with 'danger' threatening from the drives. Thus it can be used as defense [rather: *is* one in the wide meaning, and *is not* in the narrow meaning—N.L.], though it is not always and often not only a defense [rather: never, in the narrow meaning—N.L.] as it takes care . . . of the nondefensive [narrow—N.L.] functions of the ego too. . . . Neutralization . . . can [rather: does—N.L.] serve defensive [wide—N.L.] purposes . . . beyond the . . . case in which . . . neutralized aggression . . . [is] used in countercathexis."[220]

99. That uncertainty with regard to a statement is due to factors beyond the speaker's control may be suggested even when one could easily suspect that the ambiguity of words is at fault. Some severe irregularities in the child's development of autonomy, observes Hartmann, "*apparently* belong to what B. Rank . . . has called the '*fragmented ego*' ":[221] While the author's work is recalled, the definition (if any has been given) of her coinage is not reproduced; presumably the reader's familiarity with the two words composing the new term will guide him correctly. As to Freud's "concept" of the repetition com-

pulsion "*in its proper sense*," "I *doubt*," declares Hartmann, if it is applicable to "automatisms"—though "*perhaps*" a "*domesticated form*" of that "concept" "*could* be."[222] Do the contributions of the sexual and aggressive drives to self-preservation "constitute" a "*drive*"? "I should *hesitate*," Hartmann declares, to "speak of" them thus.[223]

100. Still, an awareness that what makes one "hesitate" with regard to a contention is the obscurity of some words within it may express itself in pleonasms, quotation marks, and the replacement of real by intellectual objects (Chapters 15 and 18). While there is, the authors set forth, no question that idealization both of the self and of objects occurs before the superego has come into existence, "the question is" whether such early idealizations possess that "special character" which "*permits us to describe them as a 'system' or 'agency.'*"[224] Should one at this point start looking for evidence so as to arrive at an answer, or rather not first reformulate the question so that it becomes clearer what evidence is required for an answer to be given?

101. Words may be treated as if they were patients, perhaps little understood in the initial interview, but progressively fathomed as their analysis proceeds. Thus Hartmann moves *toward* defining a coefficient of "adaptation" so that it would be at its maximum if no increase in deprivations provoked any decrease in enjoyment and achievement, and at its minimum if even the slightest increase in difficulty made those founder. But he approaches such a *stipulation* under the guise of a strenuous inquiry into the nature of a "concept." Adaptation, he affirms, "is only capable of definition . . . with reference to . . . environmental settings." By itself, the state of equilibrium achieved by someone "tells us nothing of his capacity for adaptation"; specifically, an unhampered capacity for achievement and enjoyment "has nothing . . . to tell us concerning the capacity for adapting oneself," just as, on the other hand, disturbances in that capacity "are not to be evaluated . . . as a sign of failure in adaptation": all of which "I . . . mention . . . because it is occasionally overlooked." For the "indispensable factor in assessing an individual's powers of adaptation" is rather his relation to a "typical average [sic] environment"; of this "we must take account" in elucidating "the concept of adaptation,"[225] in exploring the fastnesses of this difficult terrain. "The term 'self' is not too well-defined in analysis," note the authors, adding as geographers might have about New Guinea some time ago, "or rather, only some of its aspects are well defined," such as "self-representation"[226]—which presumably stands in a relationship to "self" (does it not contain the same letters?) similar to that between, say, the Sepik River area to New Guinea as a whole.

102. When pondering "the sense in which [a word is] . . . best defined,"[227] its definition may, implicitly, already be taken for granted,

as an event among others. While "intelligence has various definitions" and, for instance, some authors "stress its adaptive character," "it would," Hartmann advances "nevertheless . . . be a . . . mistake to assume [sic] that a person's adaptability is proportionate to his intelligence"[228]—already defined, then? When Hartmann, proceeding toward a definition of "rationality," shows that "it is . . . misleading to call 'rational' all behavior that serves self-preservation, and 'irrational' that which runs contrary to it," he points to one source of this error: "It is, of course, true that rationality [this time without quotation marks—N.L.] is typically used for the purpose of self-preservation"; however, "it can also be used in the service of, for instance, self-destruction":[229] But is the word yet to be defined not here treated as if it had already received its meaning? Considering in a discussion of "the ego concept" Freud's "earlier theory" where ego cathexis meant "cathexis of one's own person," Hartmann reminds us that "ego tendencies are . . . frequently object-directed": which creates a "difficulty" for the "earlier theory"[230]—*if* "ego" is already taken as defined (in the sense desired by Hartmann).

103. One may react to definitions as one does to hypotheses about what goes on in patients (Ch. 9, 33). As to the possibility of "narcissism" meaning "the libidinal cathexis of the ego (as system)"— i.e., as to the stipulation that the latter eight words may be substituted where the former single word occurs, and vice versa—Freud's abandonment of an early contention (that the original reservoir of libido is the ego) "implies," according to Hartmann, a "*detachment*" from the "*formulation*" that narcissism "*is to be* defined" in the way recalled at the beginning of this sentence.[231] Observing that the word "psychoanalysis" refers to a therapeutic technique, to a method of investigation, and to a body of facts and theories, Hartmann notes that any knowledge gained by Freud's method of investigation "we would *certainly consider* as psychoanalytic," and that even related procedures, such as the application of psychoanalytic insight to data of child observation, "*many of us would today consider*" as "*included*" in "analysis."[232] Not only do "we assume," Hartmann declares, "that a process similar to that of sublimation of libido exists for aggression," but in addition "we *assume* . . . that this transformation of energy . . . *might be designated as* neutralization." It is *both* "these assumptions" that "permit. . . ."[233]

104. One may pass from talking about words to envisaging hypotheses about events without an apparent sense of hiatus. Having spoken about the "good object" and the "bad object"—both in quotes—the authors add a footnote: "These *terms and similar considerations* are familiar from the work of Melanie Klein."[234] Indeed, "to define" and "definition" may be used as synonyms for "to affirm" and "affirmation." Beginning to discuss "the crucial situations in an

204

individual's development"—"there are typical phases of conflict either between . . . or between . . . which regularly occur"—the authors announce that they are going to "*define* [them] more closely."[235] From this usage one may, again without an apparent sense of difference, pass to the older language. Having remarked that "it would be quite difficult . . . to *define* . . . a developmentally extending 'autonomy of the superego' from the ego," the authors insist: "We do not *assert* that . . . [the] development [of the superego] . . . tends to go in the direction of a growing detachment from ego influence."[236] "These *definitions* (*or characterizations*) . . ." says Hartmann when discussing "rationality."[237]

105. One tends toward affirming the truth or falsehood of definitions (Ch. 2, 23), though usually avoiding these words themselves (*see* Chapter 19). If certain events are called "rational," we obscure, Hartmann points out, "*the specific psychological meaning of the term*";[238] and yet, it would seem to me, there is no dominant usage in this case. When "narcissism" is taken to mean "libidinal cathexis of the self, not of the ego" it is "*strictly* defined."[239] Sexuality and aggression are, among all the drives, those that come closest to fulfilling "*the demands psychoanalysis makes on a concept of drive.*"[240] That we are used to judging the strength of the ego on the basis of its behavior in typical situations, to Hartmann "would imply" that ego strength "*can be formulated only* in terms of" relations.[241]

106. The quality, as it were, of definitions, it is implied, depends both on the level of knowledge (Ch. 2, 21) and on the felicitousness of "assumptions." Observing that "we learn . . . to operate with *improved* definitions of the id and the ego," the authors surmise ("it seems") that "this improved definition is *facilitated by the assumption* that both these organizations are products of a process of differentiation. . . ."[242] The more knowledge there is, the more precise can definitions become. As to the degree to which the words "health" and "pathology" can be "correlated with" clinically manifest conditions, "I should like to insist once more," declares Hartmann, "that we shall obviously be in a better position" to do so "when we have been able to advance further in . . . the analysis of adapted behavior [the preferred *definiens* for the words in question—N.L.]."[243]

26 | Insights Depend on Definitions

107. Inversely, knowledge depends on definitions.

On a few occasions the possibility is envisaged that it may not. Recalling a variety of affirmations on whether genital libido can be sublimated, and the uncertainty as to whether narcissistic libido possesses this capacity, Hartmann adds that "these and related questions do not necessarily enter the definition of sublimation."[244] Must object libido first be transformed into narcissistic libido before it may be neutralized? If "narcissistic libido" means libidinal cathexis of the ego, then, Hartmann explains, yes; for neutralization is mediated by the ego. But if "narcissistic libido" means libidinal cathexis of the self, we will be inclined to say that a change to "narcissistic" cathexis is not a prerequisite of neutralization. Thus the author conveys that it is irrelevant for the content of hypotheses which definition is chosen: in both cases one can, though in differing words, affirm that neutralization is (1) always mediated by the ego, (2) not always preceded by an increase in the libidinal cathexis of the self. Allowing a reader to perceive this, the author accents the opposite: The question is "not easy to decide,"[245] while he precisely shows that it is.

108. Mainly, in fact, the authors convey how heavy the consequences are of choosing one word over another, and one meaning of a given word as against some differing denotation. "I avoid the term 'free,' " Hartmann explains in another rare moment of detachment from vocabulary, "since . . . it has acquired so many connotations that it . . . [leads] to misunderstanding."[246] But such is not his reason for

206

avoiding—for a moment—a word in which he is usually interested, "health." As the commonly used "criteria" of health are "colored" by *Weltanschauung*, "I believe, *therefore*," he explains, "that for the time being we will have to forego the formulation of a . . . concept of health, lest we unwittingly base . . . the formation of the concept on our own . . . goals"[247]—and thereby, consummating the damage, influence the formation of theory!

109. Accepting a certain definition of an esteemed word may be sensed as affirming a high role of the event designated. If in "the most common definition" the word "sublimation" refers to a deflection of the sexual drive to more valued aims, "the advantage of this approach," according to Hartmann, "was that it . . . *clearly stated* that the highest achievements of man . . . *often* . . . have their origin in libidinal tendencies."[248]

110. Accepting a definition may be felt as affirming that there is noticeable difference (whatever that is) between events included in the referent thus created and others. Recalling the "earlier" definition of "sublimation"—designating "culturally or socially valuable achievements only"—Hartmann observes that it "*assumes an essential difference* between some striking sublimatory [sic] achievements, and other, less obvious ones"—whereas "the . . . process we want to define [sic] is probably the same in both cases."[249]

111. Accepting a definition referring to several classes of events may be sensed as denying that there are relations of cause and effect between them. Observing that "genetic determinants of the supergo have often been termed its forerunners, or forestages, or primordia," the authors declare that "there is nothing to be said against any of these terminological distinctions . . . as long as one *sees* these factors only as genetic determinants and not as parts of the . . . superego":[250] If they were the latter, they could presumably no more be the former with regard to other events designated by the *same* word; let there be no intellectual incest.

112. Accepting a definition designating a particular configuration of elements may be felt as affirming that it is only in that combination that these elements occur. Hartmann recapitulates the sequence of definitions conferred upon "sublimation" from a beginning when the word referred to a change that affected each of three aspects of a drive— the mode of its energy, its object, and its aim—to an end where only the first kind of change is thus designated, the word now simply denoting "a change in the mode of energy, away from an instinctual and toward a noninstinctual mode." What of it? Much, as only now the correlation between this class of changes and the two other classes mentioned (variations in aim and in object) "has . . . become a topic of empirical research, *being no longer prejudged, as it was, by* too narrow

a definition."[251] Thus the early definition appears to be sensed as an affirmation that mode, object, and aim of drive do *not* appear in multiple combinations—an affirmation that appears both as obviously false and evidently unconnected with the definition in question, once it is *written out*, but which can plausibly be *suggested* to have been held by one's predecessors. Comparing a wide definition of "successful" defense—designating merely that ". . . defense . . . has been performed" —with a narrower one—referring also to "health" preserved or re-established—Hartmann warns that the latter *"would threaten every study"* of the relations of defense to health *"with the danger of begging the question."*[252] That is, if the sequence of letters d-e-f-e-n-s-e in what I called a narrow meaning guarantees "health" by definition, then it becomes impossible, or at least difficult, to consider whether there is, in humans, in fact always "health" when *the rest* of the referent of the word "defense" is present. It is on the same ground that Hartmann proposes, when it comes to define "sublimation," to eliminate all references to normalcy or abnormality, so as *"not to prejudge the question"* of the relationship between the disinstinctualization of energy and health:[253] Once one has decided to *say* "sublimation" only when one also says "health," it becomes unfeasible to *observe* whether there aren't cases of disinstinctualization of energy combined with "disease."

113. To deprive an event of a prestigious word to which it has become accustomed and thus entitled is to deny that event. Having recalled that "ego functions, e.g., thought and action," may be oriented toward the self, but also toward the outer world, Hartmann reaffirms that "ego functions are not all self-directed, as would be implied if we were to use in their description only a narrow concept of narcissism":[254] If that "concept," whatever it be, and its "use," whatever that be, would entail that the pertinent acts oriented toward the outer world would not be called "ego functions," it is not that they would just be otherwise named: they would be denied.

27 | Grounds for Choosing Definitions

114. The choice of a definition for a major word having sequels of such magnitude—one may be decidedly *for* or *against* one—can be made on one or more of several types of grounds that are rarely stated in explicit fashion.

115. Choose the definition that has maximal productivity: a postulate whose characteristics are the same as those of the rule to select the construct that possesses that excellence (cf. Chapter 22). It has been said, Hartmann recalls, that the definition of "instinct" is, after all, just a matter of convention. But, he observes, while this is true, "in a sense," "still, not all . . . concepts of instinct are equally helpful."[255].

116. As with any factor of production, the productivity of a definition, it seems to be believed, is apt to vary with the combination of factors into which it enters a tool among tools. Hence it is to be expected that in an efficient intellectual universe a variety of meanings will coexist for any crucial term (*see* Ch. 1, 2). It may simply be that, looking at many kinds of events, one may never want to forego a particular word. "The aspects of the *ego* we see . . . from the angle of resistances," Hartmann notes, "are not necessarily the same as those which are in the foreground in the study of . . . psychosis, and neither the one nor the other of these groups of aspects will . . . coincide with that part of the ego which becomes visible in the . . . observation of children. Thus, partial *ego* concepts developed. . . ."[256] It may well be, notes Hartmann, that for different fields of observation and for different

methods of approach "the use of somewhat [sic] different concepts of
. . . drives may prove expedient."[257] "If," for instance, "what we call
instinctual drive in analysis . . . differs . . . from most definitions of
instinct used by biologists, this is . . . partly due to the fact that Freud's
. . . main interest was in human psychology, while the . . . data of the
biologists pertained mainly to the other species . . .":[258] Such is the
attachment to the adjective "instinctual" that Hartmann does not
even consider foregoing it by having different words designate the diverse
events to which he alludes. (Apparently the value of the corresponding
noun is smaller, as the author proposes to do without it for humans.)

117. When analysts recognized that some conditions, concomitants, and consequences of disinstinctualization are not affected by the
degree to which its aims and objects are syntonic with the ego ideal,
while the word "sublimation" was then restricted to domains *highly*
syntonic in this regard—"art, religion, etc."—it was, Hartmann implies, out of the question to leave that word in the state one then found
it and to have "sublimation" become a species of the new genus "dis-
instinctinctualization." Rather "it was necessary to broaden the concept [of sublimation]"; it had to be done, though "some of you feel
uneasy with" such extending. The "process of disinstinctualization"
could not be talked about, it seems, before it had "entered the definition," of sublimation becoming "the most important single factor"
among "several" that "at one time or another" did so. Thus "the
conceptualization of 'sublimation' . . . changed," and yet there was
permanence: The changing "conceptualization" was one of an immut-
able sequence of letters.

118. Just as with constructs, allegations about the productivity of
definitions are not apt to be accompanied by attempts at proof. It will
simply be declared that "all definitions of ego strength will prove
unsatisfactory as long as they . . . leave out of consideration," say,
intrasystemic factors.[259] It is rare for a "question" of this kind—e.g.,
"the question whether we fare better if our concept of adaptation includes" the survival of the individual only, or that of the species as
well—to be judged "difficult."[260]

119. If it is, progress in knowledge may be predicted to make it
less so. Having recalled the group of tendencies that comprises strivings
for what is "useful" egoism, self-assertion, etc., and having proceeded
to "suggest that we term these and similar tendencies 'ego interests,' "
Hartmann wonders whether or not "it might prove practical to include
in the concept of ego interests" other groups of ego tendencies of an
"otherwise similar" nature, the aims of which do not center around the
self; for instance those whose aims are centered around other persons
or around things; or those that are striving toward aims originating in

the superego, but taken over by the ego; and, finally, interests of the ego in mental functioning itself. However, for the present he abstains from deciding on such inclusions "in this field so little known to us."[261]

120. For to confer upon a string of lowly charged words a highly charged and briefer name is a serious act (see Chapter 10, paragraph 37). Envisaging "the freeing of many abilities from close connection with one . . . instinctual tendency," Hartmann notes that "we could describe [it] analytically as the emergence of the ego."[262] "Various forms of disorganization of thought characteristic of schizophrenia," he affirms, "can be described in terms of the disturbance of . . . [ego] functions." "What I had in mind here," the author recapitulates after a certain amount of such describing, "is to delineate in terms of . . . ego functions a phenomenon that Freud discovered long ago,"[263] but on which added intellectual value is thus conferred. Considering the normal development in which "the contents of the ego ideal are recognized not as aims that have been magically reached, but as demands and as direction givers," the authors advance that "the development we just described . . . can well be called a . . . trend towards growing 'autonomy' of the superego's functions. . . ."[264] Observing that "a function that has (partly) been developed as defense against the instincts may become an independent aim of the ego," Hartmann declares that "this is a . . . case of change of function (italicized in the text—N.L.]," "a term familiar to biology."[265] Recalling that "a number of functions of the ego . . . develop largely outside of the reach of psychic conflict," the authors observe that "Hartmann . . . actually speaks of a sphere of the ego free from conflict."[266] Noting that "the keeping apart of the two [words and things] belongs to that state . . . that we call the secondary process," "that is," Hartmann shows, "why Freud could describe what happens to words in schizophrenia [words are treated as if they were things—N.L.] as their being subjected to the primary process."[267] Reminding his readers that "adaptation may come about by changes which the individual effects in his environment . . . as well as by . . . changes in his psychophysical system," Hartmann concludes that "here Freud's concepts of alloplastic and autoplastic change are apposite."[268] "I have mentioned," Hartmann recalls, "ego functions opposing each other," and adds: "We may well describe . . . [such events] as intrasystemic conflicts."[269]

121. Without proper naming no insight is complete. In 1911, Hartmann observes, Freud already "deals . . . with a number of [what Hartmann calls—N.L.] ego functions," such as consciousness, thinking, attention, judgment, action. However, "what was later to become the distinction of ego and id" (correct names) was "still represented" as "an opposition of ego drives and sexual drives."[270] That is, "from the

point of view of explicit conceptualization," Freud then "[dealt] not with the development of 'the ego,' but with the ego drives":[271] The difference is large.

122. A *broad* definition of a central word may, it is felt, hinder the production of statements about *sectors* of its referent. Having observed that to "consider" every inborn mechanism an instinctual drive would "presuppose" the "broader" definition of that word, Hartmann warns that such a "conception" would "bypass rather than explain the special position of these apparatuses."[272]

123. On the other hand, the allocation of a prized word to designate a clearly prominent class of events is seemingly believed to be a necessary condition for making statements about that class. Recalling Freud's statements that egoism "is" the individual's aiming at advantage (while the word narcissism also designates libidinal gratifications), Hartmann observes that "with these statements Freud opened a wide field of potential research." Yet, "unfortunately he did not conceptualize it," because (if I understand the author) he accorded high rank only to the word "narcissism," and not to "egoism." What was the result? "The near complete neglect in psychoanalysis . . . of self-interest."[273]

124. If a less obtrusive class of events is not included in the referent of a central word, it will surely suffer. Those "concepts of sublimation" that do not refer to ego functions are "less suitable for the advancement of ego psychology."[274]

125. There is apt to be a propagation of impropriety from word to word. If a "concept of health . . . disregards . . . the conflict-free sphere [of the ego]," then "the concepts of ego strength, rank order and equilibrium cannot be satisfactorily delineated."[275]

126. Proper naming may not only be an indispensable factor for producing future knowledge; it may enlighten right away. Having observed that "the term neutralization refers . . . to the process by which both libidinal and aggressive energies are changed away from the instinctual and towards a noninstinctual mode—or to the results of this change," Hartmann affirms that, "with the help of this" (not appellation, but "conceptualization") "we can unambiguously describe the distinction of . . . instinctualization . . . and neutralization."[276] Here, to "describe unambiguously" presumably, though ambiguously, describes more than introducing an abbreviation (the one word "neutralization" for the twenty-seven words with which the author defines it).

127. Instead of justifying a definition by its productivity, one may have a sense of deriving it from reality itself (just as with constructs; cf. Chapters 22 and 24); respecting, for instance, the boundaries found in the world. Without having given a definition of "superego"—after all, at this late date the referent of such an elementary and central word

should not have to be spelled out to an audience of analysts—and hence without having had to show why it is the only admissible one, the authors insist that certain events just do not belong to the superego. The "genetic determinants" of that "system"—such as Ferenczi's "sphincter morality"—simply are "not . . . parts of the . . . superego." To make this distinction is "particularly necessary" when the events in question "*seem . . . in some way or other* 'similar' to what we *recognize* as superego function":[277] In four ways—look at what I italicized— we are told that there is but a semblance of similarity; an appearance that should not induce us into error as to where the border runs.

128. The referent of a definition should comprise *all* the essential features of the subject matter envisaged. Affirming about a system of thoughts that it is "reality-syntonic," Hartmann observes, may mean, first, that these thoughts are true and, second, that they lead to adapted behavior. Now, "clearly," the second property has "the greater . . . biological significance"; and "*thus*, we ought not to *judge* whether or not action is reality-syntonic solely by the criterion that it is based on a good understanding of reality": If an action is thus based, it still may have consequences that do not further survival. There are countless examples of this; hence "a *narrow view of the term* 'reality-syntonic' [making it refer, when applied to beliefs, to truth alone—N.L.] *would underestimate the . . . role of* action *and overestimate the importance of* understanding":[278] Once more, to accept a definition of a word is sensed as tantamount to affirming certain properties of the world.

In this vein one may enunciate requirements for a "concept," declaring that "no concept of . . . is satisfactory which does not con- sider the . . .," " no definition of . . . would I consider complete which does not refer to the . . .," "all definitions of . . . will prove unsatis- factory as long as they leave out of consideration the...," "any definition of . . . must include the. . . ." For the word "ego strength," for instance, such inclusions comprise, possible synonyms included: "non conflictual functioning," "the intrasystemic factor," "the autonomous functions" of the ego, their "interdependence," their "structural hierarchy and especially . . . how far they are able to withstand impairment through . . . defense," "the extent to which the energies of the various ego functions used are neutralized."[279] A definition of *a word*, it seems, is a compendium of crucial insights about . . . something; I cannot say, *that word's* referent, as it is precisely that which has to be chosen. Thus an "attempt to formulate a definition" of, say, "health" is an "attempt to arrive at a theoretical concept" of it,[280] an effort to achieve "a conceptualization aiming at . . . basic processes."[281] A definition should "emphasize an essential relation," as is the case for Freud's "later" definition of "sublimation" with regard to the "relation between creativity and ego."[282]

213

129. The act of defining then becomes the consummation of inquiry (see Chapter 2, paragraph 20). "Hendrick's study," observes Hartmann, "is a step towards . . . a definition of ego strength."[283]

130. Thus it may be too early to attempt a definition of a word that may nevertheless be central to one's current discourse already. "The contribution that I myself have been able to make," Hartmann observes, "does not yet enable us to formulate a concept of mental health in . . . unequivocal . . . terms."[284] When "Glover suggests a definition [of sublimation] which includes displacement together with the change in the mode of cathexis," he is reminded that "the relations between . . . displacement . . . and . . . energy transformation . . . are . . . in need of further study."[285]

131. Progress in knowledge leads to advance in definitions. "Think," Hartmann recalls, "how the conceptualization of aggression has changed [since the beginning of psychoanalysis], until finally aggression *was realized to be, and defined as* one of the basic instinctual drives":[286] It is not conceivable that there might have been *progress in propositions* containing the same central word of *constant meaning*.

132. One may start with a sparse (and implicit) definition of a crucial word; then discover conditions, concomitants, and consequences of the class of events it covertly designates; and thereupon feel impelled to enrich the word's meaning by introducing these relationships into it (see Chapter 2, paragraph 22). Not to do so may appear as unusual conduct: "We find in Freud's later work new ideas on the subject," Hartmann observes about sublimation, "which, however, he has not . . . used for a redefinition of 'sublimation,' "[287] as he should have and as Hartmann does; for "early concepts of sublimation . . . did not account for the clinically essential differences between sublimation and sexualization."[288] Having discovered the magnitude of the role played by "the subordination of . . . psychic tendencies . . . under the ego's organizing function," Hartmann affirms that "this will better *describe* what we *call* healthy behavior," better, presumably than if this phenomenon were omitted from the "definition" of "health."[289] Discussing that same "definition," Hartmann sketches a development. When analysis in its infancy became acquainted with the conflicts that give rise to neuroses, "it seemed a relatively simple matter to *define* mental health and mental illness." But by now one has learned that conflicts that had been believed to be pathogenic exist also in healthy people (so the word whose "definition" is sought is already defined? *See* paragraph 102 above) and that the choice between health and illness is rather determined by temporal and quantitative factors, by the ego's functions of adaptation, achievement, "etc." Knowing all this, we advance *propositions* on the relations between these factors and health? No, "we . . . make these functions . . . the *touchstone of the concept* of health."[290]

133. A definition given to an important word should be such that it will designate an event of high frequency. Having recalled that as a member of a group the individual may accept moral standards that as a private person he would reject, Hartmann observes that this superego cleavage "is *characteristic* enough to be considered by Waelder as a basis for *defining* the groups just dealt with (as against what may be called 'associations')."[291] "Freud," the authors note, claiming for "definitions" what would go without saying for hypotheses, "established his definitions of the psychic systems after . . . scrutiny of his clinical material. That material suggested that in a typical psychic conflict one set of functions is more frequently on 'the one side' than on 'the other side' of the conflict. . . . The relatedness is one of frequency."[292]

134. According to yet another implicit postulate the definition of a word may have to be such as to preserve the truth of a particular sentence to which one is attached and which happens to contain that word. Thus Hartmann, apparently taking it for granted that "in a large field of human activity *successful* functioning depends on *sublimation*," deplores our being "used to saying [presumably: defining—N.L.] that in sublimation ego aims are substituted for instinctual aims, which may be accompanied by a change of objects." "Is it really *true*," he asks us to consider, "that it *depends* only on the aims (and objects) whether or not we can *speak* of sublimated activity?" If it were, he seems to suggest, "sexualization of ego functions" would be a species of "sublimation." Now, as such sexualization beyond certain limits interferes with proper functioning, it would no longer be true that where there is "sublimation," there is "stability" of ego functions. But, apparently, that text should be kept true; an objective that can be assured by changing the definition of one of the words composing it (the only one, it so happens, which it is feasible to change much), namely "sublimation."[293]

135. While in this case the protection of a sentence requires a novel definition of a word that in any event has no dominant meaning in ordinary speech, one may—though only rarely—approach the awareness that if a word is to be used that does possess such a meaning, that meaning should, for the sake of convenience, be preserved. A reason, explains Hartmann, why some "concepts" of "health" are "too narrow" is that they underestimate the variety of personality types that "*must practically speaking, be considered* 'healthy' . . ."[294]—which, I take it, means: . . . which are usually called that.

28 | Variants of Tautology

136. "Shifting the accent too exclusively" either on maturation or on object relations gives, in Hartmann's judgment, a "one-sided picture" of development:[295] If the picture were not that, would we still call the shift of accent in question "too exclusive"? It is, in the authors' opinion, "relative independence" from both the objects and the ego that "constitutes" the superego as an "organisation distinct" from the id and the ego:[296] If the superego weren't that, would we still say that it enjoys "relative independence"? The superego, the authors recall, does not reach "full development" if the overcoming of the oedipus has not, in Freud's words, been "completely successful":[297] If the superego has not advanced *that* far, would we yet speak of the liquidation of the oedipus as *that* "successful"? Recalling that while many ego functions inhibit gratification of instinctual needs, the ego can also indicate the way to aggressive action against the outside world, the authors affirm that "in contradistinction . . . the superego is specifically suppressive":[298] To be sure, as, presumably, nonsuppressive unconscious moral demands made on oneself are *said* to be of the "ego-ideal". His "hypothesis" that "countercathexis is fed by neutralized aggressive energy," follows, according to Hartmann, "if we assume" that "aggressive energy is . . . bound in the service of the ego's defensive actions":[299] Is being thus bound not a synonym for "countercathexis," and would that energy still be in the ego's "service" if it were not "neutralized"? Envisaging individuals who belong to different personality types (according to one of the usual typologies), Hartmann considers the frequency with which

216

we might expect their external behavior and motivation to be equal on the basis of such a typological diagnosis only, and compares that frequency with the corresponding frequency "in regard to a given institutional structure": the phenomena in question will in the latter case be "more frequently" equal—on condition that, in the individuals concerned, "the relationship to reality is unimpaired."[300] But were the latter frequency not higher than the former, that is, if "institutional structure" had no impact on the persons involved, would we still designate their "relationship to reality" as "unimpaired?" In the instances quoted, we seem to be told that if a situation designated by one set of words obtains, the same situation indicated by another string of terms occurs.

137. Having recalled that from a certain point on in childhood anxiety acts as "a *signal*" that "warns of changes to come," the authors affirm that anxiety "can operate" in this fashion "only when the child has learned to anticipate the future":[301] Indeed, when the child is still unable to do so, it cannot—in other words—receive a "warning of changes to come," that is, a "signal." There remains the information that the neonate cannot anticipate the future, while many older children can: something capital but well-known enshrined in a bit of theory. "As long as the child values momentary pleasure gains more highly than future gains," Hartmann points out, "*rational* planning of his actions will be . . . incomplete":[302] Quite so, for when we affirm that it is, we have in mind, among other things, precisely such a pattern of valuation. In "*superego* regression," the authors advance, while as a rule ideal aims or imperatives or both have changed, "something of their structure is preserved":[303] Were it not, would the regression still be one of the "superego?" "As *ego development* proceeds, abstraction from the concrete situation becomes possible":[304] Did it not, would the ego still enjoy "development"? (We are, as in an instance cited above, left with an essential and homely truth: as time passes, abstraction . . . becomes possible—unless it does not). In the "*healthy*" adult, explains Hartmann, the partial reversibility of ego functions is not incisive enough to create "serious trouble":[305] Would he still be "healthy" if such trouble befell him?

138. "Taking into account the nature of other people," asserts Hartmann, "involves" something else: "an achievement in *objectivation*."[306] In contrast to the key words of the sentences discussed in the preceding paragraphs, the meaning of the term I underlined is obscure; still, it would be difficult (if one wants to avoid becoming odd) to confer upon that term a definition that would not include in the word's referent the "taking into account" in question. The "closer," Hartmann surmises, the neutralized aggression used by ego or superego is to the "instinctual condition" of that energy, the higher the "degree to which

the primary process has been replaced by the secondary process."[307] Once again, there is no explicit definition of the degree of "closeness" in question—but, were one to attempt to formulate one, it would be hard to avoid having that term designate, among other events, precisely the degree of "replacement" mentioned by Hartmann as a phenomenon with which the former is merely "correlated," and, to boot, only "probably" so.

139. The implicit definition of a word that a sentence merely exploits under the guise of alleging relationships between events may be one that is in this fashion being *proposed* rather than recalled. It is, so Hartmann tells us he *"thinks,"* a step in the child's acceptance of "the reality principle in a wider sense" that he learns to "integrate expectancies of outer consequences with those concerning inner ones":[308] But is it not precisely this capacity that the author proposes to designate as the principle in question "in a wider sense"? Action, he also affirms, *"can"* be "truly reality-syntonic" only if it considers both the outer and inner reality of the actor and their interaction:[309] Is this a law of events or not rather the enunciation of a coinage? Proceeding to *"state our views"* on the aim of sadistic impulses, the authors show that "they *have to be* differentiated" from other aggressive tendencies directed against objects. For the element that *"characterizes"* sadistic aims is pleasure not only from the discharge of aggression and from destruction, but also from the infliction of pain, the suffering or humiliation of others. Sadism, *"therefore,"* *"can be viewed only in the context of"* an already developed and complex object relation"[310]—that is, only when such a relation obtains will the authors—a decision they herewith enunciate —use the word "sadism."

29 | Combating the Awareness of Tautology

140. The reality principle—renouncing uncertain pleasure for the sake of a later, but assured, one—"clearly presupposes," according to Hartmann, "two . . . *ego functions of the greatest importance*—postponement and anticipation."[311] Now that principle does not seem to presuppose that these two activities are ego functions or that they are of importance. It does presuppose just them. But if somebody were to say, starkly, that renouncing present for future pleasure "presupposes" postponement and anticipation, he might perceive that "renouncing" and "postponing" here designate the same event, and that to act for the sake of the future includes "anticipating" it. The superfluous words I italicized reduce the chance of this discovery being made. "The recognition of inner demands," the authors propose, "broadens *the field of objective* cognition of inner reality, *of self-knowledge*":[312] Cross out the unnecessary (to meaning) words I have italicized, and you may no more want to pronounce the sentence. Having recalled that we are used today to defining "defense" in general terms, Hartmann announces that in speaking of a "particular" defense mechanism, he will add a statement about its "specific characteristics *and functions*":[313] Eliminate the last two words, and silence may replace this sentence too, as the difficulty of being "particular" without being "specific" may then overwhelm us.

141. Anticipation, declares Hartmann, participates in every "action" to some degree.[314] Unless the reader were to understand "some" as including precious little, he will be surprised and dismayed—or im-

219

pressed—as it is all too easy to think of a contrary case—until he dis-covers, if he does, that the author seems to withhold the name of "action" from an event devoid of anticipation. The deviant use of a common word produces a sentence both novel and invulnerable, avoiding the usual trade-off between these two desirable characteristics.

142. Talking about operations of the mind (cf. Chapter 15) may help avoiding the recognition that a sentence is but about words. If words are treated as if they were things—by patients—this is, Hartmann explains, "*looked at from* . . . [*the*] *point of view* [*of ego functions*]," a "loss in the representational function of the ego which . . . allows differentiating the signs from what they signify":[315] Without the introduction of "point of view" there might have been a clearer view of what is asserted here: If words are treated as if they were things (noted in this simple English), they are thus treated (laid down with vocabulary of conspicuous Latin derivation).

143. One may use locutions to which we are accustomed from sentences indubitably bearing upon events even, or precisely, when no such reference is present (*see* Ch. 3, 37). At a certain moment in the development of psychoanalysis, Hartmann recalls, "it was *realized* that all drives are part of the . . . id":[316] Surely, then, it could not have been a matter of changing the (implicit) definitions of "id" and/or "drive." "The vulnerability of the schizophrenic ego to frustrations from with-out," according to Hartmann, "*indicates*" that "its relation to reality" —"the object-directed functions"—"*must*" have been damaged:[317] But does the word "vulnerability" not designate here the schizophrenic ego's propensity to react to frustrations from without by withdrawal of cathexis from reality? And when such a propensity obtains, is not—in other words—the ego's "relation to reality damaged"?

144. More particularly, one may affirm that a relationship does not hold in all cases: Then we can be certain that it is one between events, not words. Envisaging the individual in a world in which traditional goal structures and standards of conduct have collapsed, and confronted with the task of substituting rational calculations and a new organization of his aims for behaviour built on traditional patterns, Hartmann sur-mises that before his ego can reestablish a "balance" among goals, as well as between ends and means, "adaptation *may* suffer."[318] Had he claimed instead that it *does*, one might have been more moved to ask how it could help so doing in the absence of "balance": not by the nature of things, but by the meaning of words.

145. The same effect is achieved by reducing certainty rather than frequency. An aggressive response toward an external danger is normal, Hartmann recalls, while a sexualized one threatens pathology; thus, an aggressive response is more frequent. Then, *if* defense against internal danger is "modeled" after defense against danger from without,

it is *"possible,"* the author suggests, that the use of neutralized aggression in internal defense is more regular than that of neutralized libido.[319] Had he (correctly) claimed this event to be, in the circumstances, certain rather than merely possible, it might have been perceived that the certainty flows from the meaning of a verb, "to be modeled after." It is not flatly, either, that Hartmann asserts any "neutralization of drive energy" to "change the balance between the instinctual and the noninstinctual forces": He merely "thinks" that one "may" assume this.[320] If outer frustration has provoked aggression for which the vicissitude that "predominates" is that of being used in countercathexes, then, the authors claim, it is *"likely"* that guilt *"can"* be "avoided":[321] Had they noted that to the extent that one destiny of that aggression "predominates" any other *is* "avoided," it might have been perceived that these are two names for the same event. For an infant already to engage in "activities" towards "objects," but not yet to distinguish between the two, is, Hartmann judges, a "transitory step" between "simple discharge" and "action"—*"probably."*[322] Had he, as he could have, affirmed that the stance in question *is* such a "step," it might have become more apparent that it is so by virtue of the meaning of an adjective: "transitory." (Where the "probably" might have been appropriate is for the assertion that infants—always? sometimes? under what conditions? The slant of the sentence as it stands makes it possible to avoid such detail—do at some point perform "activities," which are neither "discharges" nor "actions"; that is, where "objects" are involved—hence, these activities are not "discharges"—but where these objects are not distinguished," which, presumably would produce "actions.") "The *assumption* is made," the authors declare about certain ego functions invested with fully neutralized drive energy, "that these autonomous functions are less threatened by regression":[323] Would they still be "autonomous" if they were more threatened?

146. Indecision about what rules to set for the use of a word whose present employment is little regulated may appear as uncertainty about what goes on in patients. Observing that reality testing of the inside is never perfect even in the normal person, Hartmann qualifies: "with the exception . . . of the . . . 'fully analyzed' person . . ."—*"maybe"*[324] —where the resolution of doubt might occur, maybe, by one's decision either to include the perfection in question into the referent of "fully analyzed person" (an expression whose present ambiguity is acknowledged in the author's quotation marks), or to exclude it from that term's meaning. In the former case, the "exception" is established (through language), and only in the latter case would uncertainty (pending, as the phrase goes, further research) be in order.

147. If a word is presented as designating a cause of an event, it

surely can't be a synonym of the word naming that event! Occasionally, Hartmann notes—recognizing this mode—we encounter statements *"ascribing"* any failure to "lack of adaptation." Affirming that such statements "beg the question: What makes a person succeed or fail . . .?"[325] The author conveys the sense (no more) that the events designated by the word "failure" are also among those named by the term "lack of adaptation." The authors themselves, however, advance—for instance—that if the attitude of one defeated is not only "self-destructive," but also "libidinized," then it will be, with regard to the victor, one of "pleasurable submission":[326] Is this a sequel to "libidinized self-destruction" or just a nontechnical way of talking about (all or some of) it? When there emerges, in early childhood, a distinction between the self and external objects, "we *infer*," the authors state, that "narcissistic cathexis has been transformed into object cathexis":[327] a condition of that event or its other name? That reality testing is impaired when objects have a strong value accent, Hartmann observes, "may be partly *accounted for*" by the fact that "the superego . . . has its roots in layers of the personality governed by the primary process":[328] But when we affirm that it does, do we not, "partly," have that very impairment in mind? Full object relations, that is, constancy of the objects independent of need, Hartmann shows, *"presuppose"* "neutralization of libidinal as well as aggressive energy"[329]—perhaps because we have decided to call "neutralized" only an energy that remains faithful to an object independent of need. A lasting object relationship, say the authors, expressing the same point, *"depends"* on "neutralization of libido":[330] Apart from affirmations that derive from meanings of words, this merely seems to remind us that you can't have fun with somebody else *all* the time. That the child's attachment to those he loves outlasts deprivation is for the authors a *"consequence"* of the "replacement of the pleasure principle by the reality principle":[331] Or is it not rather a part of what we designate by the latter term? When early identifications and early object relationships take the place of contents and functions of the superego, this, according to the authors, is "a *result*" of "superego regression"[332]—or perhaps what is meant by it? Alluding to the low degree to which the commands of the schizophrenic superego are obeyed, the authors "surmise" that "much [sic] of what has been described as characteristic of the schizophrenic's superego" is *"due to"* "the low level of integration between ego and superego, [this comma presumably preceding a synonym—N.L.] to the lack of that coordination which is normally establised, at least in the adult, between ego and superego functions":[333] But is it not precisely the high level of violation of the schizophrenic's superego by his conduct that makes us *say* that the level of integration between his ego and superego is low, that there is a lack of coordination between them? The authors recall that the severe character of demands and expected punishments that we find in some forms of "superego regression" is related to early object relations taking the place of later ones, but that usually the real objects of those earliest stages of development have not been as cruel as the regressed superego is; and the authors "think" that in this situation a change from a more to a less neutralized mode of aggression used by the superego "should be considered" as "an additional *causative factor*":[334] But is some such expression as "reduction in the degree of neutralization of the superego's cathexis" not just another name for what is also designated by some such expression as "excess of the regressed superego's cruelty over that of early real objects"? "What started in a situation of conflict may . . . become part of the nonconflictual sphere," Hartmann shows, "*through* what one could call a 'change of function' ":[335] But do we not, precisely, *call* something that starts with conflict and continues without it subject to a "change of function"? A partial awareness of this is, in fact, expressed by the authors: Observing that with the passage of time in normal development the striving after perfection of the ego ideal becomes relatively independent of the objects and of the ego ideal's instinctual precursors, this, they declare, is "something . . . which we may well *describe as or attribute to* a 'change of function,' *a term used in describing* ego development (Hartmann, 1939)."[336]

148. If one can indicate patients for whom a statement would be false, then it surely does not turn on words only! And if one merely approaches such an indication, one already suggests that more than meanings of terms are involved. Discussing how it is that "I have called action an ego function," Hartmann conveys the sense (no more) that actions might be imagined that would not be of the ego (which would make his act of "calling" say something about events): In every behavior upward of a certain age, he reminds us, we can trace the influence of all three psychic systems. Indeed, there is a variety of types of action from the point of view of the influence the systems exert upon it. Thus, while the formation of action is normally accomplished by the ego, other of its characteristics may derive from the id or the superego. The stimulus that sets action going may be found in one of the other systems as well, and the driving force of action may be supplied by any one of the systems. Action may predominantly serve the ego or instinctual need; it may also be mainly in the service of the superego. Thus Hartmann; but he never goes so far as to tell us what an "action" would look like which would not be an "ego function." And moving toward this unreachable assertion, he also veers away from it. It is, he advances, neither "unnecessary" nor "impossible" to "correlate

functions" (presumably, such as "action") with "systems" (such as "ego") in a "definite" fashion, though one which is only "more or less" so. Thus action, finally, is, in some fashion, of the ego.[337]

149. Oscillation between meanings is a further mode of shielding what is true by definitions: When one or more of the words involved admit of several referents, each of them may entail a different status of the sentence in question. Having affirmed that the psychoanalytic interview is a "field situation" (without indicating what it would have to look like *not* to be one), having evoked a patient whose initial complaint is about lack of interest in his work, and having observed that in the course of his analysis such lack may shift to the treatment that he will then want to discontinue, the authors envisage that at this point "*the field is restructured* by a transference interpretation."[338] The assertion arouses interest, I believe, by virtue of a *strong* connotation of the undefined locution I italicized, which would make the sentence read, in translation: At this point a transference interpretation will have high impact. But a question then arises: Will it *always* have such an impact? To affirm that would make the sentence interesting, but also render it vulnerable. Or *often*? All too familiar. Here is where the coexistence of a *weak* connotation of "the field is restructured" with the just discussed strong one helps out: In that second meaning we have (implicitly) decided to apply the name of "restructured field" to the analytic interview whenever one of a series of events has occurred, one such being, precisely, a transference interpretation. Now we have obtained a sense of certainty (justified merely with regard to *language*, to be sure: but it is not inevitable that one be aware of that) which has eluded us as long as we addressed ourselves to what happens in *patients*; a sense of certainty that we may be able, unaware, to transfer to the engaging and hazardous affirmation that, in the situation sketched, a transference interpretation will *always* move the patient profoundly. We have thus managed to avoid (at the price of confusing language and reality) the distressing trade-off between the worth of an affirmation and its certainty. The setting up of the "ego ideal," the authors claim, is—they say, in a vein discussed above (cf. Chapter 15) "can be considered"—a rescue operation for narcissism, and the "ego ideal" continues to have this effect once the superego has developed.[339] This is interesting as long as we are swayed by a *sparse* implicit definition of "ego ideal," designating merely certain aspirations one harbors for oneself, regardless of one's estimate of the degree to which one lives up to them. Of course even then it would be unexciting to affirm that the presence of such aspirations *sometimes* makes one feel better about oneself, but worthwhile to advance that it *always* does so. Worthwhile—and, once more, hazardous. Here again, the acceptability, in current language, of a *rich* implicit definition may come to the rescue of (perhaps

224

not only the patient's, but also the analyst-writer's) narcissism: The authors, in fact, talk about "the child's self-esteem *and* ego ideal development," and note that in the development of the ego ideal "self-idealisation . . . [plays] a role"[340]—all of which hints at an expanded meaning of "ego ideal," now including one's own favorable reactions toward having such an "ideal" in the sparse meaning, and now also comprising beliefs that one is living up to its demands. But then "ego ideal" has come to *designate* aspects of what is ordinarily called "narcissism." Here we acquire the sense of certainty that we may transfer to the interesting, but dubious, assertion that being demanding of oneself *always* helps feeling well about oneself.

150. The protective oscillation may occur between various meanings not of a word referring to *patients*, but of one about the *nature of the statement* pronounced. That word may permit sensing one's affirmation to be about language, or about the world, or about both (in a way one avoids describing); or it allows one not to choose between these possibilities.

151. A regressive sexualization of morality, the authors advance, is "an *essential* characteristic" of moral masochism:[341] Is it that we have safely decided not to name a state of soul one of "moral masochism" unless that sexualization is present? Or is it that we boldly advance a law of nature according to which that regression obtains whenever moral masochism (now otherwise defined) occurs?

152. An organization of the organism (a term not defined, but put between quotation marks in the text—to tell the reader that it awaits definition?), Hartmann claims, is "a *prerequisite*" of successful adaptation:[342] because, arbitrarily, we would not speak of the latter without the former, or because the latter might, but just doesn't, occur without it?

153. The capacity to neutralize large quantities of aggression may, the authors cautiously advance, "constitute" one of the "*criteria*" of ego strength (the latter term once more between quotation marks):[343] Is "criterion" a synonym for "element of definition," or for "indicator"?

154. Alternatively, the authors surmise, the internalization of nonneutralised aggressive energy may be "the *hallmark*" of a weak ego:[344] a synonym for "criterion," calling for the same question?

155. Considering "the differences" between "sublimation" and "sexualization," Hartmann suggests that "one could try" to "*relate*" them to the following: the preponderance of the secondary or the primary process; the degree to which the functions in question are ego-syntonic; whether suppression of the function leads to anxiety; how likely it is that the ego activity changes into instinctual gratification; "and so on."[345] While it is difficult to discuss the last factor, all the others are, in current usage, "*relevant aspects of that distinction*"—

but in any one of two senses: elements of current implicit definitions of the two words in question; or factors surmised to be associated with the referents of these words which, then, do not include them. The first sense furnishes us certainty; but of nothing more than having made a decision on our own use of words. The second does not assure truth, but it does make us address ourselves to patients. That expressions such as "to relate" and "a relevant aspect of a distinction" in current usage have both of these meanings again allows us to avoid choosing between safety and achievement. Considering "attempts" to "*relate*" automatisms procuring reality mastery to "the repetition compulsion," Hartmann recalls that Freud "introduced" the latter as a "*characteristic*" of the instinctual drives, and that [presumably for that reason—N.L.] our "applying" it to a "remote field" such as the mastery of reality leaves "uncertainties"[346]—about what is, or should be, designated by a certain word, or about what laws govern human nature?

156. At one time, Hartmann recalls, Freud "*identified*" self-preservative tendencies with ego drives[347]—did he announce that the two, when used by him henceforth, were synonyms (a sense perhaps suggested by "ego drives" being within quotation marks in this passage) or had he discovered a law (if so, which?) linking two classes of events?

157. Freud and others, Hartmann also reminds us, have often "*equated*" narcissism (now it is this word that is between quotation marks) with the libidinal cathexis of the ego[348]—to which it is difficult to give another meaning than: They have often employed the word "narcissism" to refer to the libidinal cathexis of the ego. In a similar vein Hartmann observes that Melanie Klein "equates" the capacity to cathect ego activities with libido "with" the capacity to sublimate.[349]

158. Such straddling may also occur in talking about sentences of others that one does not accept. Developing the "objections" he feels "obliged" to raise against certain "definitions" of the words "mental health" and "mental illness," Hartmann shows that these "conceptions" do "approach the problem too exclusively from the angle of" the neuroses, "or rather" that they are "formulated in terms of" contrast with the neuroses. For in these "conceptions" phenomena (mechanisms and phases) with which we have become familiar from neuroses are "relegated to the realm of" the pathological; health is "characterized" as a condition in which these elements are absent.[350] The author does not face the question whether that "relegation," this "characterization," are by stipulation about language or through discovery about patients.

159. Having noted, in the passage I quoted a moment ago, that Melanie Klein "equates" the capacity to cathect ego activities with libido "with" the capacity to sublimate, Hartmann continues: "*She also thinks*" that libidinal fixations on speech and pleasure in movement are preconditions of the capacity for sublimation:[351] Thus the first

226

sentence which does not bear on events (*see* paragraph 157 above), is assimilated to the second, which does (*see* paragraphs 104 and Ch. 8, 28). The integration into the ego of functions belonging to the other psychic systems, Hartmann claims, "presupposes" three things: ego strength; relative freedom from anxiety; intactness of the organizing function.[352] There is no doubt that the second factor refers to events *other* than those designated by the "integration" in question; not so for the first and the third between which it is placed and to which it lends strength. Differences in "the type of action," Hartmann maintains, "correspond to" differences in the following: the ego level directing the action (level of integration and differentiation, "and so forth"); the organization of the motives; the type of goals; the organization of the means:[353] Some of these factors may refer to events *not* designated by "type of action," while others presumably do not live up to this condition—and can use the support they receive from being close to those near to patients.

160. A given turn of talk, while obscuring that a sentence bears on words only, may also reveal this. Noting that the child learns to make a distinction between his activity and its object, Hartmann reminds us that from then on, "*metapsychologically* speaking" there is "a difference between the cathexis of an object-directed ego function and the cathexis of an object representation."[354] For him, this is an instance of the difference between metapsychology and—what shall I say?—psychology. But in "metapsychologically *speaking*" there is also the "speaking": What has been presented to us is the same event designated in two languages. Envisaging the case in which one who has been defeated renounces his superego for that of the victor, Hartmann affirms that "then *we can speak of*" masochism of the ego in relation to the superego.[355] In contemporary usage the locution I put between quotes is taken to express an operation of the mind (cf. Chapter 15); but what does it say, literally? Again, that we can speak of a given event in more than one tongue. The outbursts of violence of the schizophrenic superego, Hartmann declares "*may be described*" as a modification of its energy that brings its cathexis closer to the fully instinctual mode:[356] Indeed, why not use this set of words rather than another? As long as *no constant object relation* existed for the infant, the authors note, "we could speak of" an *oscillation between attitudes related to objects that were kept apart*:[357] perhaps it is all a matter of keeping two synonyms (which I italicized) apart.

161. The struggle between the desire to deny that a sentence says nothing about patients and the pressure to become aware of this may become visible. (In the instances to follow I shall emphasize with one line those words that seem to me mainly to admit, and with two lines those that appear largely to deny.) Having recalled that we find instances of successful adaptation achieved by regression, Hartmann

asks himself "why it is so often the case that adaptation can only be achieved in these regressive detours?", and answers: "Probably . . . [the ego] is evidently by itself incapable of guaranteeing an optimum of adaptation."[358] In the case of sexualization, the author advances, "we often say that an ego function has . . . been invested with a 'sexual meaning.' " In the case of sublimation, too, "we may find" determinants of a sexual character.[359] At one time, Hartmann recalls, "Freud identified the self-preservative tendencies with 'ego drives,' " and "the cathexes proceeding from them he called 'interests'. . . ." Today, however, "we no longer speak of 'drives of the ego'. . . since it was realized that all . . . drives are part of the . . . id . . .; this change in theory necessitates a reformulation also of the phenomena Freud had in mind in speaking of 'interests.' "[360] "Tentatively," the authors declare, "we are inclined to assume that the capacity to neutralize large quantities of aggression may constitute one of the criteria of 'ego strength'. . ."[361] one admission against many denials, but that one being the parting shot.

30 | Hidden Repetitions

162. Having quoted Freud as affirming on the one hand, for a certain case, that the superego "knew more" than the ego about the id, and, on the other hand, that the superego is influenced by processes that "have remained unknown" to the ego, the authors ask themselves "whether Freud meant to convey . . . the same meaning in the two sentences quoted, or whether he intended by the use of the word 'knowing' to give the second [here, the first—N.L.] additional significance. . . ." This, they answer "seems hard to decide"[362]—and unusual to inquire into, as is perhaps expressed by the fact that the authors in

their full text wonder not whether the meaning of the two sentences is "the same," but whether it is "*precisely* the same." So unusual is precision about the relationship between meanings that follow each other; which are no doubt, in the habitual locution, close to each other; and with regard to which it ordinarily seems impertinent to inquire whether they are "precisely the same" or different—as if the crucial difference were not between difference and sameness, but rather between no and small difference on the one hand and large divergence on the other hand.

163. When undeclared synonyms are used, a passage (in which I shall italicize them) may be sensed as richer in content than if designations had been kept uniform:

> [In 1926 Freud described] the function of the ego under the impact of *perceived threats. Danger* may come . . . when instinctual demands increase. . . . [The] increase in instinctual demands may . . . create *conflict* with the environment. . . . In each such case the function of the ego is related to . . . *a condition of imbalance* in the total situation.[363]

Having observed that "in an environment where there is a . . . premium on conformism, the ego may enforce . . . neglect . . . of . . . moral valuations," Hartmann adds, without hinting at repetition, that "in such instances social anxiety might . . . [be] stronger than the . . . moral system."[364] Having recalled that "there are activities that *can adequately be performed only* if the higher ego functions . . . are temporarily kept in abeyance," Hartmann goes on to affirm that "the impossibility of transitorily switching of these functions may . . . *interfere with successful adaptation*:"[365] Many readers, I would guess, will not ask themselves what the relationship between these two sentences is, and then consider the possibility that the meaning of the second repeats that of the first. Incorporation, the authors recall, "is . . . a *genetic precursor* of identification; and the latter is *formed after its model* [I would rather say, formed after it—*or*: modeled after it—N.L.]":[366] Few readers, I would again surmise, will reflect upon the "and" in this sentence and envisage the eventuality that what follows that conjunction designates the same event as what precedes it. "We may say," affirms Hartmann, "that the *stability* of sexualized ego functions [is] . . . *less secure* [than that of sublimated ones] and that they *more easily follow the pull of regressive tendencies*":[367] As this "and" also the remark just made can be applied. At one point the authors enunciate three sentences:

S_1: As the child grows, he learns to control his drives.
S_2: As the child grows, the differentiation between id and ego becomes ever more complete.

229

S_3: The child's defenses against drives maintain that differentiation.

with two transitions between them:

T_1: (between S_1 and S_2): "this means";
T_2: (between S_2 and S_3): "and."

The reaction of many readers will not include an awareness of the possibility that some of the events to which any one of these sentences refers are also events that another one of them designates: that directing defenses against drives (S_3) is another name for (some or all) ways of learning to control them (S_1); which is in turn a name for (some or all ways of) differentiating between id and ego (S_2).

164. That a sequence of sentences is a repetition of just one point can be hidden from awareness in the manners discussed above with regard to single sentences turning upon words only.

If the language of the first sentence is common, what follows may be technical. "One distracts a child best by loving attention," the authors observe, only to continue: "Cathexis directed towards action is thus transformed into object cathexis."[368] "At the end of the first year," they note, "the child has formed lasting object relations": "transient [cathexis has been partly transformed] into permanent cathexis."[369] Essential for the undisturbed functioning of the ego, Hartmann reminds us, is the degree to which its activities have become "independent from their origins." "*And so is*," he continues, "the degree to which they are protected against regression and [sic] instinctualization."[370] After having recalled that the child learns to make a distinction between his activity and the object toward which it is directed, Hartmann proceeds to the presumably more important affirmation that this "represents [is?—N.L.] one aspect of 'objectivation' [a synonym for: making a distinction between self and nonself?—N.L.], which is an ego contribution [a synonym for: "to learn"?—N.L.] to the development of object relations [a synonym for: distinguishing between activity and its object?—N.L.] and an . . . element in the institution of the reality principle [taking account of objects includes distinguishing them from oneself?—N.L.]."[371]

165. Presumably affirming a positive correlation between the level of cathexis of major persons ("objects") and that of other entities ("reality"), Hartmann declares that "contact with reality is also based on object cathexis," and goes on to claim that "*therefore*" "withdrawal from . . . object relations may result in a loosening of the ego's attachment to reality . . .":[372] repetition appearing as inference.

230

166. Words expressing a relationship between sentences may both deny and admit the possibility that the latter repeats the former (*see* paragraph 160 above). "Individuals," observe the authors, "whose superego has remained more open to change than is commonly the case—*that is to say*, when the demarcation line between ego identifications and superego identifications is less strictly drawn than we usually find. . . ."[373] But then, we have all read about, for instance, paranoid personalities, *that is to say*, individuals in whom conflict around homosexual tendencies is intense . . . .: Once more, the same words may designate different objects (here, different relations between sentences).

167. When hidden repetition plays a role *between* sentences, it is apt to occur also *within* a statement, even if its meaning does not turn upon words only. The authors discuss "[the] *key* identifications which form the *core* of the superego,"[374] and the phase "before the *superego* has developed *as a separate agency*."[375] (The implied suggestion of a non-"separate" superego is not developed when it comes to approach— nothing beyond that happens—defining the word.) Hartmann envisages the older child's attempt "to master *reality* in an *alloplastic* way," as well as his learning "to develop *autoplastically* the state of affairs in his *psychic systems*."[376]

168. Such repetition is facilitated by the fact that one meaning of "or" is: "in other words." The cathexis of the self, the authors insist (keeping a tautology hidden also with the help of a concealed pleonasm), is by no means "*identical with or limited to*" the cathexis of the ego:[377] One may, if unquestioned, enjoy a sense of there being two, and, if challenged, withdraw to—one. The span of movement may be larger: Hartmann discusses the ego's achieving, with regard to its functions, "*synthesis*, or *integration*, or *organization*,"[378] which is more satisfying than synthesis, synthèse, sintesi; or integration, intégration, integrazione; or organization, organisation, organizzazione.

SECTION 4: WHAT IS NEW HERE BEYOND THE WORDS?

31

Fighting the Awareness of Just Restating

169. Words whose omissions would not seem to impoverish the meaning of a sentence may facilitate its being pronounced. That the oral, anal, and phallic phases influence the superego may be taken for granted; yet it is worth recalling that "*on the side of the drives* the phallic phase as well as the *earlier* oran and anal *libidinal* phases influence *the general and individual features of the system* superego."[379]

170. "Danger," observe the authors, in passing "*i.e.* . . . . changes that tend to evoke feelings of *helplessness* . . .":[380] The reader may conceive an exhilarating sense of being told about a surprising conquest of psychoanalysis. Indeed, one classical finding is probably recalled here: that a danger (in the ordinary meaning of the word) with regard to which I, consciously have a sense of mastery may induce a sense of helplessness deeper down. But this capital and familiar finding is given a strikingly new garment by the "i.e." in the sentence quoted which implies either that *every* danger (in that word's common usage) induces an unconscious sense of helplessness—surely novel and certainly false—or that the authors have resolved to use the word "danger" only when the latter condition obtains.

171. Conferring upon a familiar word a peculiar meaning—sometimes by an explicit statement, which at least the reader is apt to have forgotton soon afterward—may furnish freshness (*see* Chapter 8, paragraph 29). Having reserved the word "action" for acts under at least a certain degree of control on the part of the "ego," Hartmann can claim that the replacement of "motor discharge" by "action" is "an essential

element in Freud's theory of ego development,"[381] rather than an event that it is difficult for a naked eye to miss. Proposing to restrict the word "aggression" to designate only those acts intent upon damage whose targets are well delineated by the one who commits them, the authors note about early infancy that the motor discharges then observed "which we are used to considering as aggressive discharges" are "not directed against an organized world"; [382] as if they had overcome a weird belief that they were, rather than merely discontinued, a more generous dispensing of the word "aggression."

172. That, enraged by another, I may proceed to hurt myself if I do not lash out at him, is classical; but it is worth recalling that "the *economic function* of the *external source* of unpleasurable feelings is . . . [in part] its *function* as *catalyst*, i.e. . . . [as rendering possible] the discharge of otherwise self-destructive energies aroused by the existence of this *external source.*"[383] The more I believe I am living up to my aspirations, the better I feel about myself? Yes, and Edith Jacobson has shown that "the degrees of self-esteem *reflect* the *harmony* or *discrepanacy* between *self-representation* and *the wishful concept of the self.*"[384] All men are talkers (except those who aren't). Rather, "*verbalization* is part of the *function* of the *apparatus* of all men. . . ."[385] It matters to know just what it is in me that I feel so good about: "In this *context* [which is not pertinent here—N.L.] another point might become *relevant*, though little is known about it so far, namely, the habitual or *situational representation* of the various *localizations* of narcissism in the *self image.*"[386]

173. Such is the attraction of difficult words that they tolerate proximity to the simple ones that might have sufficed (*see* Chapter 1, paragraph 12). When a patient (we have already encountered him), who has come for analysis complaining that he lacks interest in his work shows affect in the hour when discussing events in the office, and when the analyst then draws his attention to the "contradiction" thus displayed, it might appear all too evident to note that "the patient has been stimulated to observe similar contradictions." But it is stimulating to hear that when this happens, "*the structure of the field* is changed."[387]

174. One may be plain to start with, and then learned. Having observed that "a healthy ego must . . . allow some of its . . . functions . . . to be put out of action occasionally"—something not too difficult to translate into an evocation of common experience—Hartmann continues for specialists only: "This brings us to the *problem . . .* of a *biological hierarchy* of the ego's *functions* and to the *notion* of the *integration of opposites. . . .*"[388]

175. Inversely, after expressions that are difficult one may permit oneself simplicity. Having observed about the "verbal element" in the analytic situation that one "structural function of . . . [this] process"

is due to the fact that in the development of the child the "fixing of verbal symbols" is one main road toward "objectivation," Hartmann can say about the similar role of such "fixing" for patients: "It facilitates the patient's way to a better grasp of physical as well as psychic reality."[389]

176. One plain expression may be accompanied by others, both fastidious and simple, designating the same event; which creates a sense of complexity about what is asserted. Acquiring aspirations for himself, a child starts believing that by the very act of so doing he lives up to them, and gains only later the insight that this is not so: "In the place of wishful thinking and of the distortion of inner reality—a distortion which is connected with the . . . forerunners of ego ideal functioning— . . . later . . . the contents of the ideal are recognized not as aims that have been magically reached, but as demands and as direction givers."[390]

177. What several attractive words drawn from a substantial list can achieve—as I have tried to show in the preceding paragraphs —can be accomplished by a single term if it be one central in theory.

The chance of a child's responding aggressively when interrupted in his activity is greatest when he is just learning what he is doing: worth saying if one can add that "we find this plausible" not just from experience, but "since we might assume" that during practice absorption is most intense? No, that "*cathexis* is most intense."[391]

While we are apt to take it for granted that some events in us that are not desires are closer to desires than others, we will yet be impressed when we see Hartmann "assume that the optimal functioning of different ego activities (e.g., defenses on the one hand and thought processes on the other) is dependent on different shades of *neutralization*."[392] Pleasure from another is not uninterrupted? Rather, "the formation of a lasting object relationship depends on the partial neutralization of libido." When you are attacking him too much, your relation with him will end? In a relationship "discharge of aggressive energy is limited."[393]

Though it may be evident and capital that, as time passes in childhood, "abstraction from the concrete becomes possible," it might appear pertinent to note that it does so as "*ego* development" proceeds.[394] When sick in soul, dreaming, or on the couch, I do not dispose of all my skills? "That under certain conditions the ego's achievements can be reversible, we see in neurosis, psychosis, in the dream, in analysis."[395]

To be sure, I may sense or recall that under stress I am apt to do less well than usually in some respects, but to keep up my habitual performance in others—in truth, "we . . . have ample clinical evidence of the fact that even in the 'normal adult' not all *functions of the ego* achieve the same degree of stability."[396] Catatonics may be incapable of elementary performance? "In catatonic states . . . motor activity loses even residues of ego functions—its coordination into deliberate acts."[397] It may surprise us less to hear that during the second half of his first year the child becomes capable of "anticipation of events" than to have it demonstrated to us that such "operations" are "a central function of the ego [not that any other, as far as I recall, is ever called peripheral—N.L.]."[398] While readers might take it for granted that in any act in which a drive is not satisfied overtly, it may be gratified covertly, they will still be interested to learn that in the child "the development of new ego functions, like for instance that of acting in the outer world, may open up new avenues for direct and indirect . . . gratification of instinctual tendencies."[399] Morality is apt to be opposed not only to lust and cruelty, but also to cold and discreet selfishness? "There are both ideals and positive and negative imperatives which oppose not the drives but . . . ego functions"; "a more subtle demarcation of one's 'rights' and 'duties' in relation to those of other people is one of the results of superego formation." Thus "some [self-interests] will prove superego-syntonic, and others not." As a matter of fact, "thinking of ontogenesis,"—having thought of it, one may return to what is both capital and elementary—"among the prohibitions which the parents impose on the child from early childhood on, there are many that concern the child's self-interests."[400]

178. Central words of analytic theory (which, in the quotations to follow, I shall mark by a single line) may be joined by terms from the advanced vocabulary of the human sciences at large (double line). Wanting to affirm that with normal development one's ideals for oneself and one's moral prohibitions come closer together than they were at the start, and avoiding any statements about details of that process, the authors advance that "the ego ideal's precursors . . . lead to . . . the ego ideal in a strict sense, namely the ego ideal as a function of the superego. The contents of the ego ideal and the contents of the moral prohibitions [presumably a synonym for "superego"—N.L.] are brought into close contact [here we recognize the implicit definition of "ego ideal": aspirations for oneself, if their closeness to moral prohibitions goes beyond a critical level—N.L.]. . . . The ego ideal and the moral restrictions are gradually integrated, and assume the central position [what other components assume peripheral positions?—N.L.] in what has been called a person's 'moral system.' "[401] If man were mindless, his chances of survival would be smaller? Yes, "the functions of the ego, . . . the ego's aspect of regulating the relations with the environment and its organizing capacity in finding solutions fitting the environmental situation and the psychic systems at the same time . . . become of primary importance for self-preservation in man."[402] More particularly,

knowledge may be useful: "Objectivation, another function we attribute to the ego, in helping to develop our knowledge of the external world, is . . . instrumental in the organization of action."[403]

179. Having been suitably translated, a plain point can thus be talked about with words appropriate to advanced theory. The neonate does not anticipate; thus he does, among other things, not sacrifice present pleasure for the sake of future satisfaction, not foreseeing how having the former might reduce the chance of getting the latter. In richer words, the transition from the pleasure principle to the reality principle is rendered possible by the formation of an ego function, that of anticipation. And now:

> Various theories have attempted to explain the relation of the two principles. . . . No explanation is satisfactory unless we assume that the transition from one principle to the other is rendered possible by [never mind what—N.L.] . . . which enters the process as an independent variable. . . .[404]

180. In another mode, an event too obvious to be enunciated starkly may become speakable if one also alludes to the acts of mind (cf. Section 15) supposedly connected with its being mentioned. One might not want to bother recalling that education aims at socialization, and still desire to affirm that "*from the general biological point of view* . . . education aims . . . at . . . socialization."[405] That education may have goals beyond preventing neurosis seems all too plausible; less so, perhaps, that "the goal of education *cannot be satisfactorily defined in terms of the concept of* neurosis-prevention alone."[406] Though the discovery that hurting is fun has been made by many laymen, it is for the specialist to arrive at "the realization that the discharge of aggression and the destruction of objects *may be considered* pleasurable per se."[407] Recalling that the superego has not been there from the beginning, while the drives and the ego have, the authors do not infer that this is why regression of the superego has less of a span, but rather that "this is one reason why regression is *harder to conceptualize* with respect to the superego than with respect to the drives and the ego."[408] We would readily believe that the adult's pleasures would be smaller than they are had he not, apart from maturing, also learned since birth; but it seems worth noting that "since the formation of the ego *can in part be described as* a learning process . . . *one might say that* in man the gratification of . . . drives is guaranteed by learning."[409] The ego aims, among other things, at interfering with the expression of drives? That is, "a large sector of the ego's functions *can also be described from the angle of* its inhibiting nature"—a focusing on the activities of the theorist, which is, in this case, balanced by an envisagement of essences:

"Defense is a . . . *expression* of . . . [the ego's] inhibiting *nature.*"[410] The child develops not only in psychosexual respects, but also with regard to aggression, object relations, ego functions? Yes, to be sure. But it can be put differently: "*Descriptions of* developmental *problems will not only have to refer to the data concerning* psychosexual development; *they will also have to include data on* the development of aggression, on that of object relations, and at least some of the key functions of the ego."[411] Adult character is determined by the development of ego, of drives and of object relations? This is not the only way it can be said: ". . . a *satisfactory description of genetic considerations must simultaneously take into account* the development of the ego, the instinctual development and that of object relations. *Only on this basis does characterology become valuable. . . .*"[412] If I am infatuated with myself, I may so be with regard to something other than my sexual prowess— or: As narcissism may be either instinctual or neutralized, "*a description from the angle of* narcissism *does not account for the distinction between* 'sexual overestimation' [why the quotes?—N.L.] of the self, as we find it, e.g., in megalomania, and other forms of self-cathexis."[413]

181. It is in such fashion that a plain statement, rather than being avoided or seasoned, can, having been made, still be enhanced. Talking in the analytic hour, Hartmann reminds us, in reasonably simple language (1) facilitates the patient's grasp of physical and psychic reality, (2) becomes the object of transference analysis, (3) furnishes emotional discharge, (4) is influenced by the superego. And then: '*This is to say* that the different aspects of speech . . . as *described by psychologists and philosophers*, become *coherent and meaningful if viewed from the angle of our structural model. . . .*"[414]

182. References to intellectual operations may be combined with advanced words from the human sciences so as to render the evident speakable. In an analysis there are two persons and a few rules? Yes, the psychoanalytic interview "*can reasonably be described as* a *field* situation in which two people react to each other within conditions established by rules of procedure."[415]

183. Central words of analytic theory (one line) may be associated both with words of other theory (two lines) and talk about processes of the mind (wavy lines): "We now are prepared to approach one type of conflict that arises in earliest childhood: the conflict with the object. . . . The discussion of conflict with the object introduces the psychological reality in which the child lives and develops. . . . In a more general sense, however, it introduces the role played by the continuum of indulgence and deprivation to which the child is exposed." That is,

    . . . contact with his environment imposes upon the child unavoidable deprivations.[416]

184. The type of sentence that I discussed in Section 3, Chapters 28, 29, 30—it looks as if it bore on events, but on inspection appears to turn on words—can be used to protect an affirmation that does concern the world, but hardly increases our knowledge. The transition from the pleasure principle to the reality principle—a momentary pleasure, uncertain in its results, is given up in order to gain an assured pleasure at a later time—"cannot," Hartmann asserts, "be derived from the pleasure principle alone": The anticipation of the future "enters the process as an independent variable."[417] In other words, a child does not sacrifice present gratification on behalf of anticipated satisfaction, unless he is capable of anticipation—an affirmation true by virtue of the meanings of the words composing it, but suggesting another one true by all to evident evidence: Not capable of anticipation at birth, a child usually acquires the ability for it somewhat later.

185. One may avoid the awareness of saying something obvious by alleging a cause of it, which on inspection turns out to be a renaming of it (*see* Chapter 3, paragraph 37; Chapter 11, paragraph 54). The growing child takes into account, in his relations with others, what he learns about the world outside? Rather, "what *the evolving reality principle has taught him* about the world outside."[418] A child's aggressive response to being interrupted is more intense when the interruption is aggressive? To be sure; but this becomes worth saying if it is "understandable" in a sense other than that which would be conveyed by a layman's use of this adjective in such a context. What happens, in fact, in the case envisaged is that the one who interrupts "becomes doubly bad"; in other words, the child dislikes not only being interrupted, but also an adult's bad feelings toward him. Now, as a "bad object" (in quotation marks—still a British import in 1949) such an adult "*exercises an appeal*" to the child's aggression, "*attracts*" it, "*thus inviting*" it.[419] But are these three assertions (presumably of identical meaning) designating anything but the event itself that they render "understandable"?

186. If a statement is made with excessive restrictions, the awareness that, stripped of them, it would be unsurprising, may be subdued. To account for the dynamic interrelationships of an individual's characteristics genetic principles are required? Of course, but it is more intriguing to consider that "*most* psychological typologies, *especially* . . . [those] not based on genetic principles . . . do not account *fully* for the . . . dynamic interrelationships of an individual's characteristics."[420] To be sure, one is then unlikely to note that there are thus a *few* psychological typologies not based on genetic principles that *do* account fully for dynamics (who are these competitors of analysis?); but the presence of words conveying complexity and caution has rendered the statement more attractive. Imagining that one is living up to one's aspirations for

oneself is different from soberly assessing to what extent one falls short of them? Yes, but it is more arresting to learn that "[the] wishful concept [of the self] does *not fully* represent the aim-setting function of the ego ideal."[421]

187. Alternatively, emphasis rather than understatement may shield against the intimation of knowing it already: There must be reason for stress. ". . . education *undoubtedly* aims at . . . socialization."[422]

188. That effort has been expended on research or theoretical analysis creates the presumption of a valuable pay-off. As everybody with whom I am in touch for some time, will at times hinder my desires and enrage me, my relation with him is apt to come to an end unless I can subdue my bad feelings toward him? That, I may believe, I know; but did I know that "the formation of a permanent object relation is, *as has been shown elsewhere*, dependent on the capacity of the individual to bear frustrations," and that "*we now add another condition*: Such permanent object relation is also dependent on the sublimation of aggression"?[423] The neonate is not yet capable of the "pleasure at the suffering or humiliation of others" by which the authors define "sadistic impulses"? Rather, "there *is little doubt* that in *observing* the child's relation to his mother, *we can actually study* the transition from the discharge of aggression in a general sense to that . . . discharge which we here consider as sadistic."[424] The more a mother succeeds in convincing her child that he will be rewarded a bit later for giving something up right now, the better will he take it? Or, "*there can be little doubt* that the better assured the child is that indulgence will follow postponement of demands, the more easily will the deprivation be tolerated"; in fact, "*Benedek*, in this connection, *stresses* the importance of . . . confidence."[425]

189. If an obvious point is linked with one less so, the quality of the latter may be diffused onto the former. That, beyond a certain level, the directing of libido toward the self is unpleasant, is one of the great findings of analysis—which can be used for affirming about "an analogous hypothesis with regard to aggression" not that the latter is, in contrast, unsurprising, but rather that it is "even more plausible":[426] —all too true to boot. Having, with respect to "self deceptions," after some analysis arrived at the plain point that they "can in many cases be traced to . . . the superego," the authors enrich that statement with the assertion that this is the case "more often" than for "deceptions about the outside world":[427] interesting, and unsupported.

190. While a few aspects of the relationship between two classes of events may be obvious, their precise connection may be obscure; a situation that may itself be obscured by words suggesting that more is asserted than is. The less pleasant adults, in the child's belief, make life for him, the more mixed his feelings toward them will be: This may

become the assertion that the child's ambivalence toward his first love objects *"corresponds"* to "their position within the *continuum* leading from indulgence to deprivation"—which suggests two quantified variables and a function giving us the position on the former if we know that on the latter. That we do not, alas, have such insight, is perhaps expressed through the authors' saying that *"one might say"* the "correspondence" in question to obtain.[428]

191. Making a point that is all too true, one may suggest (not declare) that according to some (not named) another statement can be inferred from it; one may then—correctly—indicate that no such inference can be made, and that the supposedly inferrable point is in any case false: Thus the initial assertion is rescued from a sense of excessive familiarity. Having affirmed at some length that various aspects of the ego are among the determinants of the formation of the superego, the authors warn that "we say this without wanting to imply that the energy commonly used by the superego is neutralized to the same degree to which, e.g., the energy-feeding intellectual processes is."[429]

192. That the superego may stimulate repression is elementary; not so that "in the cases" where that is the case "we could describe this . . . as 'a dependence of one form of aggressive relation (between ego and id) on another one (between superego and ego) . . .' ":[430] while no new insight on relationships between events is (yet) gained, indicating a class of which a familiar relationship is a member, though an obvious one, replaces the sense of familiarity by that of novelty.

32 | Emancipation From Classical Prejudice

193. One may proclaim truths that common sense has presumably never doubted, but which were perhaps sometimes—as a rule, implicitly —denied when analysis was young. One may do so without either recalling the earlier negations or what has made for their ceasing: the arrival of evidence or the onset of sobriety? The new pronouncements are agreeably shocking, as they contain the very words—the unchanged central terms—hitherto associated with the now abandoned denials. "Growth," the authors announce, "is not limited to the sequence of zones of predominant erotogeneity." For "it includes the unfolding of ego functions, the development of thought from an archaic phase to one in which concrete thinking is . . . supplemented by . . . more and more abstract concepts. . . ."[431] There are "several reasons," Hartmann explains, "why not only the differences between ego and id, and between ego and superego, are relevant, but also differences in the ego itself . . . the cooperation and antagonisms between its various functions."[432] The authors seem eager to break down a live (but, if so, undeclared) superstition according to which a "function," if it belongs to the "ego," is never affected by any of the "functions" belonging to the "superego," and vice versa. Noting that "the distinction between 'being a function of' and 'being accessible to the influence of' has not always been clearly made," they illustrate: "The fact that we attribute internal perception to the ego . . . does not imply that internal perception could not come under the influence of superego functions"; in fact, "the superego may both stimulate and interfere with . . . the knowledge of inner reality."[433]

Recalling that, in Freud's words, a neurosis may vanish if the subject becomes involved in the misery of an unhappy marriage, loses all his money, or develops a dangerous organic disease, the authors add that "powerful identifications," too, can produce such changes: "Certain observations lead us to suspect [this]." But have observations on conversions to this effect not been available for long? Perhaps they were neglected, as they concern persons "whose superego has remained more open to change than is commonly the case."[434] Access to these phenomena was barred, it seems, as long as one believed in the proposition against which the authors inveigh (implicitly) when they declare that "with the setting up of the superego as a separate agency its development has not come to an end."[435] Freud having allegedly remarked *alles muss man können*, it becomes interesting to discover that *manches muss man müssen*: that "the 'must' and the 'inability-to-do-otherwise' are not always criteria of pathology"; in fact, that "the normal ego . . . must . . . be able to must." Thus "we conclude" that the normal ego is able to yield to musts: no discussion as to why this "conclusion" came in the century's second third rather than its first. When and how did the "facts" that the contrasting "oversimplified conceptions of health disregard"[436] first become available?

194. It may be appropriate to reject (implicitly) the (no doubt equally implicit) belief that what has not been talked about in analytic writings does not exist, even when patent facts are involved. "Naturally," the authors declare, "it is not meant that during the oedipal phase only the superego develops":[437] Are there then any who affirm that those aspects of the child on which, say, Piaget has focused (apart from moral feelings), hardly change during the years in question? Having quoted Freud to the effect that "if the ego has successfully resisted a temptation to do something that would be objectionable to the superego, it feels . . . its pride increased," the authors advance into new terrain: "Pride does not necessarily remain tied, as a kind of recompense, to . . . resisting temptation. It can become a lasting . . . aspect of a personality." Also, "pride is . . . not limited to moral pride." My dots replace: "clearly"; but it is not clear why this, presumably, was not clear before.

195. The liberation from classical prejudice, the discovery of starkly present facts that had been barred from view is apt to be expressed not with a smile about human limitations, but with satisfaction about analytic advance. That the increase of guilt, as a consequence of frustration, is not a "regular" (which in the context, I believe, means: invariable) occurrence—it had apparently and strangely been held to be that—may be presented as a discovery by virtue of "clinical observations" (no reference) with which "we are impressed."[438]

196. It seems natural that pertinent evidence, though easily accessible, just will not be perceived or presented as long as it would overthrow a reigning sentence: Attention to it has to wait for a revolution in the palace of theory. Freud, the authors recall, started from the idea that the *id* is the sole carrier of hereditary traits, and only later became aware of the fact that "there was no reason to assume" that the *ego* is not built upon hereditary predispositions. It was an "impact of this [latter] point of view" that "the study of interaction between constitutional and environmental factors was initiated . . . by Margaret Fries (1946)"; it was "as a result of this approach" that an insight could be gained which now confirms (modified) theory rather than invalidating it: "It appears" that "even the earliest interaction between mother and child may be . . . determined by the child's earliest [that is, hereditary—N.L.] reaction patterns." "There seems little doubt, then," the authors conclude, without a smile about the limitations of fact-finding in the past, but with pride in the prospective productivity of recent theory, "that research . . . will be considerably facilitated by the assumption that hereditary factors . . . play their part in the formation of all organizations."[439]

3 3 | The Fact of Interdependence

197. The mere affirmation *that* every aspect of the psyche influences all others and is affected by them may seem satisfying (*see* Chapter 2, paragraph 59); it does not seem to arouse too much impatience about not having discovered *how* (where one has, the sheer allegation of interdependence is unlikely to be often made); nor misgivings about the

ease with which such sentences may be multiplied. That personality is structured, Hartmann declares, "is bound to influence" the formation of symbols;[440] the two processes, differentiation of psychic structure and relation of the self to external objects, are "interdependent";[441] factors in the nonconflictual sphere "codetermine" the ways of conflict solution, and are "in turn influenced" by the latter;[442] ". . . we . . . may expect" (indeed) that the ego's growing independence from the instinctual drives "influences" the formation and elaboration of the superego[443]; the anticipation of danger and the objectivation of outer and inner reality "play a role" in the resolution of the oedipal conflict.[444]

198. The properties and impact of any part of the psyche vary with its context: instead of this truth being once-and-for-all affirmed, it is ever anew declared in changing incarnations. The coordination of the parts of the organism and [sic] of their functions "differs" on the various levels of development;[445] "one might say" (to be sure) that a specific structure of stimulus-response correlation is "characteristic" of a specific phase through which the child goes;[446] identifications and projections made at a time when the demarcation of self and object is not yet fully established "are not quite the same" as those on a higher level.[447]

199. For such content there are modes of shielding with which we have become familiar.

The environment acts upon the ego? No, "*differences* in the environment act *directly* upon the *development* of ego *functions*."[448]

200. Object relations are affected by the ego? Rather, "satisfactory 'object relations' *can only be assessed if we also consider* . . . ego development."[449]

201. Defense influences and is influenced by ego? Yes, "*there is no doubt, and I mentioned it before,* that defense is . . . under the influence of other processes in the ego and, on the other hand, that defense intervenes in a . . . variety of . . . processes in the ego; *this I discussed as an essential aspect of developmental psychology.*"[450]

202. In a distinctive mode, sentences of the type here considered may be shielded by introducing manifestly indeterminate elements into them. The defensive functions "influence" those ego tendencies that keep up contact with reality "*and so on.*"[451]

203. Words may appear that suggest the *nature* of a relationship where only the *presence* of one is affirmed. According to the statement just quoted the defensive functions "influence *in various ways*" those ego tendencies which. . . . The ratio of active and passive, of male and female components prior to the Oedipus complex "helps to shape *in a definite way*" the form which it takes.[452] We have knowledge of "*parallel*" development in ego and id;[453] we know that what is pleasure and what is not "*parallels at least to some extent*" the development of

245

the ego.[454] Every step in the formation of the object *"corresponds to"* a phase in psychic differentiation.[455] The goals of an individual's actions *"mirror"* his relationships with the outer world, but also his instinctual drives, his interests, his moral demands, the state of his mental equilibrium, and so forth.[456] The synthetic and differentiating functions of the ego are *"definitely correlated with"* the control of instinctual drives.[457]

34 | The Fact of Causation

204. A statement that at first sight seems to affirm relations between classes of events may, on inspection, turn out to assert merely that *there are* causes for a certain phenomenon: An event may be related to a series of events so comprehensive that it is, at the very least, not clear what is left out. Psychic differentiation, according to the authors, is determined by "the maturation of the apparatuses which later come under the control of the ego," and by "the experiences that structure the psychic apparatus."[458] Now maybe, for the authors, there are, or could be, maturing apparatuses that do not ever come under the ego's control, as well as experiences that do not structure the psychic apparatus. But it is not clear that there are such; it may be that nothing that could conceivably "determine" the event the authors envisage (psychic differentiation) is excluded from their brief but forceful list.

205. That this is so seems to be indicated in the case of some such lists, as we have already seen above (paragraph 202), by the fact that they end with an "and so forth." While ego interests, Hartmann observes, are often rooted in id tendencies, they are also determined by the superego, by ego functions, by other ego interests, by a person's

relation with reality, by his modes of thinking, or by his synthetic capacities, "*etc.*"[459]

206. When there is emptiness from too many causes, words about causation may abound. It is, for the authors, "the . . . general prerequisites, or more specific . . . psychic determinants" of superego formation that "can be found" in object relations, or in the development of the ego and the instinctual drives.[460]

207. Or lists of causes may lack items whose absence confers specificity, but would, if challenged, perhaps not be continued. If the authors, considering child development, claim that "parental response will tend to vary . . . according to the stage of libidinal and ego development of the child, according to the manifestations of aggression, according to the individual predispositions of the parents, but also according to prevailing social norms," [461]do they really mean to affirm that the parents' response is insensitive to the development of their children's *superegos*?

208. One may convey that a list of causes that seems exhaustive does in fact not comprise all conceivable ones, without indicating how it falls short of that. As far as the child's early experiences in learning are concerned, psychoanalytic hypotheses, the authors explain, tend to take into account "*mainly*" four factors: first, the stage of maturation of the apparatuses; second, the reaction of the environment; third, the tolerance for deprivation; and fourth, the various types of gratification afforded by the processes of learning and the satisfactions that can be obtained as consequences of mastering.[462] Where is the stage of libidinal development, and that of the superego's? Either included in one or the other of the four factors—in which case the list may be exhaustive after all—or not; and that, I suppose, would not be specificity, but oversight.

SECTION 5: WHAT HAVE WE LEARNED ABOUT THE EGO RECENTLY?

35 | How Do We Know This Is Ego?

209. During the first quarter of the century, Hartmann recalls, "ego psychology came . . . to be looked on by analysts as . . . outside real analysis. . . ."[463] Now that it is inside, how to decide whether a certain aspect of a patient is of the "ego?"

It is customary to make such a decision without indicating just what particular properties of a "function" are designated by affirming that it is of "the system" ego.

210. One may be content with an allusion to the existence of such a definition: "Our view is to attribute to one psychic system functions which . . . have *something essential* in common. . . ."[464] The "demarcation" of "substructures" in "Freud's model of psychic personality" was, according to Hartmann, based on the fact that he found *"greater coherence"* among some functions than among others.[465] If Freud "conceived" of the superego as an agency among whose functions he "included" the ego ideal, it is because he saw the moral prohibitions and the strivings toward the ideal as *"closely related."*[466]

211. Even when divergences and variations in the attribution of a certain "function" to a certain "system" are discussed, one may avoid statements indicating the meaning of such an act. "In Freud's work," the authors recall, "there are . . . certain activities which at one time are *described* as ego functions, and at other times as superego functions." Thus "Freud had originally *assigned* reality testing to the superego. . . . Later . . . he says this is 'a point which needs *correction*,' and he adds: 'It would *fit in perfectly* with the relations of the ego to the world of

perception if reality testing *remained* a task of the ego. . . .' " When the authors advance that "Freud's change of mind in *attributing* reality testing first to the superego and later to the ego belongs . . . to those changes in the *conception* of the superego that are the . . . outcome of . . .," one may expect that we will learn what *events* we are *designating* when we are "attributing" functions to systems; but no: The quotation I broke off ends with ". . . of ego psychology." In the same vein the authors put forward the "suggestion" to "*assign* to the ego still another one of the functions which Freud had originally *attributed* to the superego . . . [namely] internal perception. . . . Freud himself sometimes spoke—and we think *convincingly*—of inner perception as a function of the ego. On the other hand . . . as late as . . . 1932 . . . he *allocated* self-observation to the superego. . . ."[467]

212. Despite, or because of the lack of explicit directions, such decisions may be made assertively. "*Clearly*," Hartmann notes about "intelligence," it "belongs to the ego."[468] "Intentionality," he declares, "is among the first achievements of the child *we would not hesitate* to characterize as *true* ego functions."[469] That a certain function is of a certain system may be pronounced in a fashion that suggests that the system is a badly charted territory in which a new mountain range has been discovered. "The *recognition* of the synthetic function," recalls Hartmann, "*made* the ego, which had always been considered an organization, now also an organizer of the three systems of personality."[470]

213. In contrast to such assurance, one may be mild about accepting or rejecting the statement that a certain function is of a certain system: as if the function were as yet incompletely observed; as if such reports as had been collected about it rendered it probable that full information would show it to belong (or not to belong) to the system in question— and yet no indications are given as to what evidence is available, and which lacking. "It would be *difficult*," Hartmann judges about the process of generalization, formalization, and integration of moral values, "to attribute what I have in mind here to the superego. . . . It *rather* corresponds to what we *know* of . . . the ego."[471] Recalling Freud's assertion that the holding up of ideals is of the superego, the authors "*feel reasonably sure* . . . that . . . [this] is the *most plausible* answer to the question concerning the structural position of the ego ideal."[472] The group of tendencies that comprises strivings for what is "useful," egoism, self-assertion, "etc.," declares Hartmann, "*should it seem reasonable*, be attributed to the . . . ego."[473]

214. One may simply declare that a statement of the type here discussed is uncertain, without indicating why that is so and how it could become less so. The capacity for anticipation "*seems to be*" a feature of the ego.[474] If the ego surely controls perception of the outer

world, it is only *"probably"* that it controls that of the self.[475] Self-scrutiny with reference to the authentic quality of moral values is *"very likely"* a function of the ego.[476] And if, as recalled above, it is "clearly" that intelligence "pertains to the ego," "I would *hesitate* to equate it [whatever that might mean—N.L.] . . . with the ego."[477] Attribution of function to system remains an act both delicate and opaque.

36 | The Ego Is Independent

Heredity

215. In varied words the authors declare that there is heredity to the "ego."

"Not all the factors of . . . development present at birth," Hartmann affirms, "[are] part of the id."[478]

"The development [of the ego]," he advances, "is traceable not only to the impact of reality and of . . . drive":[479] "The apparatus serving perception, motility and others that underlie ego functions . . . are not created by the [instinctual] needs."[480] The tendencies to gain pleasure and to avoid unpleasure "cannot fully account for . . . the reality principle";[481] "memory, association, and so on are functions which cannot possibly be derived from the ego's relationship to instinctual drives or love objects."[482] "The ego . . . [is] more than . . . a by-product of the influences of reality on . . . drive."[483]

At birth, and before "there exist . . . dispositions for future ego functions."[484] "Ego development . . . is partly based on . . . maturation,"[485] a "maturation [that] follows . . . laws which are . . . part of our inheritance."[486]

"The apparatus serving perception, motility . . . as well as those that account for . . . memory are partly inborn";[487] "the differentiation between ego and id . . . is . . . in part an innate character . . .";[488] among the factors which from birth on modify the ego is "congenital . . . equipment."[489]

Thus, "the ego . . . has a partly independent origin";[490] "the development of ego functions enters the process as an independent variable".[491] There is an "autonomous area" of the ego,[492] a "partly autonomous development of the ego",[493] for "we may call autonomous factors the elements . . . of the ego which originated in . . . [its] hereditary core"[494] and, finally, speak of the ego's "primary autonomy".[495]

216. Just precisely what beliefs about patients are denied with such diversity and insistence? How might patients look if their egos possessed no "primary autonomy?" Not raised, the question is not answered.

217. Sometimes the implicit definition of "maturation" appears to be expanded so as to include slowness—which permits opposing Melanie Klein, but hardly concerns heredity: "Keeping in mind the role of maturation in ego development may . . . help us to avoid one pitfall of the reconstruction of mental life in early infancy: . . . the interpretation of early mental processes in terms of mechanisms known from . . . later maturational stages."[496]

218. Perhaps, to stress the existence of a "hereditary core" in the ego is sensed as important because a classical prejudice is thus corrected (cf. Section 4, Chapter 32). "In quite a few passages," Hartmann recalls about Freud, "he . . . states that the . . . reality principle is due to the influence of the external world on the individual"—thus presumably denying that "the development of ego functions . . . [enters] as an independent variable into the . . . [process] described. . . ."[497] In fact, as the authors remind us, "Freud started from the idea that . . . the id is the sole carrier of hereditary traits".[498]

219. One might, in hind view, smile at such an affirmation, and observe once more how great insights are apt to have a price that one only later can cease paying.

This is not the authors' mood (cf. paragraphs 193 and 195 above). They still treat seriously what by now should appear as obviously false which permits them to reprint doubtful reasoning: The id, Freud first affirmed, is the sole carrier of hereditary traits, *since* the ego "constitutes," at the start, that part of the id that is "modified by . . . experiences": which might mean that the moment we know the same aspect of a patient is hereditary, we also know that we are not going to *call* it a part of his "ego".

Instead of noting with relief that an early error—perhaps useful, and certainly substantial—has been corrected with delay, the authors express satisfaction about the ultimate conquest of the always evident. "Freud's statement of 1937 [from which I just quoted—N.L.] and Hartmann's (1939) distinction between the ego and the physiological apparatus at the ego's disposal [the first presumably modified by experience and the second hereditary—N.L.]," the authors declare without apology, "represent a broadening in psychoanalytic approaches to psychology"; in fact, "for another sector of psychoanalytic propositions they establish the interaction of innate and environmental factors." On the same page, still, the authors remark that "the ego equipment of an individual, his intelligence, prowess, skills . . . are *obviously* in part due to hereditary factors."[499]

220. Hartmann's words seem imbued with a sense of science advancing against current obstacles, too, when he undertakes to "assume" that differences in the time at which grasping, walking, and the motor aspect of speech appear, do "enter into . . . ego development as a partly independent variable."[500] What gives the authors' statements on this matter zest is the implicitly affirmed *presence* of opponents who would not only in general fashion deny maturation, but specifically contest that what "makes the transfer from the pleasure principle to the reality principle possible" are "maturational changes proceeding during the second half of the first year" that render the child capable of "anticipation of future events [sic]."[501] But who these contemporary adversaries are we do not learn.

Irreversibility

221. Partly independent in origin, the ego enjoys the same quality in operation; again, there are many names for it.

"The results of . . . ego development may be . . . irreversible. . . ."[502]

There is "resistivity of ego functions against regression."[503]

Or "stability vis-à-vis inner or outer stress."[504]

Ego functions have "distance from ego-id conflicts or . . . from . . . regressive trends."[505]

They may achieve "virtual independence from conflicts and . . . regressive tendencies," or "relative independence . . . from id pressure."[506] They are "independent factors";[507] finally, they enjoy "secondary autonomy."

222. Which grows with growth: with the passage of time there is "growing independence from the immediate impact of stimuli,"[508] "better protection against instinctualization and regression."[509]

None of this for the neonate: "The apparatus serving perception, motility and others that underlie ego functions seem, in the infant, to be activated by instinctual needs."[510]

Little of it in childhood, when "ego activities show . . . a tendency to get reinvolved in the . . . instinctual demands that contributed to their development";[511] "newly acquired ego functions show a high degree of reversibility in the child."[512]

Still, change, if slow, is massive: "the . . . ego . . . evolves . . . by freeing itself from the encroachment of . . . instinctual tendencies."[513]

223. Once more, who ever has denied any of this? How would patients look if it weren't true?

224. And who among analysts has asserted the opposite [whatever that would clinically mean], making it worthwhile for the authors to note that "there can be no question of 'absolute' independence in . . . [secondary] autonomy"?[514]

225. In truth, that "the ego gradually gains a comparative independence from immediate outside or inside pressure" is, as Hartmann observes on a single occasion, "*a fact that one is used to considering as a . . . trend in human development*"—"though," he notes, "*usually not in this terminology*":[515] Might the usefulness of the "concept" "secondary autonomy" be to render acceptable stress on what otherwise goes without much saying?

226. As for statements into which this "concept" enters, "the degree of [secondary] autonomy [of the ego] is," according to Hartmann, "*correlated* with . . . ego strength."[516] The latter term remaining undefined, I am unable to ascertain whether the truth of the sentence follows from implicit meanings or from common observation; while the use of a word with prestige from statistics conveys the sense of a finding obtained with effort—a sense also communicated when "the degree of secondary autonomy," "closely linked up with . . . ego strength" as it is, appears as "*probably* the best way to *assess* it."[517]

227. "Secondary autonomy [of the ego]," the authors also advance, "is *correlated* with the investment of certain ego functions with fully neutralized drive energy."[518] "Secondary autonomy," Hartmann declares, "is . . . *dependent on* neutralization." "In the course of development," he shows, "[the] cathexes [of ego functions] . . . [are] neutralized, *and* they . . . gain a certain degree of autonomy vis-à-vis the instinctual drives."[519] While the authors mention the case in which there is a high degree of neutralization with a low degree of autonomy,[520] they do not note the obverse possibility; and I wonder whether the (undeclared) rules for "asuming" high neutralization are not such that asserting the high secondary autonomy of an ego function *entails* assuming a high degree of neutralization for its cathexis: at one point the authors refer to "the degree to which ego activities are . . . autonomous, *i.e.,* . . . the degree to which the ego's . . . cathexis is neutralized."[521]

254

228. Declaring that when the ego uses neutralized energy, the latter is either "drawn from *ad hoc* acts of neutralization" or "provided by . . . [a] reservoir of neutralized energy at the ego's disposal,"[522] Hartmann affirms a negative correlation between the ego's level of secondary autonomy, and the ratio of "ad hoc" over "reservoir" procurement of neutralized energy.[523] But we are told nothing about how to ascertain, in any given case, the value of that ratio.

229. With an "increase in autonomy of the ego," the authors surmise, "we may expect a diminution of . . . magical thinking,"[524] that is, thinking with affinity to id and superego: perhaps because we would not call an ego addicted to such thinking highly "autonomous."

230. More generally, there is, according to the authors, a negative correlation between an ego function's level of secondary autonomy, and the ratio of primary process characteristics over secondary process ones in its operations—perhaps for the same reason?

231. Sometimes we may not have to hesitate whether to adjudge a sentence a tautology or a truism. "The extent to which identification may lead to regression depends," according to the authors, "on the degree of the ego's autonomy":[525] to be sure, as the "autonomy" in question (the one called "secondary") *designates* resistivity to, among other things, regression.

232. On the other hand, when a statement is clearly about patients, it may also obviously lack novelty. The higher a person's capacity to function normally in the face of adverse circumstances within and outside himself, the lower the chance that he will become a schizophrenic: "One would expect," observes Hartmann—one would, indeed—"that the . . . preservation of . . . ego functions could be related to the degree of secondary autonomy which these functions have reached in the course of childhood development . . ."[526]

Aims of One's Own

233. Talking about "secondary autonomy of the ego" often, the authors but rarely speak about the ego's "aims." "That the ego sets itself aims," Hartmann mentions in passing, "was emphasized by R. Waelder long ago (1930)."[527] "Ego aims," we learn, "may lie in the direction of id tendencies; they may be opposed to them . . . ; the third group are . . . aims the ego . . . sets itself . . .";[528] but about these we hear no more, nor do we get a glimpse of what the assertion in question denies, i.e., what patients would look like if their egos did not set themselves aims.

255

234. The authors seem divided between a desire to affirm the ego by attributing independence to it and a wish to safeguard both the domains of the other "systems" and the person's unity by limiting that attribution. Envisaging the ego, they declare it "an independent organization"; considering id, ego, and superego, they maintain that these "are . . . not . . . independent parts of personality. . . ."[529]

235. But through time independence seems to be gaining. "The question whether all energy at the disposal of the ego originates in the instinctual drive," Hartmann declares at one point (1950) "*I am not prepared to answer.*"[530] Later (1955) he does assert "the *possibility* . . . that part of the mental energy [at the disposal of the ego] . . . belongs from the very first to the ego, or to the inborn precursors of what will later be . . . the ego functions, and . . . to those apparatus that come gradually under the influence of the ego. . . ."[531] At the end (1964) he has achieved certainty that "part of the energy which the ego uses *is not derived* (by way of neutralization) from the drive but *belongs* from the very first to the ego, or to the inborn precursors of what will later be . . . ego functions." Then "we may speak of it as primary ego energy."[532]

37 | The Ego Is Rich

236. While in the past the functions of the ego were "incompletely described," at present, the authors observe, it is generally "*realized*" that "*the realm of the ego*" is "wider":[533] The possibility of a word

having changed its meaning is implicitly denied, and accepted only that of a continent's size having been underestimated.

237. In passing, the authors refer to subdivisions of the ego about which one almost never hears. Suddenly calling for more study of *"functional units"* (presumably not a synonym of "ego functions"), Hartmann recalls that "I spoke of one such unit within the ego: the nonconflictual sphere":[534] the reader is more likely to have learned that it exists than that it is a "unit of functioning" on a par with "the counter-cathexes," "the dealings with reality," "the preconscious automatized patterns" and "the organizing function."[535]

238. But back to "ego functions." Instead of a definition, an allusion to one: "Ego functions have some . . . characteristics in common some of which I mentioned today, and which distinguish them from the id functions;[536] the latter, a rare expression; and no such function is, I believe, ever named.

239. Instead of an enumeration, a claim that it would be imprac-ticable. "A catalogue of ego functions would be rather long," explains Hartmann, "longer than a catalogue of functions of either the id or the superego." Little wonder that "no analyst has ever endeavoured a complete listing of ego functions," and that it is not "among the aims of my presentation to do so." In fact, "I shall mention only some of the most important ones."[537] Correspondingly, the authors limit themselves to recalling "our view which considers perception, thinking, defense, *and so on*, as functions of the ego";[538] and even when they merely envisage "those functions [of the ego] which make a stable balance of the agencies [ego and superego] possible," they continue: "*e.g.*, . . . [the] organizing function or . . . neutralization."[539]

240. Observing that if "a thought content can be cathected, . . . so can the activity of thinking," the authors, instead of simply ending a neglect of this capital and obvious point, present the advocacy of considering it as a notable advance: "We propose to make a distinction which promises to be helpful in clarifying a number of theoretical and clinical questions. . . . We expect that the approach to these questions will be facilitated if we follow a suggestion made by one of us (Hart-mann, 1953) in regard to the ego: we should differentiate contents and functions more clearly than is commonly done; in addition, it is advis-able to distinguish . . . the cathexes of contents from the cathexes of functions."[540]

241. "One set of ego functions among others" is to be called "ego interests."[541] "The group of tendencies which comprises strivings for what is 'useful,' egoism, self-assertion, *etc.*"—"these *and similar* tendencies" are named "ego interests";[542] "for instance, those concern-ed with social status, influence, professional success, wealth, comfort

and so forth."[543] That is, tendencies whose "aims center around one's own person."[544]

I have not found any hypothesis about them.

242. There are "ego apparatuses," never defined. They seem to be a class not overlapping with "ego functions": Defense mechanisms may be patterned after preliminary stages of ego functions "*and*" after processes characteristic of the ego apparatus;[545] self-preservation is based on the interaction of ego functions, "*but also*" on that of ego apparatus;[546] a number of functions of the ego "*related to*" the apparatus at its disposal develop largely outside of psychic conflict.[547]

243. Apparatuses are seldom named. "The image of the body, one of the apparatuses of the ego. . . ."[548]

244. The influence of maturation as against development, the authors seem to suggest at one point, is higher for the ego apparatus than for the nonapparatus ego: "In . . . [the ego's] growth . . . maturational factors [are] operating most clearly . . . where the apparatuses are concerned . . ."[549]—a sentence that my lack of knowledge about what "apparatus" designates prevents me from examining.

245. At the beginning of life, the authors explain, the maturation of apparatuses that serve motility, perception, and thought "proceeds without the total organization we call ego": "Only after ego formation will these functions be fully integrated."[550] That is, only when they are that, only when there is—presumably a synonym—a "total organization" of which these functions are elements, only then, according to an implicit and here revealed definition, do the authors agree to speak of "ego": a central word that should have an exacting sense. At other times the desire to make the ego coeval with the id wins out over the wish to render it finely structured; then the authors recall that if "the superego 'has not been there from the beginning' (Freud)," "the instinctual drives and the ego have."[551] There remains, behind the tautology cited at the beginning of the preceding paragraph, the truism that whatever "ego" elements, or forestages thereof, the neonate has, are little "integrated," and usually become more so with the passage of time.

38 | The Ego Is Powerful

246. "For a considerable time," the authors observe about an individual's predispositions to meet crucial situations, "the reference to the instinctual demands dominated the discussion of these predispositions." With regard to "the capacities" with which an individual is equipped in coping with pressures, "there is no hesitation to refer [to them] in clinical descriptions," but "this point of view is . . . new in theoretical discussions."[552]

247. The liberation from the classical prejudice against "capacities" is accompanied by the emancipation from the classical preference for pathology: if "it has long since been recognized what the study of the normal owes to pathology," "it is also true that in order to understand neurosis . . . we have to understand . . . the healthy person . . ."[553]

248. In theory, too, where id was, ego shall be. Displacement, a redirection of drive? Rather "a . . . form of learning. It widens the child's experience and is a . . . basis on which the integration and differentiation of experiences may be built."[554]

249. Sentences for which it is difficult to indicate by what clinical events they would be invalidated affirm the ego above other "systems." According to Hartmann the ego "might," presumably in distinctive fashion, "find energies of the id or the superego *at its disposal*." For instance, "action will frequently *draw on* the energy *reservoir* of the other . . . units of personality":[555] Just how would patients have to behave for this assertion to be false?

259

250. One of the "formulations . . . [that] would have been unthinkable on the basis of the preceding theory," Hartmann affirms, concerns "the *relation* of the pleasure and reality principles":[556] an allusion, presumably, to the circumstance that the term "an act conforming to the reality principle" designates, among other things, an act of anticipation, that is, in Hartmann's *language,* the exercise of an "ego function."

251. "Differences in intellectual development, in motor development and so on," Hartmann claims, "affect the child's coping with conflict." That is, common sense and nonanalytic psychiatry have, in this regard, not been proved wrong? Rather, "in our clinical work we observe daily how" this is so[557] without, however, hypotheses about the "how," being advanced. But has this not been *observed* in *clinical* work for decades, even in extreme anti-ego times? Surely, but only now can it be *talked about* in *"theory"*—and, as I noted above, with pride about advance rather than with dismay about delay. In the same way the authors discover (for "theory") that the degree of maturity (autonomy) that the child's ego has reached at the time his superego is formed "appears to be relevant" for that formation, where only the opposite— that it has turned out to be irrelevant—would be worth saying if one were less moved to declare liberation from classical prejudice. "More specifically," the authors continue, the level of development of the intellect and of language, "for instance," "must be considered": There are "relations" between the auditory sphere and the superego (but what new insights into them have we gained recently? And do they, whatever may have *caused* their discovery, have "theoretical" *premises* in "ego psychology"?); the capacity for self-observation is a "precondition" (by definition, perhaps?) of superego development; and the degree of objectivation achieved in inner and outer perception and in thinking an "essential factor" behind it:[558] perhaps, again, not by virtue of a recently discovered law of nature, but rather in view of the habitually entertained meaning of the term "superego development"?

252. The incorporation into theory of the evident (and capital) may induce formulations that hover between common sense, in a weak meaning, and radical revision of analysis in a strong one. A person's stability and effectiveness, observes Hartmann, are affected not only by the plasticity or strength of drive, the tolerance for tension, "etc." It is rather by "the *purposive* coordination and rank-order of functions . . . *within* the ego" that they are "*decisively* influenced": There is "*primacy of the regulation by intelligence.*"[559] Has reason regained the dominion it lost in the nineties?

39 | The Ego Is Also Harmonious

253. With reason advancing, conflict recedes. Proclaiming that the classical neglect of nonconflict has ceased— "the description of a country . . . includes besides its . . . wars . . . its peacetime traffic across the border ... the peaceful development of its populace, economy, social structure, administration, etc."[560] Hartmann implicitly attributes to predecessors the affirmation that nonconflict does not occur: "*Not every* adaptation to the environment, or every learning and maturation process, is a conflict." Confronting the prejudice that everything is, it becomes appropriate to enumerate (incompletely) the denied manifold: "I refer to the development *outside of conflict* [underlined in the text— N.L.] of perception, intention, object comprehension, thinking, language, recall phenomena, productivity, to the . . . phases of motor development, grasping, crawling, walking. . . ."[561]

254. Statements about the conflict-free sphere mostly affirm that it is vast and powerful; that insight into it should be gained; that it is being gained (not presented). Hartmann calls attention to "the conflict-free sphere's contributions to . . . defense (and resistance), its contributions to the displacement of the aims of instinctual drives, and so on."[562] He observes that "not only the 'negative' aspect of the ego . . . but also many other . . . ego functions . . . become . . . a . . . concern of the analyst."[563] He declares that "we are interested in what manner and what extent . . . defense . . . [is] regulated by those ego functions which are not . . . involved in . . . conflict."[564] He suggests that "the . . . study of . . . psychoses . . . must . . . take into account . . . [the] conflict-free

sphere"; "none of these problems can be completely resolved in terms of instinctual drive and conflict."[565]

255. As to particular points, all I have noted is the hypothesis that "the shift of energy from one ego function to another one seems easier achieved among the nondefensive functions":[566] Defense is stickier than nondefense?

40 | The Ego Procures Pleasure

256. While ego functions do inhibit gratifications of instinctual needs, "the ego," the authors observe, "can", in addition, "indicate the way to aggressive action against the outside world":[567] a statement that might not have been felt worth making if it could not contain "ego". (The decline of libido in relation to aggression is expressed in the fact that there is no parallel assertion about it being guided by the ego.)

257. Discontinuing yet another classical neglect, or liberating oneself from a further prejudice of earlier times, one discovers that for the developing child "the mastery of difficulties, the solving of problems becomes a novel source of delight. . . . Thinking itself yields gratification."[568] One recalls that Freud himself "repeatedly commented on the advantages the ego provides for instinctual gratification"[569]—perhaps not radically inferior to those furnished by the id?

258. *The pleasure from the functioning of the ego compensates, in part, for the loss of pleasure from the result of its functioning, which thus becomes acceptable* (a valuable point, it seems to me): As "organized thought and action, in which postponement is of the essence, can become a source of pleasure,"[570] "the potentialities of pleasure gain . . . play a paramount role in the acceptance of the reality principle."[571]

262

259. *It may not be the ardent drives that press the cautious ego, but the lively ego that quickens the sluggish drives* (an interesting case): "Ego functions . . . often . . . exert an appeal . . . on their . . . determinants."[572]

260. The "developmentally important role" of the child's enjoyment in the exercise of a recently learned function, Hartmann surmises, can be traced partly to the fact that through maturation and learning "a series of apparatus in the nonconflictual sphere of the ego . . . become available" to the child:[573] having received pleasure from something the child has recently become capable of learning is an incentive for it to learn what becomes accessible to it next?

41 | The Ego Is Distant From Drive

261. There are, Hartmann declares, "gradations" in the neutralization of energy, i.e., gradations of the extent to which energy retains characteristics of sexuality or aggression.[574] In fact there are "*many shades*" of this kind,[575] or rather, "*any number*" of transitional states between full and zero neutralization,[576] a "*continuum*" from fully instinctual to fully neutralized energy:[577] To that "probability," in fact, "both clinical experience and theory point,"[578] a convergence on which no details are given.

262. In this infinity Hartmann singles out four points, formulated with regard to aggression, but presumably obtaining also for libido.[579] In ascending order of neutralization: the "unmitigated" drive; the aggression the superego uses toward the ego (it is classical that this

aggression is close to drive); that which the ego uses toward drives (it is equally classical that this aggression is farther from drive than the preceding one); and the aggression in nondefensive ego activities, showing the "highest" degree of neutralization.[580]

263. Classical points about sublimation (of libido) are, according to the authors, equally true for neutralization (of libido and aggression). While an increase in the ego's "neutralized" cathexes is, Hartmann observes, not likely to cause pathological phenomena, its being swamped by "insufficiently neutralized instinctual energy" may have this effect; and this is "equally true where not libidinal, but aggressive cathexes are being turned back . . . upon the self. . . ."[581] The "nature" of "good object relations" is, Hartmann advances, "neutralized,"[582] rather than sublimated. "Sexualization *or aggressivization* [that is, deneutralization —N.L.]" of ego functions leads to their disturbance,[583] while it is "neutralization" rather than sublimation, that plays a "decisive part" in the mastery of reality.[584]

264. Some activities are usually farther removed from drives than others: "different degrees of neutralization are commonly provided for different ego functions."[585] "It seems that the ability for *higher* mental functions is dependent . . . on the *degree* to which the ego's . . . cathexis is neutralized."[586] (Or is it that we *say* that the latter is "neutralized highly" when an ability of the kind mentioned is high?) An executioner is apt to be cruder in his aggression than a legislator: "it is not unlikely that the direction-giving function of the superego works with a higher degree of neutralization of aggression than its enforcing function."[587] You may be more or less ferocious in serving given ideals: The authors note "the possibility that there exist variations, partly independent of the contents, in the mode of energy used by the superego."[588]

265. Reaffirming the classical point that the superego's cathexis is in part derived from aggression, the authors seem to suggest that the presence of the word "neutralized" in their formulation makes their assertion different; but they do not indicate in what respect. "*It is well-known*," they recall, "that . . . *modified* aggression is used by the superego."[589] As if they were making a different point, the authors observe that "we are inclined to consider the contribution of *neutralized* aggressive energy to the . . . superego to be at least as important as that of libido."[590]

266. More particularly, the authors hint that prior to the discovery of "neutralization" all internalization of aggression was affirmed to be "self-destructive." Now we know better: "Self-destruction is not the only alternative to aggression being turned outward; neutralization is another alternative";[591] "not all internalized aggression leads the way to destruction of the self,"[592] though when aggressive energy is internalized "without neutralization," "the incentive to some kind of self-

destruction may [sic] exist."[593] "*We may venture to say*," the authors declare, that if in the balance between libido and aggression a shift toward aggression takes place, such a shift need not necessarily interfere with the individual's emotional stability:[594] as it was, by implication, believed before "neutralization" was discovered. We are not told whether analysts at that time were aware of expecting more pathology than occurred.

267. The ego's cathexis, the authors affirm, is largely neutralized aggression; and the latter is largely ego cathexis. While the authors do not deny the presence of sublimated libido in the ego's cathexis, they are not apt to talk about it.

Stressing the novelty of the affirmation that the ego is supplied with neutralized aggression, the authors show that when outer frustration provokes aggression that cannot be discharged, it may be used in the ego's countercathexes (defenses) against the drives; and this explains "clinical observations . . . (which) seem to indicate that the increase of guilt, as a consequence of frustration, while . . . often observable, is not a regular occurrence."[595] We are (as I said in the preceding paragraph), not told whether these observations began to be made but recently, and, if so, why; whether the earlier belief that in the conditions indicated guilt always arises had prevented their being made; whether earlier analysts had been aware of a discrepancy between expectations and observations.

268. In schizophrenia, affirms Hartmann, there is but a low capacity to "shift" neutralized energy to the point where it is "needed":[596] There is no indication of the types of clinical observations that render this assertion "probable."[597]

269. Having called a low level of neutralization of ego cathexis (which he assumes for schizophrenia) "dedifferentiation" of ego, Hartmann proceeds from this unusual meaning to a customary one by speaking about "differentiated" object relations in contrast to "incomplete demarcation or fusion" between self and object, as well as between ego and id. Conferring three implicit definitions upon the same word permits suggesting a hypothesis for which evidence is not brought forward. "This *dedifferentiation* of the ego [the low level of neutralization of its cathexis—N.L.]", the author starts out, "*means* that . . . *differentiated* . . . object relations . . . and [sic] . . . objectivation . . . can no longer be maintained; in their place we find incomplete demarcation or fusion of self and object, and lack of *differentiation* also between ego and id."[598] All three levels envisaged—that of the ego's capacity to neutralize aggression, that of demarcation between self and nonself and that of delimitation between ego and id—are, one would indeed expect, rising with the passage of time in normal developments; which makes it possible to suggest, without declaring the hypothesis, that an

increase in the first is a *condition* for an enhancement of the second and third. The suggestion once conveyed with the help of a transitory triple meaning of "dedifferentiation," one may abolish that very dedifferentiation in the designation of events: "Speaking of reality testing, I said before [in the passage just discussed—N.L.], that its *dedifferentiation . . .* may be related to *deneutralization.*"[599]

270. *If the schizophrenic's capacity to neutralize energy is low*—perhaps by heredity[600]—*and if the psyche has certain other properties ascribed to it by the authors' constructs* and mentioned in the preceding paragraphs of this section, *then*—as the authors point out—*various characteristics of schizophrenia* (elements, I would add, of that word's definition, *or* events correlated with its referent) *are "explained"* (a valuable point, I would believe):

1. As *defenses* are cathected with neutralized energy, they will in the schizophrenic be *weak in relation to drives* (amounts of energy will remain on the side of the drives instead of weakening it and reinforcing the side of the defenses), "which describes . . . what we . . . find in schizophrenia."[601]
2. *The superego will be cruel.*[602]
3. *The superego will be weak,* "endowed with . . . little power to enforce its commands," given (1) and the fact that it is "defenses on whose function the enforcement of superego commands depends."[603]
4. *Libido detachment*—one of the defenses that "demand a lesser degree of neutralization"—*will "prevail."*[604]

However, what has to be "assumed" in order to "explain" these four phenomena, is, in contrast to the authors' assertions (1) not that the capacity to neutralize *aggressive* energy is impaired, but that the power to deinstinctualize *energy* is limited; (2) not that "[the] process of neutralization takes places *through mediation of the ego,*"[605] but that, wherever it takes places, it is *impaired.*

271. Considering the possibility of a covariation between (1) the capacity to neutralize aggression, and (2) the fusion of "residual" aggression and libido, the authors observe that "it is suggestive to assume" such a relationship:[606] Here an "assumption" is already "suggestive" when it "explains" *one* event (the difference between schizophrenics and others with regard to the fusion in question) rather than *more than one,* as in the preceding paragraph.

42 | A First Balance Sheet

272. Previous knowledge of "ego functions" was, Hartmann recalls, "somewhat shadowy";[607] Freud's study of them in *Two Principles of Mental Functioning* (1911) was "not yet . . . in the framework of the set of propositions which we call ego psychology today."[608]

Since then "a more differentiated knowledge of the development and the functions of the ego has evolved";[609] we can now, on many an occasion, proceed "in a direction which will enable us to penetrate more deeply into the realm of ego theory."[610] In fact, "ego psychology" has reached a "new level,"[611] there has been a "vast broadening" of insights,[612] and "new vistas have opened up."[613] "Our knowledge of the complexity . . . of human motivation . . . has come to a point at which . . . it has become as difficult of access to most nonspecialists as are the later developments of the physical sciences."[614]

273. Throughout the preceding pages I have italicized those acquisitions that appear valuable to me. They occur in:

Paragraph 62: An inference that the authors might have drawn concerning aggression upon being interrupted

Paragraph 63: The potential for pathology of aggression as against libido

Paragraph 258: Pleasure in functioning and the reality principle

Paragraph 259: The ego stimulating drives

Paragraph 270: Sequels to the impairment of the capacity to neutralize in schizophrenia.

Notes to Part Three

1. Heinz Hartmann, Ernst Kris, and Rudolph M. Loewenstein, *Papers on Psychoanalytic Psychology* (New York: International Universities Press, 1964), p. 76.
2. Heinz Hartmann, *Psychoanalysis and Moral Values* (New York: International Universities Press, 1960), p. 30.
3. Hartmann *et al.*, p. 136.
4. *Ibid.*, p. 37.
5. *Ibid.*, p. 7.
6. *Ibid.*, p. 71.
7. Heinz Hartmann, *Essays on Ego Psychology: Selected Problems in Psychoanalytic Theory* (New York: International Universities Press, 1964), p. 192.
8. *Ibid.*, p. 201.
9. *Ibid.*, p. 60.
10. *Ibid.*, p. 82.
11. *Ibid.*, p. 295.
12. Hartmann *et al.*, p. 152.
13. Hartmann, *Essays*, p. x.
14. *Ibid.*
15. Hartmann *et al.*, p. 142.
16. Hartmann, *Essays*, p. xii.
17. *Ibid.*, p. 72.
18. Hartmann *et al.*, p. 138.
19. *Ibid.*, p. 140.
20. Hartmann, *Essays*, p. 198.
21. Hartmann *et al.*, p. 136.
22. Hartmann, *Essays*, p. 315.
23. Hartmann *et al.*, p. 134.
24. *Ibid.*, p. 129.
25. *Ibid.*
26. *Ibid.*
27. *Ibid.*, p. 88.
28. *Ibid.*
29. *Ibid.*, p. 134.
30. *Ibid.*
31. *Ibid.*
32. *Ibid.*, p. 88.
33. *Ibid.*, pp. 134–135.
34. Hartmann, *Essays*, p. 291.
35. Hartmann *et al.*, p. 143.
36. Heinz Hartmann, *Ego Psychology and the Problem of Adaptation* (New York: International Universities Press, 1958), p. 6.

37. Hartmann *et al.*, p. 133.
38. *Ibid.*, pp. 129–130.
39. Hartmann, *Essays*, p. 319.
40. Hartmann *et al.*, p. 88.
41. *Ibid.*, p. 130.
42. *Ibid.*
43. Hartmann, *Essays*, p. 320.
44. *Ibid.*, p. 301.
45. *Ibid.*, p. 320.
46. Hartmann *et al.*, p. 132.
47. Hartmann, *Essays*, p. 175.
48. *Ibid.*, p. 66.
49. *Ibid.*, pp. 177–178.
50. *Ibid.*, p. xii.
51. *Ibid.*, p. 142.
52. *Ibid.*, p. x.
53. *Ibid.*, p. 100.
54. *Ibid.*, p. 105.
55. Hartmann *et al.*, p. 152.
56. Hartmann, *Essays*, pp. 64–66.
57. *Ibid.*, p. 226.
58. Hartmann *et al.*, p. 159.
59. Hartmann, *Essays*, p. 152.
60. Hartmann, *Ego Psychology*, pp. 67, 71.
61. Hartmann, *Essays*, p. 93.
62. Hartmann *et al.*, p. 158.
63. *Ibid.*, p. 140.
64. Hartmann, *Essays*, p. xii.
65. Hartmann *et al.*, p. 164.
66. Hartmann, *Essays*, p. 192.
67. Hartmann *et al.*, p. 169.
68. *Ibid.*, p. 124.
69. Hartmann, *Essays*, p. 171.
70. Hartmann *et al.*, p. 147.
71. *Ibid.*, pp. 147–148.
72. *Ibid.*, p. 95.
73. Hartmann, *Essays*, p. 146.
74. Hartmann *et al.*, p. 89.
75. *Ibid.*, pp. 99–100.
76. *Ibid.*, p. 161.
77. *Ibid.*, p. 172.
78. Hartmann, *Essays*, pp. 165–166.
79. Hartmann *et al.*, p. 179.
80. *Ibid.*, p. 83.

81. Hartmann, *Essays*, p. 159.
82. Hartmann, *Ego Psychology*, p. 16.
83. Hartmann, *Essays*, p. 12.
84. *Ibid.*, p. 94.
85. *Ibid.*, p. 105.
86. Hartmann, *Ego Psychology*, p. 88.
87. Hartmann, *Essays*, p. 81.
88. *Ibid.*, p. 88.
89. *Ibid.*, p. 119.
90. *Ibid.*, p. 14.
91. Hartmann *et al.*, p. 137.
92. *Ibid.*, p. 134.
93. Hartmann, *Essays*, p. 157.
94. *Ibid.*, p. 123.
95. *Ibid.*, pp. 316–317.
96. *Ibid.*, p. x.
97. Hartmann *et al.*, p. 135.
98. *Ibid.*, pp. 35–36.
99. *Ibid.*, p. 168.
100. *Ibid.*
101. *Ibid.*, p. 160.
102. *Ibid.*, p. 159.
103. *Ibid.*, pp. 130–131.
104. Hartmann, *Ego Psychology*, p. 25.
105. Hartmann, *Essays*, p. 15.
106. Hartmann *et al.*, pp. 145–146.
107. *Ibid.*, p. 131.
108. Hartmann, *Essays*, pp. 110–111.
109. Hartmann *et al.*, p. 153.
110. *Ibid.*, p. 152.
111. Hartmann, *Essays*, p. 176.
112. Hartmann *et al.*, p. 76.
113. *Ibid.*, p. 179.
114. *Ibid.*, p. 169.
115. Hartmann, *Essays*, p. 231.
116. *Ibid.*, p. 203.
117. Hartmann *et al.*, p. 76.
118. *Ibid.*
119. Hartmann, *Ego Psychology*, p. 95.
120. Hartmann *et al.*, p. 168.
121. *Ibid.*, p. 153.
122. *Ibid.*, p. 156.
123. *Ibid.*, p. 40.
124. Hartmann, *Essays*, p. 106.

125. *Ibid.*, pp. 174–175.
126. *Ibid.*, p. 170.
127. *Ibid.*, p. 125.
128. *Ibid.*, p. 175.
129. *Ibid.*, p. 61.
130. Hartmann *et al.*, p. 160.
131. *Ibid.*, p. 37.
132. *Ibid.*, p. 119.
133. *Ibid.*, p. 122.
134. Hartmann, *Essays*, p. 5.
135. *Ibid.*, p. 71.
136. *Ibid.*, p. 344.
137. *Ibid.*, p. 126.
138. *Ibid.*, p. 74.
139. Hartmann *et al.*, pp. 119–120.
140. *Ibid.*, p. 36.
141. Hartmann, *Essays*, pp. 133–134.
142. *Ibid.*, pp. 132–133.
143. Hartmann *et al.*, p. 81.
144. Hartmann, *Essays*, p. 134.
145. Hartmann *et al.*, p. 122.
146. *Ibid.*, p. 39.
147. *Ibid.*, p. 79.
148. *Ibid.*, p. 145.
149. *Ibid.*, p. 94.
150. *Ibid.*, p. 140.
151. *Ibid.*, p. 141.
152. Hartmann, *Essays*, p. 79.
153. *Ibid.*, p. 192.
154. *Ibid.*, pp. 228–229.
155. *Ibid.*, p. 129.
156. *Ibid.*, p. 84.
157. *Ibid.*, p. 126.
158. *Ibid.*, p. 134.
159. *Ibid.*, p. 130.
160. *Ibid.*, p. 236.
161. Hartmann *et al.*, p. 39.
162. Hartmann, *Essays*, p. 305.
163. *Ibid.*, p. 190.
164. *Ibid.*, p. 171.
165. *Ibid.*, p. xiv.
166. *Ibid.*, p. 128.
167. *Ibid.*, p. 194.
168. Hartmann *et al.*, p. 174.

169. Hartmann, *Essays*, p. 41.
170. Hartmann *et al.*, p. 37.
171. *Ibid.*, p. 169.
172. Hartmann, *Essays*, p. 170.
173. *Ibid.*, p. 196.
174. *Ibid.*, p. 170.
175. *Ibid.*, p. 175.
176. *Ibid.*, pp. 137–138.
177. Hartmann *et al.*, p. 94.
178. *Ibid.*, p. 89.
179. *Ibid.*, p. 47.
180. Hartmann, *Essays*, p. 137.
181. Hartmann *et al.*, p. 42.
182. Hartmann, *Essays*, p. 305.
183. Hartmann *et al.*, p. 77.
184. Hartmann, *Essays*, p. 171.
185. *Ibid.*, p. xii.
186. *Ibid.*, pp. 171–172.
187. Hartmann *et al.*, p. 63.
188. Hartmann, *Essays*, pp. 175–176.
189. Hartmann *et al.*, p. 174.
190. Hartmann, *Essays*, p. 196.
191. *Ibid.*, p. 132.
192. *Ibid.*, p. 175.
193. *Ibid.*, p. 234.
194. *Ibid.*, pp. 132–133.
195. *Ibid.*, pp. 131–132.
196. Hartmann *et al.*, p. 35.
197. Hartmann, *Essays*, p. 204.
198. *Ibid.*, pp. 152–153.
199. Hartmann *et al.*, p. 151.
200. Hartmann, *Essays*, p. 132.
201. Hartmann, *Ego Psychology*, p. 107.
202. *Ibid.*, pp. 15–16.
203. Hartmann *et al.*, p. 179.
204. Hartmann, *Essays*, p. 241.
205. Hartmann *et al.*, p. 76.
206. Hartmann, *Essays*, p. 105.
207. Hartmann *et al.*, p. 161.
208. Hartmann, *Essays*, p. xiii.
209. Cf. Hartmann *et al.*, p. 75, paragraph 2.
210. *Ibid.*, paragraph 3.
211. *Ibid.*, pp. 141–142.
212. Hartmann, *Ego Psychology*, p. 80.

213. Hartmann, *Essays*, p. 244.
214. *Ibid.*, p. 84.
215. *Ibid.*, p. 227.
216. *Ibid.*, p. 238.
217. *Ibid.*, p. 166.
218. Hartmann *et al.*, p. 161.
219. Cf. *ibid.*, pp. 161–165.
220. Hartmann, *Essays*, pp. 234–235.
221. *Ibid.*, p. 178.
222. Hartmann, *Ego Psychology*, p. 98.
223. Hartmann, *Essays*, p. 83.
224. Hartmann *et al.*, p. 161.
225. Hartmann, *Essays*, pp. 15–16.
226. Hartmann *et al.*, p. 160.
227. Hartmann, *Essays*, p. 287.
228. Hartmann, *Ego Psychology*, p. 60.
229. Hartmann, *Essays*, p. 61.
230. *Ibid.*, p. 287.
231. *Ibid.*
232. *Ibid.*, p. 319.
233. *Ibid.*, p. 142.
234. Hartmann *et al.*, p. 76.
235. *Ibid.*, p. 23.
236. *Ibid.*, p. 167.
237. Hartmann, *Essays*, p. 49.
238. *Ibid.*, p. 61.
239. *Ibid.*, p. 192.
240. *Ibid.*, p. 327.
241. *Ibid.*, p. 139.
242. Hartmann *et al.*, p. 142.
243. Hartmann, *Essays*, p. 16.
244. *Ibid.*, p. 237.
245. *Ibid.*, p. 231.
246. Hartmann, *Ego Psychology*, p. 93.
247. *Ibid.*, pp. 80–81.
248. Hartmann, *Essays*, pp. 216–217.
249. *Ibid.*, p. 224.
250. Hartmann *et al.*, p. 146.
251. Hartmann, *Essays*, pp. 216–217, 223.
252. *Ibid.*, p. 225.
253. *Ibid.*, pp. 225–226.
254. *Ibid.*, p. 192.
255. *Ibid.*, p. 70.
256. *Ibid.*, p. 157.

257. *Ibid.*, p. 70.
258. *Ibid.*, pp. 70–71.
259. *Ibid.*, p. 140.
260. Hartmann, *Ego Psychology*, p. 76.
261. Hartmann, *Essays*, pp. 135–136.
262. *Ibid.*, p. 81.
263. *Ibid.*, p. 190.
264. Hartmann *et al.*, p. 167.
265. Hartmann, *Essays*, p. 44.
266. Hartmann *et al.*, p. 21.
267. Hartmann, *Essays*, p. 190.
268. Hartmann, *Ego Psychology*, p. 26.
269. Hartmann, *Essays*, p. 138.
270. *Ibid.*, p. 241.
271. *Ibid.*, p. 285.
272. Hartmann, *Ego Psychology*, p. 102.
273. Hartmann, *Essays*, p. 286.
274. *Ibid.*, p. 221.
275. Hartmann, *Ego Psychology*, p. 81.
276. Hartmann, *Essays*, pp. xii-xiii.
277. Hartmann *et al.*, p. 146.
278. Hartmann, *Ego Psychology*, p. 66.
279. Hartmann, *Essays*, pp. 140, 145, 146.
280. *Ibid.*, p. 14.
281. *Ibid.*, p. 225.
282. *Ibid.*, p. 224.
283. Hartmann, *Ego Psychology*, p. 16.
284. Hartmann, *Essays*, p. 18.
285. *Ibid.*, pp. 224–225.
286. *Ibid.*, p. 215.
287. *Ibid.*, p. 216.
288. *Ibid.*, p. 223.
289. *Ibid.*, p. 66.
290. *Ibid.*, pp. 3–4.
291. *Ibid.*, p. 51.
292. Hartmann *et al.*, p. 31.
293. Hartmann, *Essays*, pp. 217–218.
294. Hartmann, *Ego Psychology*, p. 81.
295. Hartmann, *Essays*, pp. 108–109.
296. Hartmann *et al.*, p. 51.
297. *Ibid.*, p. 157.
298. *Ibid.*, p. 84.
299. Hartmann, *Essays*, p. 133.
300. *Ibid.*, p. 94.

301. Hartmann *et al.*, p. 45.
302. Hartmann, *Essays*, p. 58.
303. Hartmann *et al.*, p. 175.
304. *Ibid.*, p. 45.
305. Hartmann, *Essays*, p. 177.
306. Hartmann, *Ego Psychology*, p. 70.
307. Hartmann, *Essays*, p. 171.
308. *Ibid.*, p. 202.
309. *Ibid.*
310. Hartmann *et al.*, p. 77.
311. Hartmann, *Essays*, p. 242.
312. Hartmann *et al.*, p. 166.
313. Hartmann, *Essays*, p. 225.
314. *Ibid.*, p. 40.
315. *Ibid.*, p. 190.
316. *Ibid.*, p. 135.
317. *Ibid.*, p. 194.
318. *Ibid.*, p. 58.
319. *Ibid.*, p. 134.
320. *Ibid.*, p. 187.
321. Hartmann *et al.*, p. 174.
322. Hartmann, *Essays*, p. 187.
323. Hartmann *et al.*, p. 142.
324. Hartmann, *Essays*, p. 201.
325. Hartmann, *Ego Psychology*, p. 23.
326. Hartmann *et al.*, p. 74.
327. *Ibid.*, pp. 37–38.
328. Hartmann, *Essays*, p. 48.
329. *Ibid.*, p. 199.
330. Hartmann *et al.*, p. 83.
331. *Ibid.*, p. 47.
332. *Ibid.*, p. 175.
333. *Ibid.*, p. 176.
334. *Ibid.*, pp. 175–176.
335. Hartmann, *Essays*, p. 123.
336. Hartmann *et al.*, p. 166.
337. Hartmann, *Essays*, pp. 41–42.
338. Hartmann *et al.*, pp. 16–17.
339. *Ibid.*, p. 163.
340. *Ibid.*
341. *Ibid.*, p. 169.
342. Hartmann, *Essays*, p. 17.
343. Hartmann *et al.*, p. 74.
344. *Ibid.*

345. Hartmann, *Essays*, pp. 217–218.
346. Hartmann, *Ego Psychology*, pp. 98–99.
347. Hartmann, *Essays*, p. 135.
348. *Ibid.*, p. 231.
349. *Ibid.*, p. 219.
350. *Ibid.*, pp. 13–14.
351. *Ibid.*, p. 219.
352. *Ibid.*, p. 67.
353. *Ibid.*, p. 42.
354. *Ibid.*, pp. 187–188.
355. Hartmann *et al.* p. 74.
356. Hartmann, *Essays*, p. 195.
357. Hartmann *et al.*, p. 83.
358. Hartmann, *Essays*, p. 13.
359. *Ibid.*, pp. 217–218.
360. *Ibid.*, p. 135.
361. Hartmann *et al.*, p. 74.
362. *Ibid.*, p. 160.
363. *Ibid.*, p. 20.
364. Hartmann, *Psychoanalysis and Moral Values*, pp. 32–33.
365. Hartmann, *Essays*, p. 56.
366. Hartmann *et al.*, p. 151.
367. Hartmann, *Essays*, p. 218.
368. Hartmann *et al.*, p. 43.
369. *Ibid.*, p. 44.
370. Hartmann, *Essays*, p. xi.
371. *Ibid.*, pp. 187–188.
372. *Ibid.*, p. 202.
373. Hartmann *et al.*, p. 177.
374. *Ibid.*, p. 147.
375. *Ibid.*, p. 158.
376. Hartmann, *Essays*, p. 63.
377. Hartmann *et al.*, p. 131.
378. Hartmann, *Essays*, p. 176.
379. Hartmann *et al.*, p. 155.
380. *Ibid.*, p. 45.
381. Hartmann, *Essays*, p. 166.
382. Hartmann *et al.*, pp. 75–76.
383. *Ibid.*, p. 77.
384. *Ibid.*, p. 164.
385. *Ibid.*, p. 97.
386. *Ibid.*, p. 163.
387. *Ibid.*, p. 17.
388. Hartmann, *Essays*, p. 11.

389. *Ibid.*, pp. 149–150.
390. Hartmann *et al.*, p. 166.
391. *Ibid.*, p. 81.
392. Hartmann, *Essays*, p. xiii.
393. Hartmann *et al.*, p. 83.
394. *Ibid.*, p. 45.
395. Hartmann, *Essays*, pp. 176–177.
396. *Ibid.*, p. 178.
397. Hartmann *et al.*, p. 31.
398. *Ibid.*, p. 39.
399. Hartmann, *Essays*, p. 40.
400. Hartmann *et al.*, pp. 170–171.
401. *Ibid.*, p. 164.
402. Hartmann, *Essays*, p. 84.
403. *Ibid.*, p. 39.
404. *Ibid.*, pp. 39–40.
405. Hartmann, *Ego Psychology*, p. 82.
406. *Ibid.*
407. Hartmann *et al.*, p. 77.
408. *Ibid.*, p. 175.
409. *Ibid.*, p. 61.
410. Hartmann, *Essays*, p. 115.
411. Hartmann *et al.*, pp. 142–143.
412. *Ibid.*, pp. 91–92.
413. Hartmann, *Essays*, p. 192.
414. *Ibid.*, pp. 149–150.
415. Hartmann *et al.*, p. 16.
416. *Ibid.*, p. 78.
417. Hartmann, *Essays*, pp. 39–40.
418. Hartmann *et al.*, p. 158.
419. *Ibid.*, p. 81.
420. Hartmann, *Essays*, p. 94.
421. Hartmann *et al.*, p. 164.
422. Hartmann, *Ego Psychology*, p. 82.
423. Hartmann *et al.*, p. 70.
424. *Ibid.*, pp. 77–78.
425. *Ibid.*, p. 41.
426. *Ibid.*, p. 76.
427. *Ibid.*, pp. 159–160.
428. *Ibid.*, p. 40.
429. *Ibid.*, pp. 148–149.
430. *Ibid.*, p. 174.
431. *Ibid.*, p. 89.
432. Hartmann, *Essays*, p. xi.

433. Hartmann *et al.*, pp. 159–160.
434. *Ibid.*, p. 177.
435. *Ibid.*, pp. 177–178.
436. Hartmann, *Ego Psychology*, pp. 93–94.
437. Hartmann *et al.*, pp. 84–85.
438. *Ibid.*, p. 174.
439. *Ibid.*, pp. 131–132.
440. *Ibid.*, p. 97.
441. *Ibid.*, p. 77.
442. Hartmann, *Essays*, p. 165.
443. Hartmann *et al.*, p. 95.
444. *Ibid.*, pp. 157–158.
445. Hartmann, *Essays*, p. 61.
446. Hartmann *et al.*, p. 35.
447. *Ibid.*, p. 154.
448. *Ibid.*, p. 90.
449. Hartmann, *Essays*, p. 163.
450. *Ibid.*, pp. 132–133.
451. *Ibid.*, p. 202.
452. Hartmann *et al.*, p. 156.
453. Hartmann, *Essays*, p. 172.
454. *Ibid.*, pp. 83–84.
455. Hartmann *et al.*, p. 77.
456. Hartmann, *Essays*, p. 43.
457. *Ibid.*, p. 202.
458. Hartmann *et al.*, p. 77.
459. Hartmann, *Essays*, p. 137.
460. Hartmann *et al.*, p. 147.
461. *Ibid.*, p. 82.
462. *Ibid.*, p. 43.
463. Hartmann, *Essays*, p. 283.
464. Hartmann *et al.*, p. 160.
465. Hartmann, *Essays*, pp. 146–147.
466. Hartmann *et al.*, pp. 161–162.
467. *Ibid.*, p. 159.
468. Hartmann, *Ego Psychology*, p. 60.
469. Hartmann, *Essays*, p. 173.
470. *Ibid.*, p. 291.
471. Hartmann, *Psychoanalysis and Moral Values*, p. 30.
472. Hartmann *et al.*, p. 162.
473. Hartmann, *Essays*, p. 135.
474. *Ibid.*, p. 292.
475. *Ibid.*, p. 114.
476. Hartmann, *Psychoanalysis and Moral Values*, pp. 50–51.

477. Hartmann, *Ego Psychology*, p. 60.
478. Hartmann, *Essays*, pp. 119–120.
479. *Ibid.*
480. *Ibid.*, p. 167.
481. *Ibid.*, pp. 250–251.
482. Hartmann, *Ego Psychology*, p. 15.
483. Hartmann, *Essays*, pp. 119–120.
484. *Ibid.*, p. 250.
485. *Ibid.*, p. 105.
486. *Ibid.*, p. 167.
487. *Ibid.*
488. *Ibid.*, pp. 167–168.
489. *Ibid.*, p. 121.
490. *Ibid.*, p. 119.
491. *Ibid.*, pp. 250–251.
492. *Ibid.*, p. 170.
493. *Ibid.*, p. 40.
494. *Ibid.*, p. 169.
495. *Ibid.*
496. *Ibid.*, pp. 120–121.
497. *Ibid.*, pp. 242–243.
498. Hartmann *et al.*, p. 131.
499. *Ibid.*
500. Hartmann, *Essays*, p. 121.
501. Hartmann *et al.*, p. 39.
502. Hartmann, *Essays*, p. 123.
503. *Ibid.*, pp. 176–177.
504. *Ibid.*, p. 176.
505. *Ibid.*, p. 177.
506. *Ibid.*, pp. 176–177.
507. Hartmann *et al.*, p. 21.
508. Hartmann, *Essays*, p. 115.
509. *Ibid.*, p. 218.
510. *Ibid.*, p. 167.
511. *Ibid.*, p. 219.
512. *Ibid.*, p. 177.
513. *Ibid.*, p. 122.
514. Hartmann *et al.*, p. 166.
515. Hartmann, *Essays*, p. 230.
516. *Ibid.*, p. 218.
517. *Ibid.*, p. 177.
518. Hartmann *et al.*, p. 142.
519. Hartmann, *Essays*, p. 229.
520. *Ibid.*

521. Hartmann *et al.*, p. 95.
522. Hartmann, *Essays*, p. 230.
523. Cf. *ibid.*, pp. xiii-xiv, 194.
524. Hartmann *et al.*, p. 95.
525. *Ibid.*, p. 152.
526. Hartmann, *Essays*, p. 190.
527. *Ibid.*, p. 229.
528. *Ibid.*, p. 230.
529. Hartmann *et al.*, pp. 36, 37.
530. Hartmann, *Essays*, p. 130.
531. *Ibid.*, p. 236.
532. *Ibid.*, p. xiv.
533. Hartmann *et al.*, p. 21.
534. Hartmann, *Essays*, p. 145.
535. *Ibid.*
536. *Ibid.*, p. 139.
537. *Ibid.*, p. 114.
538. Hartmann *et al.*, p. 162.
539. *Ibid.*, p. 179.
540. *Ibid.*, p. 158.
541. Hartmann, *Essays*, p. 66.
542. *Ibid.*, pp. 135–136.
543. *Ibid.*, p. 64.
544. *Ibid.*, p. 136.
545. *Ibid.*, p. 124.
546. *Ibid.*, p. 61.
547. Hartmann *et al.*, p. 21.
548. *Ibid.*, p. 97.
549. *Ibid.*, p. 91.
550. *Ibid.*, p. 36.
551. *Ibid.*, p. 175.
552. *Ibid.*, p. 21.
553. Hartmann, *Essays*, p. 293.
554. *Ibid.*, p. 172.
555. *Ibid.*, p. 41.
556. *Ibid.*, p. 292.
557. Hartmann, *Ego Psychology*, p. 16.
558. Hartmann *et al.*, pp. 148–149.
559. Hartmann, *Ego Psychology*, p. 56.
560. *Ibid.*, p. 11.
561. *Ibid.*, p. 8.
562. *Ibid.*, p. 9.
563. Hartmann, *Essays*, pp. 158–159.
564. Hartmann, *Ego Psychology*, p. 15.

565. *Ibid.*, p. 10.
566. Hartmann, *Essays*, p. 233.
567. *Ibid.*, p. 84.
568. Hartmann *et al.*, p. 48.
569. Hartmann, *Essays*, pp. 244–245.
570. *Ibid.*
571. *Ibid.*, p. 84.
572. *Ibid.*, p. 177.
573. *Ibid.*, p. 83.
574. *Ibid.*, p. 129.
575. *Ibid.*, pp. 223–224.
576. *Ibid.*, p. 131.
577. *Ibid.*, pp. 223–224.
578. *Ibid.*, p. 228.
579. Cf. *ibid.*, p. 202.
580. *Ibid.*, p. 228.
581. *Ibid.*, pp. 129–130.
582. *Ibid.*, p. 199.
583. *Ibid.*, p. 192.
584. *Ibid.*, p. 235.
585. Hartmann *et al.*, p. 172.
586. *Ibid.*, p. 95.
587. *Ibid.*, pp. 172–173.
588. *Ibid.*, p. 175.
589. *Ibid.*, pp. 71–72.
590. *Ibid.*, p. 70.
591. Hartmann, *Essays*, p. 226.
592. Hartmann *et al.*, p. 71.
593. *Ibid.*, pp. 73–74.
594. *Ibid.*, p. 71.
595. *Ibid.*, p. 174.
596. Hartmann, *Essays*, p. 203.
597. *Ibid.*, p. 233.
598. *Ibid.*, p. 200.
599. *Ibid.*, p. 201.
600. Cf. *ibid.*, p. 204.
601. *Ibid.*, p. 198.
602. Hartmann *et al.*, p. 173.
603. *Ibid.*, p. 176.
604. Hartmann, *Essays*, p. 197.
605. *Ibid.*, p. 128.
606. Hartmann *et al.*, p. 70.
607. Hartmann, *Essays*, p. 149.
608. *Ibid.*, p. 241.

609. Hartmann *et al.*, p. 145.
610. Hartmann, *Essays*, p. 11.
611. *Ibid.*, p. 105.
612. *Ibid.*, p. 124.
613. Hartmann *et al.*, p. 101.
614. Hartmann, *Psychoanalysis and Moral Values*, p. 22.

Precis of Paragraphs

I: Identification

1. Sentences presenting definitions are rare.
2. An important word does, of course, have many meanings.
3. —and a significant class of events will be designated by more than one such word.
4. It is in passing that one may declare two major words to be synonymous.
5. When the opposite is suggested, the ease with which they may be regarded as synonyms after all allows one not to proceed on the hard path of differentiation.
6. Some implicit meanings could bear coming out into the open.
7. Others less so, as they fall outside of what is sensed as the word's domain.
8. —or, while remaining within it, are too weak for a respected word.
9. "Internal" images: you could omit the adjective.
10. "Internalized" images and "introjects": unconscious beliefs?
11. —or any belief?
12. Enjoy your concept and retain plain words.
13. Elucidations of words stopping short of presenting their definitions.
14. Claiming obscurity.
15. It is normal not to be sure what colleagues mean when using a major word, common between them and myself.

16. The referent of a major word can be approached only through analogies.

17. A concept should be rich.

18. Merely affirming that the various classes of events to be designated by the same word have something in common.

19. Words are interdependent.

20. Defining: the culmination of inquiry.

21. Inquiry may invalidate prior definitions.

22. Ensconcing hypotheses in definitions.

23. Definitions should be true.

24. Propositions are free.

25. There are limits to the power even of a concept.

26. You can cross it out.

27. Overcoming staleness of contention through freshness of words.

28. Proposing a strange language.

29. Designating a moderate event by a word suggesting an extreme one.

30. Merely affirming that there are relationships between major factors.

31. Avoiding a decision on a sentence, without ever beginning to indicate how it might be arrived at.

32. That the truth of an assertion follows from the meanings of words contained in it may become apparent when its demonstration is attempted.

33. Presenting an assertion about which one wonders whether it is not a tautology without sketching a world for which it would be false.

34. Qualifying a tautology as one might an assertion about the world.

35. Affirming about a tautology that it is derived from "theory" or "observation."

36. If it is not a tautology, it is wrong.

37. Designation into explanation.

38. Making an assertion safe by familiar-sounding words of unknown reference.

39. —or by the unrecognized obscurity of habitual concepts.

40. —by avoiding a claim of truth or falsehood.

41. Mutual aid between several meanings of an ambiguous word.

42. —a moderate meaning protecting an extreme one.

43. Suggesting that there is no "adoption" without "mingling."

44. Swinging between moderate and extreme meanings of an ambiguous word.

45. Combining words going in both directions.

46. Cathecting objects or their representations?

47. Preferring the inner to the outer.

48. Sheltering the affirmation that others are felt as within one.

49. Going from such an assertion about past relations to the same about present ones.

50. More on point 40.

51. The in-and-out movement of psychic particles.

52. A self being added onto another.

53. Insertion.

54. Metamorphosis.

55. Putting oneself into another's place.

56. The sense of sameness.

57. The sense of communion.

58. The sense of fusion.

59. Adoption.

60. Counteradoption.

61. Assimilation.

62. Adopting reactions toward oneself.

63. No adoption without mingling?

64. Stopping short of declaring this.

65. Taking it for granted.

66. Concluding at both adoption and mingling from the same evidence.

67. Leaving it obscure which characteristic qualifies for inclusion into the family of "identifications."

68. A proposal about words.

69. Damage-limitation by ceasing to employ abused words.

70. The use of broad words to designate domains of inquiry rather than to appear in hypotheses.

71. No identification without prior impairment of object relation?

72. The coexistence between identification and object relation taken for granted outside of "theory."

73. —while a problem there.

74. Identification without prior impairment of object relation.

75. Under what conditions does each of the possible relationships between identification and object relation obtain?

76. What are the relationships between the kind of striving abandoned and the kind of "junction" acquired?

77. Is the principal agent of prohibition always the principal target of identification?

II: Identity Arrives

1. Sentences presenting definitions are rare.
2. —which is made possible by the familiarity of the word.
3. One may merely allude to a definition.
4. Or give one which hardly reduces obscurity.
5. "Identity" sensed as obscure.
6. Treating an obscure word as if it were transparent.
7. Varied adjuncts to "identity."
8. Implicit definitions: the sense of existing.
9. —of separateness.
10. —of distinction.
11. —of permanence.
12. —of cohesion.
13. —of core.
14. —an indeterminate fraction, or all of the senses of self.
15. Employing both "identity" and a word for a particular sense of self.
16. —"identity" designating a subset of the senses of self.
17. —"social" aspects of the self.
18. —an indeterminate set of both intimate and "social" ones.
19. —what springs from within me.
20. "Identity" a synonym for: orientations.
21. —for: ego strength.
22. —for: growth.
23. —for: personality, character.
24. The sounds and letters are always the same.
25. The choice of a word is crucial.
26. Passing from one meaning to another.
27. Riskless and indecisive combat between several meanings of a great word.
28. Mingling definitions and assertions about events.
29. Asserting a very particular referent for a strong word with a rich and vague aura.
30. Work on concepts as a condition of insights into patients.
31. Being emphatic even about flagrant differences between referents assigned to the same word, or to different words.

32. Being completely aware of the possibility that a divergence in assertions may follow from a difference in definitions of the same word.

33. Deciding on a definition felt as similar to discovering an event.

34. The current chances of very large new words to appear in novel hypotheses about patients.

35. Dwelling on a word without much production of hypotheses into which it enters.

36. Merely predicting that it will.

37. "Applying a concept" may be superposing a new word on familiar ones.

38. When 35–37 are present, the push towards expanding the referent of a cherished word may prevail over the pull to limit it.

39. When a word is cherished, it may be invidious to exclude events from its referent.

40. Subsuming a humble event under a noble concept is an accomplishment.

41. A concept is rich and powerful.

42. Implying, but not showing, that the various classes of events included into the word's referent have something substantial in common other than being thus assembled.

43. Proceeding from the presence within the meaning of a word of several classes of events to the relationships in the world between them.

44. You can't dispense with concepts.

45. You can cross it out.

46. Or add it.

47. Familiar points in fancy dress.

48. Youth and old age of central words.

49. Concealed truisms.

50. Sentences that can with equal ease be viewed as being about the world and about words.

51. Sentences that mainly appear to be about reality, but are not.

52. Sentences that it is difficult to conceive to be false.

53. Sentences evidently false unless construed as tautologies.

54. The illusion of explaining.

55. Obscuring whether an assertion is about "all" or only "some," and thus hiding a truism.

56. —a tautology.

57. Not drawing vulnerable implications.

58. Fancy dress hiding weakness.

59. Asserting merely that there are relationships between factors.

60. Referring to the world under the guise of talking about intellectual operations.

61. Ambiguous words can accommodate threatening evidence.

62. Mutual aid between various meanings of an ambiguous word.

63. Desires and fears into conceptions.

64. Psychic events into identity elements.

65. It is between the latter that conflicts arise.

66. Relief and pleasure for the sake of identity.

67. The maintenance of identity, supreme objective.

68. When not in the service of identity, desires and fears are feeble.

69. They merely mask beliefs about identity.

70. The claim to be talking about identity may exceed the practice of so doing.

71. A word designating a domain of inquiry rather than a variable related to others.

72. The "gross product" of identity theory.

73. Its "net product."

74. Its limitations and justification.

75. The sense of existing.

76. The sense of separateness.

77. Imposture for separateness.

78. The sense of permeability.

79. The sense of an ineffable quality of one's being.

80. The specifiable sense of distinction from others.

81. The sense of not knowing oneself.

82. The sense of the self's inaccessibility.

83. The sense of permanence.

84. When that is impaired, the sense of separateness may remain intact.

85. The sense of permanence and the level of change.

86. —and the degree of wishfulness in beliefs about oneself.

87. The sense of unity.

88. The sense of core.

89. Relations between the core and the rest of the self.

90. Fear of expressing one's core.

91. Expressing it and being independent.

92. Excluding events from the self.

93. How vulnerable are the self's core properties?

94. How vulnerable are other senses of the self to impacts on its core proprieties?

95. Panic and elation about changes in senses of the self.

96. Levels of preoccupation with the senses of the self.

III : The New Ego

1. Small examples.
2. Not so small ones.
3. The ascent from mentioning patients to discussing concepts.
4. The importance of events resides in their influence on thought about them.
5. Discovery of relations between events as a means for abolishing lack of connection in the mind.
6. The role of a factor is important in view of the importance of a proposition related to it.
7. Examples.
8. The meaning of a statement does not depend only on itself.
9. Analysis is a system.
10. Increasingly so.
11. You can't change elements of a system.
12. You can.
13. The absence of proof that analysis is a "system."
14. Equanimity with regard to this lack.
15. More asserted than shown.
16. An inference from a truism presented as nontruistic.
17. A law as a basis for a case conforming to it.
18. Alleging derivations from theory for assertions which seem to be based on observations only.
19. Similar claims for seemingly obvious intellectual procedures.
20. Strange inferences.
21. It renders the evident less uninteresting.
22. It helps to reduce awareness of not yet having formulated a hypothesis.
23. It makes it possible not to go beyond a truism.
24. —not to furnish more indications about what it is that is being asserted.
25. —not to search for causes.
26. It aids in diminishing doubts about a hypothesis advanced.
27. —in rendering a state of indecision about it acceptable.
28. —in reducing commitment to it.
29. It replaces humble discovering by noble thinking.

30. It procures a sense of freedom.
31. It glorifies the individual analyst's freedom to choose his particular subject of inquiry.
32. It induces a sense of power.
33. Avoidance of "true" and "false."
34. The "incomplete."
35. The improper.
36. The meaningful: You can cross it out.
37. The meaningful and the meaningless: avoiding extreme positions.
38. The useful.
39. Useful for what?
40. The important thing about truth is its usefulness.
41. The useful: a word of moderation.
42. Avoiding the issue of truth.
43. Being for or against a distinction.
44. Moderation about distinctions.
45. Nondistinctions: extravagant and respectable.
46. The effort to distinguish the unconfoundable.
47. To do so is useful.
48. —requires tools, which may be distinctions, too.
49. Certainties.
50. Probabilities.
51. Indecisions.
52. —at the present state of our knowledge.
53. Common words outside of customary bounds.
54. Suggesting strong meanings which are obscure by understatements with regard to weak ones which are clear.
55. Words familiar from use, but of unknown meaning.
56. Exaggerating the degree of proof furnished.
57. Varying the estimate of proof obtained.
58. The dominance of "assumptions."
59. Meta-assumptions.
60. Confusing the impact of accepting a construct with its deductive power.
61. Does this really follow from that construct?
62. —from that construct by itself?
63. A case of success.
64. Merely claiming a construct's superiority.
65. —with regard to precisely what competitor?
66. Claiming superiority or monopoly?
67. Constructs widely differing in the sentiments they arouse, but not in the deductions they permit.
68. Claiming the mere possibility of a construct's superiority.

69. Intermediate attitudes toward constructs.

70. Indecision.

71. —for the time being.

72. Combining indecision and choice.

73. By speaking about the probability of statements being true.

74. By speaking about frequencies of occurrence for events affirmed.

75. Combining these two modes.

76. By using the language of research.

77. Combining this with contrasting words.

78. Employing words appropriate to constructs about observations, and vice versa.

79. Deriving constructs rather than deriving from them.

80. The implicit laws presiding over such derivations.

81. —the effect resembles the cause.

82. —the greater the difference in nature between an energy and a function, the smaller the contribution of that energy to that function's cathexis.

83. —whether an energy does or does not belong to the area upon which a function operates does not affect the probability of its becoming part of that function's cathexis.

84. —the smaller the difference between two functions, the higher the probability that one will draw on the other's energy.

85. —the area from which a function's cathexis is drawn coincides with that to which the function is related.

86. —the energy of an "independent" drive goes everywhere.

87. —a type of event is caused by its particular principle.

88. —what is assumed should resemble what has been observed.

89. Definitions are rarely presented.

90. Focusing on intellectual operations rather than events helps avoiding them.

91. The word defined may be a nobler synonym of what defines it.

92. The border between what is and is not included in a definition may be weakly perceived.

93. Stressing that the difference between the meanings of two words is small without indicating what it is.

94. Definitions are easily violated.

95. Taking it for granted that connotations will prevail over denotations, and yet not abstaining from the use of a word for which this is believed.

96. Abandoning the requirement of precision.

97. How much do details of meaning matter?

98. Neglecting the possibility that the difficulty of a statement is due to remediable characteristics of definitions.

99. Suggesting that this is not the case when it probably is.

100. Expressions of the awareness that it may be.

101. Treating words as if they were patients whom it takes an effort to understand.

102. Implying a definition as already given when moving toward one.

103. Treating definitions as one does hypotheses.

104. Passing between the two without an apparent sense of difference.

105. Tending toward attributing truth or falsehood to definitions.

106. Definitions depend on insights.

107. —denied on rare occasions.

108. —usually affirmed.

109. Accepting a definition: affirming a high role of the event designated.

110. —affirming much difference between what it does and does not include.

111. —denying that there are casual relations between its components.

112. —affirming that these occur only in the combination specified by the definition.

113. —denying certain classes of events outside of it.

114. Strong positions are in order.

115. Maximize productivity.

116. It is to be expected that there be a variety of definitions for a given word at a given time.

117. —and that its definition changes through time.

118. Mere claims of productivity for definitions.

119. The degree to which questions of definition can be decided depends on the level of knowledge.

120. The power of renaming a set of lowly charged words with few highly charged ones.

121. Without proper naming no insight is complete.

122. A broad definition may hinder the production of statements about parts of its referent.

123. Without a highly charged word to designate it, even a central class of events cannot be studied.

124. *A fortiori* for a less central one.

125. A vicious circle of bad definitions.

126. Instant illumination by proper naming.

127. Grounding definitions not in productivity, but in reality.

128. Compendia of insights.

129. The consummation of inquiry.

130. It may be too early to define a word in major use.

131. Progress in knowledge leads to advance in definitions.

132. Enriching definitions by propositions.

133. Referents of good definitions occur with high frequency.

134. Varying definitions so as to preserve sentences.

135. A rare regard for dominant meanings of common words.

136. If a situation designated by one set of words obtains, the same situation indicated by another string of terms occurs.

137. Drawing on the rather clear meaning of one word.

138. Limits to unsurprising meanings of an obscure word.

139. Setting forth the meaning of a word.

140. Unnecessary words.

141. The deviant use of common words.

142. Words about intellectual operations.

143. Words customarily used in sentences that are indubitably about the world.

144. Affirming that the relationship in question does not always hold.

145. Claiming uncertainty.

146. Transmuting incompleteness of definition into insufficiency of evidence.

147. Synonym into cause.

148. Approaching statements about falsification.

149. Oscillation between meanings of words about events.

150. —of words about the nature of the statement made.

151. —"essential."

152. —"prerequiste."

153. —"criterion."

154. —"hallmark."

155. —"to relate," "a relevant aspect of a distinction," "characteristic."

156. —"to identify."

157. —"to equate."

158. Straddling definition and hypothesis in the treatment of rejected statements.

159. Mixing statements about words with others about events.

160. Admitting in denying.

161. Admitting and denying.

162. A neglected matter.

163. Instances in sentences that succeed each other.

164. Reducing awareness of repetition in such a case by ascending from common to technical language.

165. —by affirming inference.

166. Admitting in denying.

167. Repetitions within a statement.

168. —with the aid of "or."
169. Unnecessary words.
170. Novel expressions.
171. Conferring a peculiar meaning upon a familiar word.
172. Difficult words.
173. —coexisting with their simple synonyms.
174. Being plain first and complicated second.
175. Becoming simple after having been difficult.
176. Multiplying designations of the same event.
177. Using central words of analytic theory.
178. —plus advanced words from the human sciences.
179. Humble matter in high frame.
180. Words about intellectual operations.
181. —as an enriching conclusion.
182. —plus advanced words from the human sciences.
183. —plus these and central words of analytic theory.
184. The aid of hidden tautology .
185. —of synonyms disguised as causes.
186. Excessive qualifications.
187. Stressing the truth in question.
188. "It has been shown that ... ."
189. Juxtaposing what is familiar with what is less so.
190. Giving the impression that more is known about a relationship than is.
191. Refuting alleged inferences.
192. Indicating a novel class of which a familiar relationship is a member.
193. The belated acknowledgment of the evident as an intellectual advance.
194. That a patent fact has not been mentioned in analytic theory does not imply its nonexistence.
195. Pride rather than a smile.
196. Naturally evidence contrary to reigning theory is unlikely to be perceived.
197. Its sheer affirmation is satisfying.
198. —as well as that of the properties and impact of any part of the psyche varying with its context.
199. Reducing the awareness of saying something so evident by unnecessary words.
200. —by talking about intellectual operations.
201. —by stressing the truth in question.
202. —by manifestly indeterminate elements.
203. —by giving the impression that the nature of a relationship is affirmed where only the existence of one is asserted.

204. Sets of causes so comprehensive that it is not clear what is left out.

205. Lists of causes ending with "etc."

206. Multiplying words about causation.

207. Lists of causes whose incompleteness would, if challenged, presumably not be maintained.

208. Conveying that a list of causes excludes some conceivable ones, without indicating which they are.

209. Deciding on whether a certain phenomenon is of the ego without indicating its distinctive properties.

210. Merely alluding to them.

211. —even when one discusses divergences and variations concerning the attribution of a "function" to a "system."

212. Assertive decisions.

213. Mild ones.

214. Indecision.

215. A variegated affirmation.

216. Not indicating what precisely is denied.

217. Confounding the fact and the tempo of maturation.

218. Emancipation from classical prejudice.

219. The belated acknowledgment of the obvious as an intellectual advance.

220. Who is being opposed in the present?

221. A variegated affirmation.

222. The normal growth of this property.

223. Who has denied this?

224. Who has affirmed "absolute" independence?

225. The new "concept" may merely render acceptable stress on what otherwise goes without much saying.

226. "Secondary autonomy" and "ego strength".

227. —and "neutralization."

228. —and drawing neutralized energy from a reservoir.

229. —and magical thinking.

230. —and the primary process in general.

231. —and regression.

232. —and schizophrenia.

233. Uncharted.

234. Discrepancies.

235. Trends.

236. Richer than we thought.

237. Sudden disclosures of major structures.

238. Mere allusions to a definition of "ego function."

239. The refusal to enumerate all such functions.

240. Distinguishing contents of functions from the latter.

296

Bibliography

ANGEL, KLAUS. "Loss of Identity and Acting Out," *Journal of the American Psychoanalytic Association*, XIII (1965), 79–84.

BEREZIN, MARTIN A. "Comments on Dr. Luquet's Paper," (*see* under Luquet—N.L.), *International Journal of Psycho-Analysis*, XLV (1964), 269–271.

BLUMSTEIN, ALEX. "Masochism and Fantasies of Preparing to Be Incorporated," *Journal of the American Psychoanalytic Association,* VII (1959), 292–298.

BRODY, MORRIS W., and VINCENT P. MAHONEY. "Introjection, Identification, and Incorporation," *International Journal of Psycho-Analysis,* XLV (1964), 57–63.

BYCHOWSKI, GUSTAV. "The Ego and the Introjects," *Psychiatric Quarterly*, XXV (1956), 11–36.

——— "General Aspects and Implications of Introjection," *Psychiatric Quarterly*, XXV (1956), 530–548.

——— "The Release of Internal Images," *International Journal of Psycho-Analysis*, XXXVII (1956), 331–338.

——— "The Struggle Against the Introject," *International Journal of Psycho-Analysis*, XXXIX (1958), 183–187.

CAMERON, NORMAN. "Introjection, Reprojection, and Hallucination in the Interaction Between Schizophrenic Patient and Therapist," *International Journal of Psycho-Analysis*, LXII (1961), 86–96.

ERIKSON, ERIK H. *Identity and the Life Cycle* (New York: International Universities Press, 1959).

——— "Reality and Actuality," *Journal of the American Psychoanalytic Association*, X (1962), 451–474.

FENICHEL, OTTO. *The Psychoanalytic Theory of Neurosis* (New York: W. W. Norton, 1945).

GAARDER, KENNETH. "The Internalized Representation of the Object in the Presence and in the Absence of the Object," *International Journal of Psycho-Analysis*, XLVI (1965), 297–302.

GIOVACCHINI, PETER L. "Transference, Incorporation, and Synthesis," *International Journal of Psycho-Analysis*, XLVI (1965), 287–296.

——— "The Frozen Introject," *International Journal of Psycho-Analysis*, XLVIII (1967), 61–67.

GREENACRE, PHYLLIS. "Early Physical Determinants in the Development of the Sense of Identity," *Journal of the American Psychoanalytic Association*, VI (1958), 612–627.

——— "The Impostor," *Psychiatric Quarterly*, XXVII (1958), 359–381.

GREENSON, RALPH R. "Introduction to a Panel 'Problems of Identification,'" and "The Struggle Against Indentification," *Journal of the American Psychoanalytic Association*, II (1954), 197–217.

—— "On Homosexuality and Gender Identity," *International Journal of Psycho-Analysis*, LXV (1964), 217–219.

GRINBERG, LEON. "On a Specific Aspect of Counter-Transference Due to the Patient's Projective Identification," *International Journal of Psycho-Analysis*, XLIII (1962), 436–440.

GRINKER, ROY R. "On Identification," *International Journal of Psycho-Analysis*, XXXVIII (1957), 379–389.

GRUEN, ARNO. "Autonomy and Identification: The Paradox of Their Opposition," *International Journal of Psycho-Analysis*, XLIX (1968), 648–655.

HARRISON, IRVING B. "A Reconsideration of Freud's 'A Disturbance of Memory on the Acropolis in Relation to Identity Disturbance,'" *Journal of the American Psychoanalytic Association*, XIV (1966), 518–527.

HARTMANN, HEINZ. Ego Psychology and the Problem of Adaptation (New York: International Universities Press, 1958).

—— *Psychoanalysis and Moral Values* (New York: International Universities Press, 1960).

—— *Essays on Ego Psychology: Selected Problems in Psychoanalytic Theory* (New York: International Universities Press, 1964).

—— ERNST KRIS, and RUDOLPH M. LOEWENSTEIN. *Papers on Psychoanalytic Psychology* (New York: International Universities Press, 1964).

HAYMAN, ANNE. "Verbalization and Identity," *International Journal of Psycho-Analysis*, XLVI (1965), 455–466.

HENDRICK, IVES. "Early Development of Ego: Identification in Infancy," *Psychiatric Quarterly*, XX (1951), 44–61.

JACOBSON, EDITH. "On Psychotic Identifications," *International Journal of Psycho-Analysis*, XXXV (1954), 102–108.

—— "Contribution to the Metapsychology of Psychotic Identifications," *Journal of the American Psychoanaltyic Association*, II (1954), 239–262.

—— *The Self and the Object World* (New York: International Universities Press, 1964).

JOSEPH, EDWARD D. "Identity and Joseph Conrad," *Psychiatric Quarterly*, XXXII (1963), 549–572.

KLEIN, MELANIE. "On Identification," in *New Directions in Psycho-Analysis*, ed. Melanie Klein et al. (London: Tavistock, 1955), 309–345.

KNIGHT, ROBERT P. "Introjection, Projection, and Identification," *Psychiatric Quarterly*, IX (1940), 334–341.

298

KRAMER, PAUL. "On Discovering One's Identity," in R. S. Eissler *et al.*, *The Psychoanalytic Study of the Child* (New York: International Universities Press), Vol. 10, 47–74.

KOFF, ROBERT H. "A Definition of Identification: A Review of the Literature," *International Journal of Psycho-Analysis*, XLII (1961), 361–370.

KRUPP, GEORGE R. "Identification as a Defense Against Anxiety in Coping with Loss," *International Journal of Psycho-Analysis*, XLVI (1965), 303–314.

LAMPL DE GROOT, JEANNE. "The Role of Identification in Psycho-Analytic Procedure," *International Journal of Psycho-Analysis*, XXXVII (1957), 456–458.

LICHTENSTEIN, HEINZ. "Identity and Sexuality," *Journal of the American Psychoanalytic Association*, IX (1961), 179–260.

——— "The Dilemma of Human Identity," *Journal of the American Psycho-Analytic Association*, XI (1963), 173–223.

——— "The Role of Narcissism in the Emergence and Maintenance of a Primary Identity," *International Journal of Psycho-Analysis*, XLV (1964), 49–56.

——— "Towards a Metapsychological Definition of the Concept of the Self," *International Journal of Psycho-Analysis*, XLVI (1965), 117–128.

LITTLE, MARGARET. "On Basic Unity," *International Journal of Psycho-Analysis*, XLI (1960), 377–384.

LOEWALD, HANS W. "Internalization, Separation, Mourning, and the Superego," *Psychiatric Quarterly*, XXXI (1962), 483–504.

LOMAS, PETER. "Family Role and Identity Formation," *International Journal of Psycho-Analysis*, XLII (1961), 371–380.

——— "Passivity and Failure of Identity Development," *International Journal of Psycho-Analysis*, XLVI (1965), 438–454.

——— "Review of David J. deLevita's *The Concept of Identity*," *International Journal of Psycho-Analysis*, XLVIII (1967), 124.

LUBIN, ALBERT J. "A Feminine Moses: A Bridge Between Childhood Identifications and Adult Identity." *International Journal of Psycho-Analysis*, XXXIX (1958), 535–546.

LUQUET, PIERRE. "Early Identification and Structuration of the Ego," *International Journal of Psycho-Analysis*, XLV (1964), 263–264.

MAHLER, MARGARET SCHOENBERGER. "Autism and Symbiosis, Two Extreme Disturbances of Identity," *International Journal of Psycho-Analysis*, XXXIX (1958), 77–83.

MALIN, ARTHUR, and JAMES S. GROTSTEIN. "Projective Identification in the Therapeutic Process," *International Journal of Psycho-Analysis*, XLVII (1966), 26–31.

MARGOLIS, GERARD J. "Secrecy and Identity," *International Journal of Psycho-Analysis*, XLVII (1966), 517–522.

MELTZER, DONALD. "The Relation of Anal Masturbation to Projective Identification," *International Journal of Psycho-Analysis*, XLVII (1966), 335–342.

MUNRO, LOIS. "Clinical Notes on Internalization and Identification," *International Journal of Psycho-Analysis*, XXXIII (1952), 132–143.

POLLOCK, GEORGE H. "On Symbiosis and Symbiotic Neurosis," *International Journal of Psycho-Analysis*, XLV (1964), 1–30.

REICH, ANNIE. "Early Identifications as Archaic Elements in the Superego," *Journal of the American Psychoanalytic Association*, II (1954), 218–238.

RITVO, SAMUEL, and ALBERT J. SOLNIT. "The Relationship of Early Ego Identifications to Superego Formation," *International Journal of Psycho-Analysis*, XLI (1960), 295–300.

ROSS, NATHANIEL. "Review of Erik H. Erikson's *Insight and Responsibility*," *International Journal of Psycho-Analysis*, XLVIII (1967), 562–568.

RUBINFINE, DAVID LAWRENCE. "Report on a Panel on Problems of Identity," *Journal of the American Psychoanalytic Association*, VI (1958), 131–142.

RUDDICK, BRUCE. "Colds and Respiratory Introjection," *International Journal of Psycho-Analysis*, XLIV (1963), 178–190.

SARLIN, CHARLES N. "Feminine Identity," *Journal of the American Psychoanalytic Association*, XI (1963), 790–816.

SAUL, LEON J., and SILAS L. WARNER. "Identity and a Point of Technique," *Psychiatric Quarterly*, XXXVI (1967), 532–545.

SCHECHTER, DAVID E. "Identification and Individuation," *Journal of the American Psychoanalytic Association*, XVI (1968), 48–79.

SEARLES, HAROLD F. "Anxiety Concerning Change, as Seen in the Psychotherapy of Schizophrenic Patients, with Particular Reference to the Sense of Personal Identity," *International Journal of Psycho-Analysis*, XLII (1961), 74–85.

——— "Review of Edith Jacobson's *The Self and the Object World*," *International Journal of Psycho-Analysis*, XLVI (1965), 529–532.

SEWARD, GEORGENE H. "Sex Identity and the Social Order," *Journal of Nervous and Mental Diseases* (1964), 126–136.

SHEVIN, FREDERICK F. "Countertransference and Identity Phenomena Manifested in the Analysis of a Case of 'Phallus Girl' Identity," *Journal of the American Psychoanalytic Association*, XI (1963), 331–344.

SUSLICK, ALVIN. "Pathology of Identity as Related to the Borderline Ego," *Archives of General Psychiatry* (1963), 252–262.

TABACHNIK, NORMAN. "Self-Realization and Social Definition: Two

Aspects of Identity Formation," *International Journal of Psycho-Analysis*, XLVIII (1967), 68–75.

WEILAND, I. HYMAN. "Considerations on the Development of Symbiosis, Symbiotic Psychoses, and the Nature of Separation Anxiety," *International Journal of Psycho-Analysis*, XLVII (1966), 1–5.

WIGGERS, HERBERT A. (reporter). "Problems of Identification," *Journal of the American Psychoanalytic Association*, I (1953), 538–549.

WOODMANSEY, A. C. "The Internalization of External Conflict," *International Journal of Psycho-Analysis*, XLVII (1966), 349–355.